Canandaigua and Canandaigua Lake

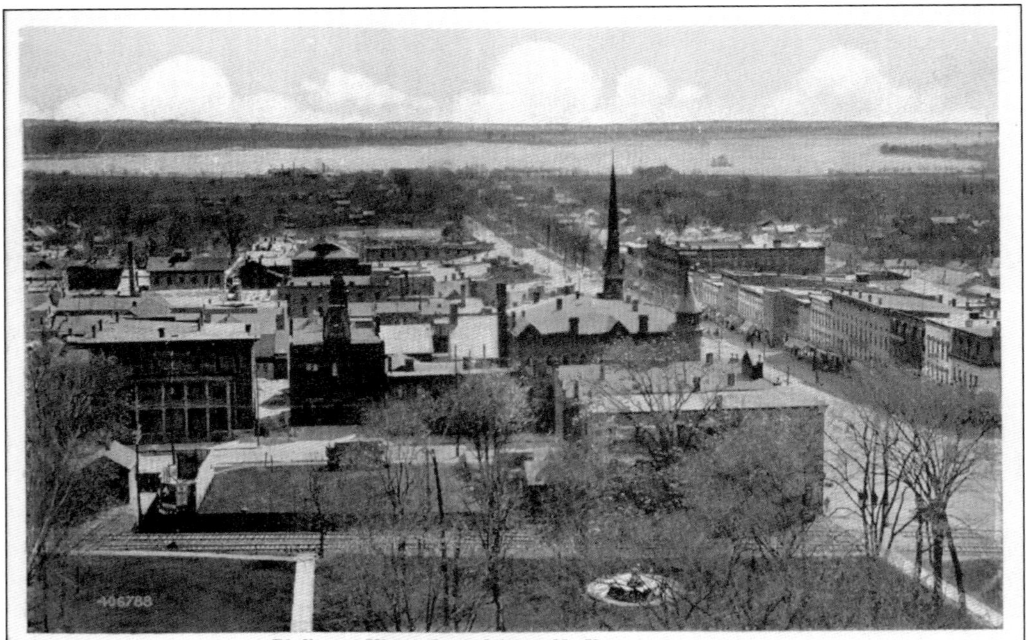

Bird's-eye View, Canandaigua, N. Y.

Canandaigua and the lake have always been linked. The lake was most likely the major reason why the Seneca people established a village here. The availability of different transportation opportunities helped Oliver Phelps decide on designating Canandaigua as the site of his first land office. This view from the courthouse dome clearly ties the lake and the community. (Author's.)

ON THE COVER: The exact location of this peaceful scene is unknown. However, it appears to be from the east side, looking toward Squaw Island in the misty distance. The small rowboat is emblematic of a quieter time on the lake before the advent of gasoline engines and large numbers of boats and cottages. (Courtesy of Ray and Barbara Henry.)

POSTCARD HISTORY SERIES

Canandaigua and Canandaigua Lake

Preston E. Pierce

ARCADIA PUBLISHING

ISBN 978-0-7385-7480-6

Published by Arcadia Publishing
Charleston, South Carolina

Printed in the United States of America

Library of Congress Control Number: 2010939086

For all general information contact Arcadia Publishing at:
Telephone 843-853-2070
Fax 843-853-0044
E-mail sales@arcadiapublishing.com
For customer service and orders:
Toll-Free 1-888-313-2665

Visit us on the Internet at www.arcadiapublishing.com

To my grandmother, Mae Elizabeth Preston Pierce, who first piqued my love of history and gave me her collection of local postcards.

Contents

Acknowledgments

Unless otherwise noted, all of the postcards included in this book come from the personal collection of the author. Throughout the process of making this book, there have been many people who have given their advice and assistance, and they deserve thanks. They include the members of the Ontario County Historical Society; Canandaigua town historian Ray Henry and his wife, Barbara; and Brighton town historian and assistant records manager for Ontario County, MaryJo Lanphear.

Bill Baneszewski and the families of the late Margery M. Elling, Charles Cooksey, and John Guyette all generously gave permission for the inclusion of their more contemporary postcards in this book. The cards of those prolific photographers give us an important perspective on the past, and the permission to use their images is greatly appreciated.

Introduction

In 1788, New England land developers Oliver Phelps and Nathaniel Gorham purchased six million acres between Seneca Lake and the Genesee River from the Iroquois people. When the New York state legislature created Ontario County on January 27, 1789, it included the entire purchase at first. That same year, Phelps established the partners' first land office in Canandaigua, the site of a Seneca-Iroquois town that was destroyed during the American Revolution. Roughly translated from the Seneca language, *Canandaigua* means "the place chosen for settlement" or "the chosen spot."

Conscious of the need for an attractive social, business, and government center, Oliver Phelps made Canandaigua a planned community from the start. Laying out the new village with a street grid and a public square, the partners required buyers to build on their property within two years. Phelps and Gorham endowed a private New England–style academy, laid out the widest Main Street in Western New York, hired a Congregational minister to establish churches throughout the area, and created a road system. Phelps actually moved to Canandaigua and served as the first judge in the new county government. The legislature permitted him to appoint many of the county officials.

Quickly, Canandaigua became an important center for water and highway transportation. Indeed, Canandaigua was an important stop on the great Iroquois path, linking the principal towns of the original Five Nations. For more than a century after 1827, Canandaigua was homeport for a succession of steamboats and scows. Turnpikes and plank roads leading to Canandaigua opened as early as the 1790s. Stage lines fanned out to other towns, delivering passengers and mail in all directions. US Route 20, a scenic transcontinental highway passing through Canandaigua since the 1920s, follows the route of the old Iroquois trail and the early Seneca turnpike. An early participant in the "good roads" movement at the start of the 20th century, Canandaigua was also the hometown of pioneer automaker John North Willys.

After 1840, Canandaigua was an important railroad junction for two early lines, the New York Central "Auburn Road" and the Northern Central Railway. From 1903 to 1930, the Rochester and Eastern Rapid Railway, an interurban trolley system, tied the town to Rochester and Geneva.

Canandaigua also became a cultural center and the hub of commercial activities for the county. James D. Bemis, the "Father of the Western New York Press," had his printing office and bookstore in Canandaigua. Bemis marketed his wares and services across Western New York. His apprentices established pioneer newspapers in many regional towns. In 1850, Bemis's son William constructed the Bemis Block, still the largest single commercial building in town. The block featured a lecture hall on its third floor where renowned speakers like Frederick Douglass, Susan B. Anthony, and Harriet Beecher Stowe addressed local audiences.

Schools played an important part in the development of Canandaigua. Endowed by Phelps and Gorham as a private school for boys, Canandaigua Academy, founded in 1791, evolved into an acclaimed public high school whose alumni have achieved distinction in many fields. In the 19th century, other schools thrived in the community, including the Ontario Female Seminary and, later, the Granger Place School for Girls. The Sisters of St. Joseph came from Carondelet, Missouri, in 1854 to operate St. Mary's School, opened in 1849. That institution still serves children in the elementary grades from the greater Canandaigua area. Finger Lakes Community College (FLCC), opened in 1968, provides a variety of new opportunities for students of all ages. The campus of FLCC also hosts the regional offices of Empire State College.

A small private library opened in town about 1813. Short lived, its members owned shares in the library corporation. The Wood Library began in 1859 as an association of people who joined to get the benefits of shared books. It was incorporated in 1868 and became a free public library in 1896. William Wood, a prominent citizen of Canandaigua, did not found the library. However, it was named in his honor in recognition of his many gifts.

Those cultural developments brought a growing number of entrepreneurs, lawyers, physicians, and politicians to Canandaigua. Many of them built impressive homes and business blocks that established the tone of the community. Many of these structures are well preserved today. The Sonnenberg Estate, now Sonnenberg Gardens and Mansion State Historic Park, is the best known of all of them. It was the summer home of Frederick Ferris and Mary Clark Thompson. Mary grew up in Canandaigua, and Frederick was part of a prominent family of New York City bankers.

A wide variety of retail and manufacturing businesses have thrived in Canandaigua and around its lake. For much of the 19th century, mills and the Mc Kechnie Brewery contributed much to the economy. The community also boasted two large brickworks. Early in the 20th century, the Lisk Manufacturing Company made Canandaigua famous for enameled kitchenware.

Canandaigua Wine Company was incorporated in 1945. Now known as Constellation Brands, the company eventually bought and consolidated Widmer, Great Western, and several other national brands. The New York Wine and Culinary Center, opened in 2006, promotes state agriculture and provides cooking demonstrations that pair local wines and produce.

In the 1960s, Mobil Chemical established a factory in Canandaigua that is now part of Pactiv, a major producer of plastic and foam products. Infotonics Technology Center, just north of the city, is a New York State Center of Excellence in photonics and microsystems.

Canandaigua National Bank and Trust Company, chartered in 1887, has grown into a financial institution of regional significance. Half a dozen other banks have branch offices in Canandaigua, continuing a tradition going back to the 1790s.

Agriculture is still important to the community. However, heritage tourism, wine tours, fall foliage festivals, skiing, water sports, hunting, fishing, and the nearby Hill Cumorah Pageant are important elements of Canandaigua's 21st-century economy, as well as its culture.

Healthcare services now account for many local jobs. Thompson Health Systems, built around F.F. Thompson Hospital, and the US Department of Veterans Affairs Hospital are the largest elements of the healthcare sector of the local economy. A wide variety of medical offices, skilled nursing facilities, and counseling centers also contribute to the size of the healthcare sector.

Canandaigua has always enjoyed a close relationship with the lake. As tourism developed and good roads circled the lake, its communities have been linked ever more closely. Gradually, steamboats gave way to pleasure boats, which are currently served by five marinas. The Canandaigua Yacht Club celebrated its 75th anniversary in 2010. Long known as the "Gem of the Finger Lakes," Canandaigua Lake continues to be a highly desirable place for summer cottages and year-round lakeside homes.

Today, old postcards are our most plentiful source of early–20th century images. They are once again a popular collector's item. When they are used for historical purposes, however, we must be careful. Many early negatives were altered or retouched by publishers. In addition, the fact that only certain places, people, and activities were shown on postcards provides a clue to the preferences and prejudices of publishers and the public.

One

Historic Homes and Buildings

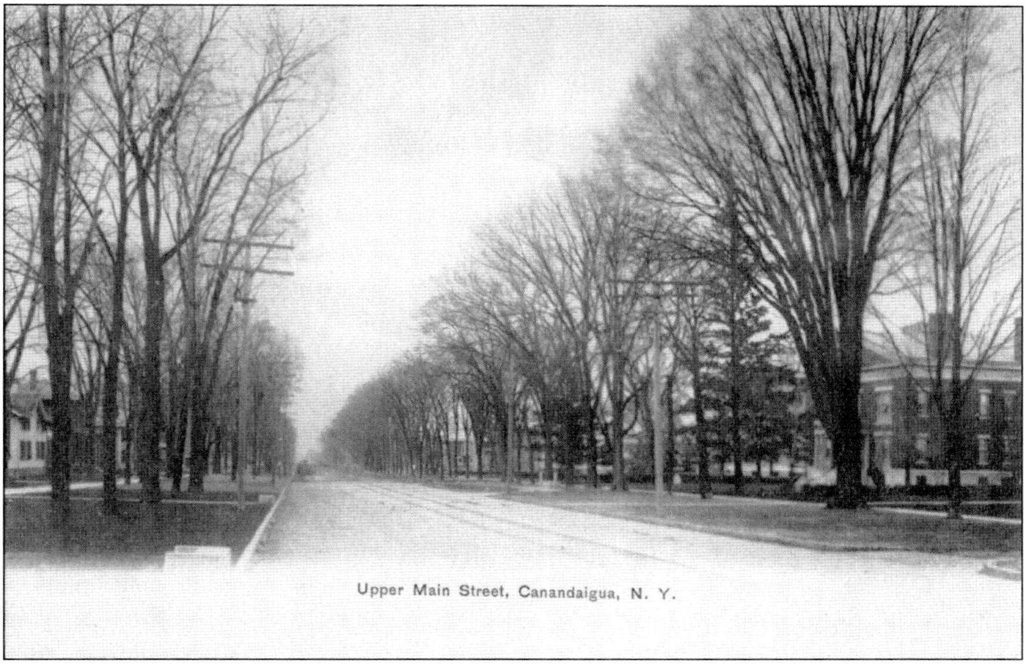

This view of North Main Street shows a wide, tree-lined avenue that is acclaimed throughout the state. Reportedly the second widest street in the nation, this view shows the grand nature of the street flanked with impressive homes and elm trees. Dutch elm disease and street widening changed this view in the 1950s.

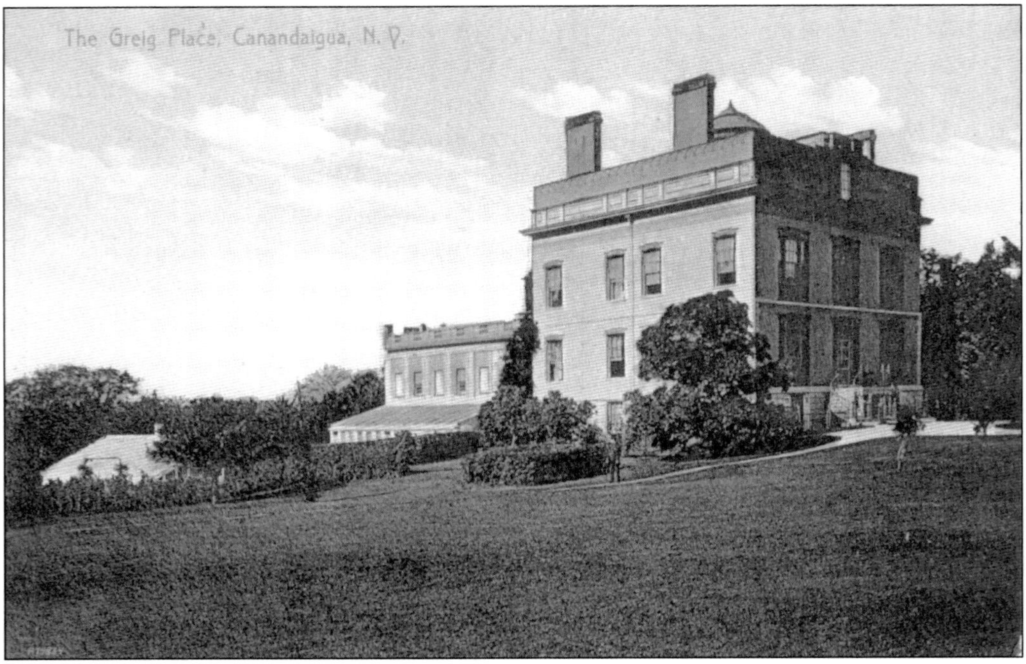

Scottish immigrant and entrepreneur John Greig built the Greig place between 1832 and 1834. The most eminent architects of London and Edinburgh approved the design for the house. The house was sold in 1889 and demolished 10 years later to make way for Scotland Road. Greig's home was one of Canandaigua's showplaces. By the time this postcard was produced, the house was probably already gone.

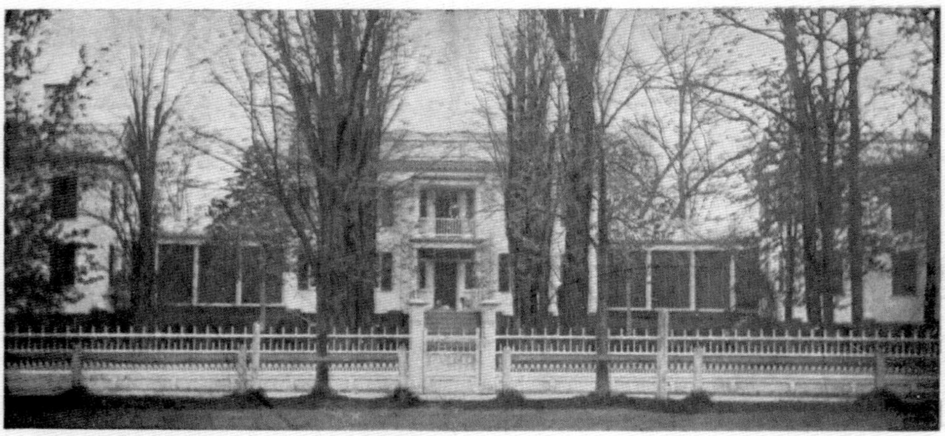

THE MORRIS HOUSE, Canandaigua, N. Y.—Built in 1793 by Thomas Morris, son of Robert Morris, the financier of the Revolution. Thomas Morris was the representative in Congress from Ontario County, which then embraced all Western New York, in 1802-3. He entertained in his Canandaigua home the refugee king Louis Phillipe, Red Jacket, Jemima Wilkinson, and every other celebrity who visited the pioneer village. The house was later occupied by Hon. Henry W. Taylor, and was finally demolished in 1900.

Here is another historical postcard that was produced after the subject was demolished. This view of the Thomas Morris house has a caption that provides all the basic information on the site. The two-wing structures were moved to Willys Place when the house was demolished. West Gibson Street enters Main Street where the main house stands in this picture, which was printed after 1907.

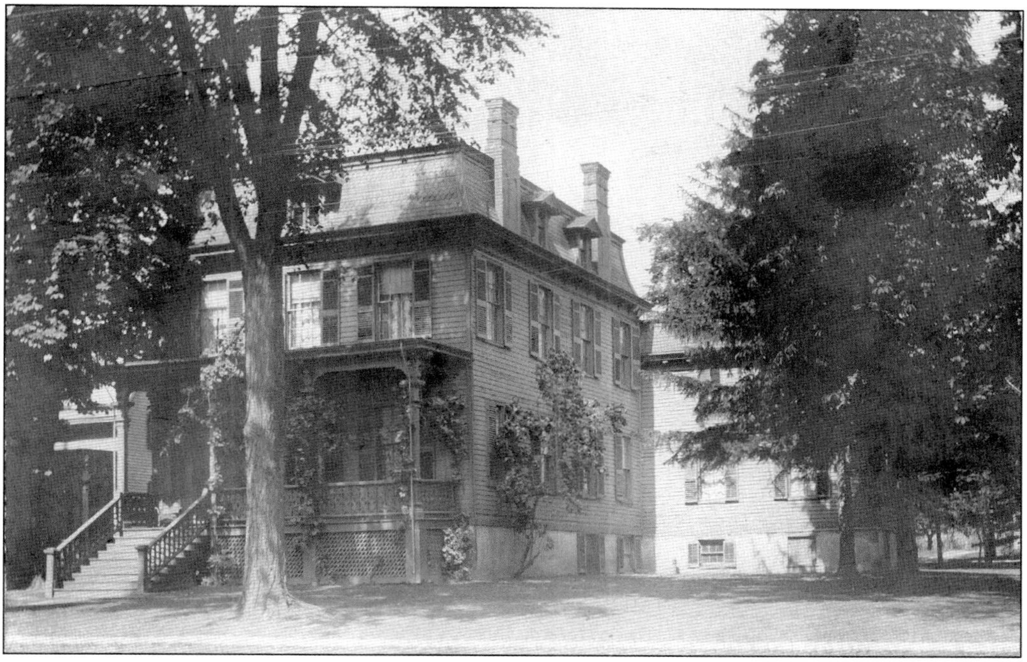

When cameras and paper designed for personal postcards appeared, anyone could become a publisher. This image shows the house built by Henry M. Field about 1840 at the corner of Park Place and Gibson Street. Reportedly an Underground Railroad stop, the house has changed little in the last century. Several prominent Canandaiguans, including Caroline Cook, Mack S. Smith, Dwight Munger, and Howard Keeney, have called it home.

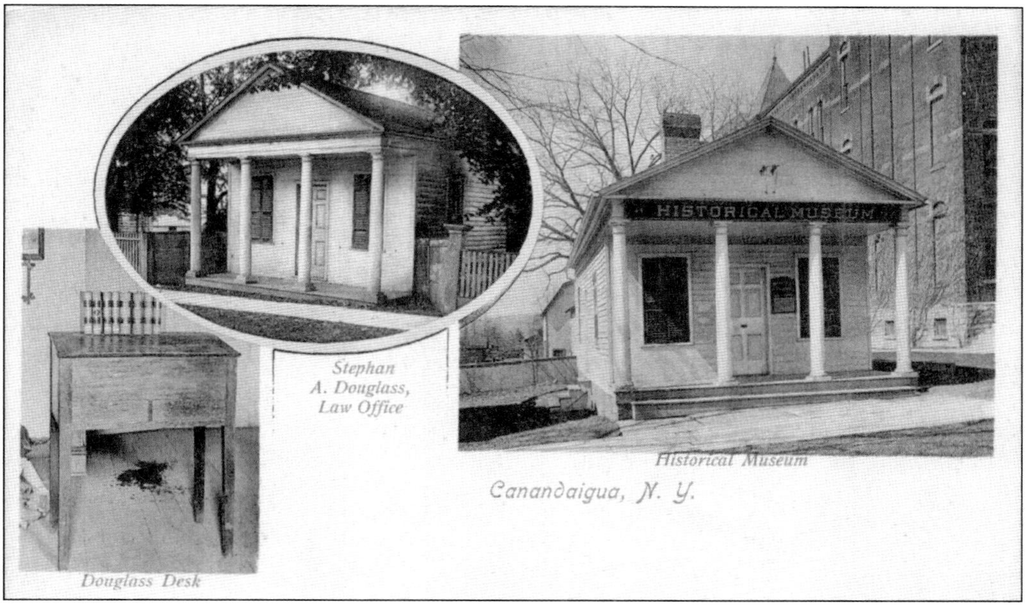

Stephen A. Douglas's law office was one of many that once dotted Main Street. It was later moved to a lot on Niagara Street. The building was moved to the grounds of the Granger Homestead in 1961, where it remains a part of that museum complex. It is similar to an office once used by the historical society that was dismantled in 1911. Douglas, the great rival of Abraham Lincoln in Illinois politics, attended Canandaigua Academy and read law here.

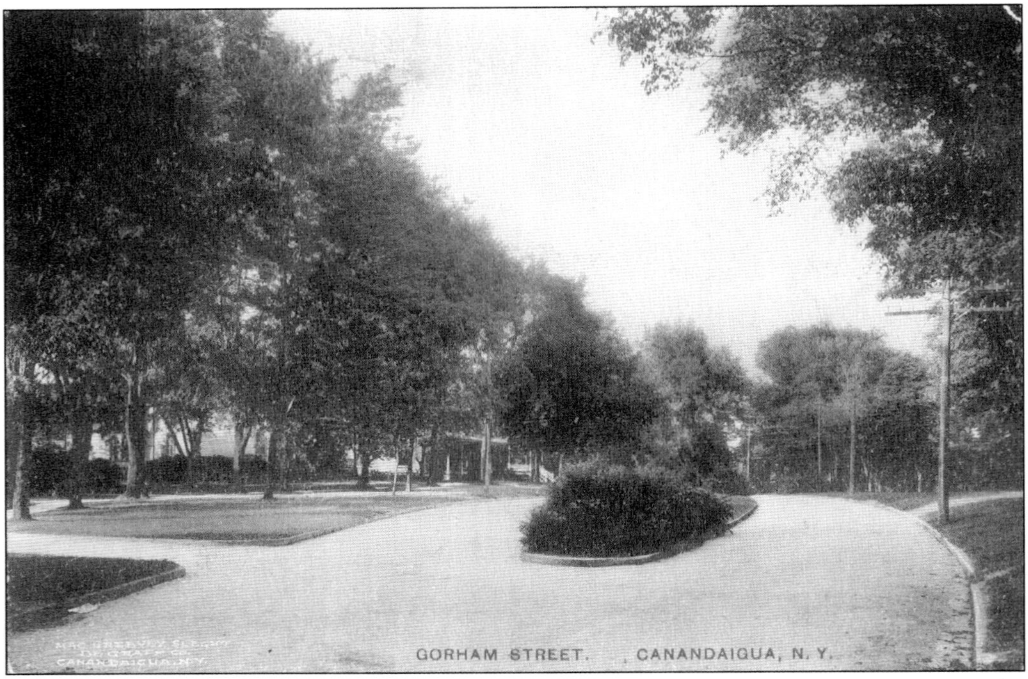

"Pickle Park" has been a feature of Gorham Street since 1904 when it was created. At the time Gorham Street was first paved with brick, a local newspaper called the creation of this parkway a long advocated municipal improvement. This postcard was probably published shortly after 1907.

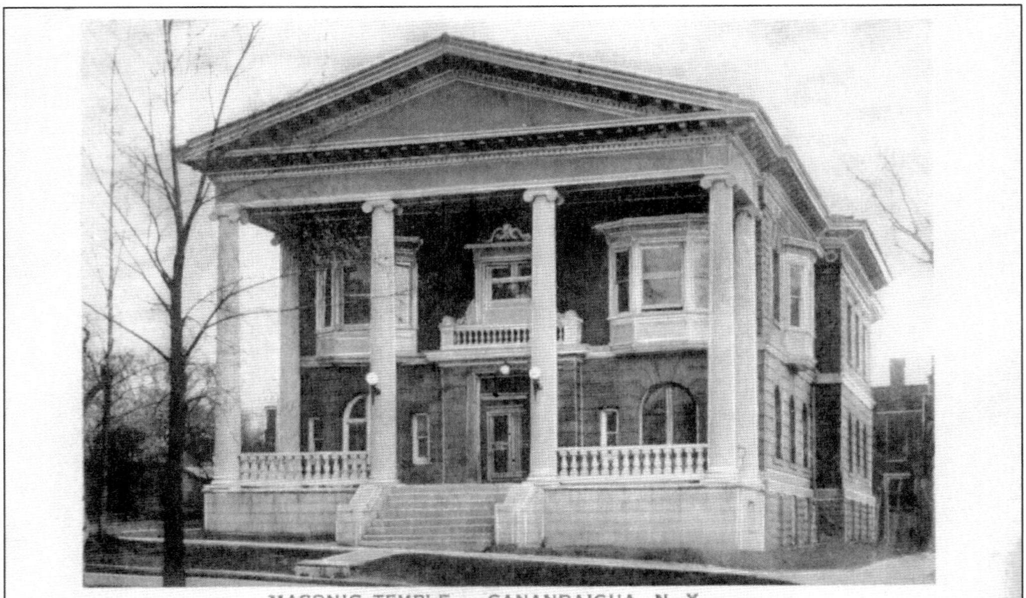

Purchased in 1920 for the use of the Canandaigua Masonic Lodge, this building also provided professional offices directly across Court Street from the county courthouse. The Masons sold it to Ontario County in 1995. When the County Municipal Building was built, Masonic Hall was incorporated into that structure, and its front was substantially changed.

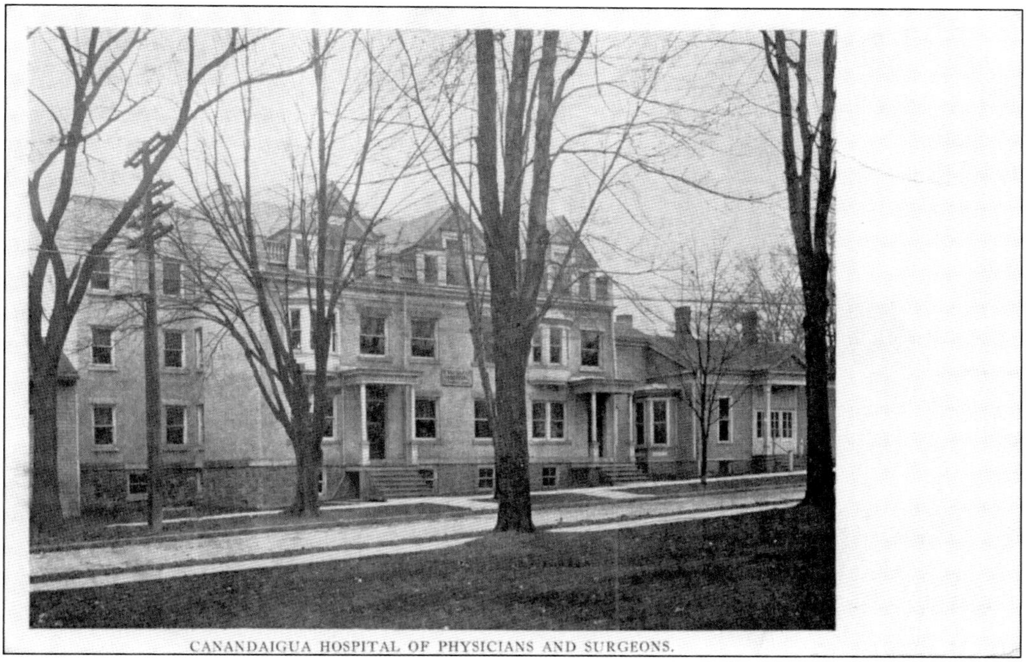

The Canandaigua Hospital of Physicians and Surgeons was opened by local physician Dr. A.L. Beahon in 1898. Modern for the time, it was small and private. A huge step forward from the residential hospitals a few physicians had previously maintained, it was never adequate but continued to operate until 1920. Since that time, the building has been an apartment complex on Gorham Street.

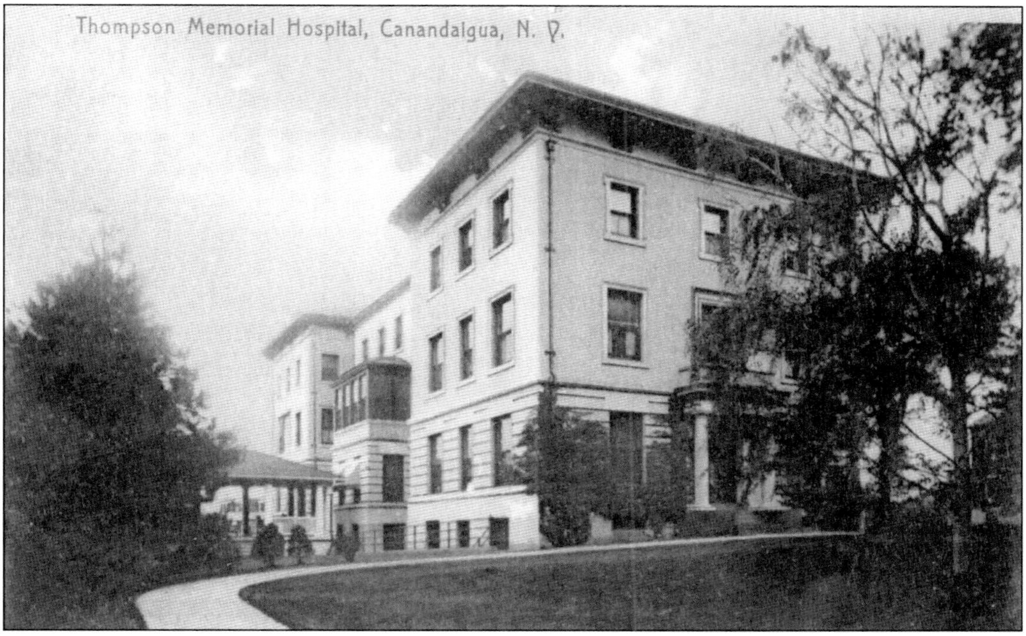

A gift to Canandaigua by Mary Clark Thompson, widow of the late Frederick Ferris Thompson, the hospital that bears his name opened in 1904. Prior to its move to a new building on Parrish Street in 1971, the original building on Main Street was enlarged several times. This unusual view of the south side is postmarked 1909 and shows the solarium. The first patient was Hiram L. Hutchens.

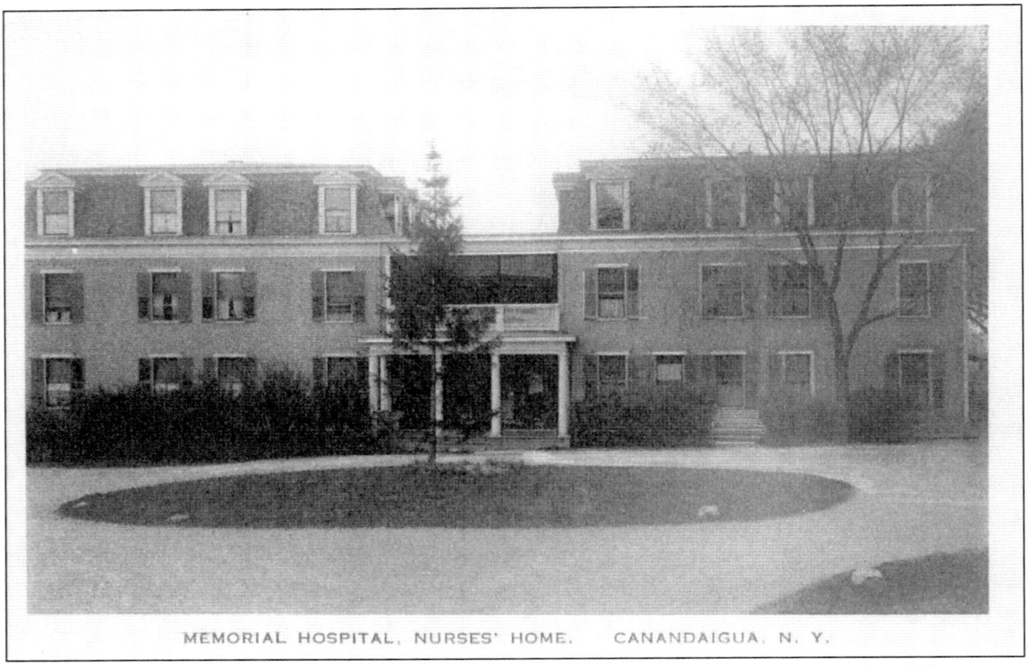

A nurses' residence was built behind Thompson Hospital in 1907. A training school for nurses opened in 1908 and doubled in size in 1911. The school closed in 1931, but this building was not demolished until 1978. It was located at the end of Wilcox Lane. The first class of nurses graduated in 1910. The last graduation in 1931 was held in the nearby First Congregational Church.

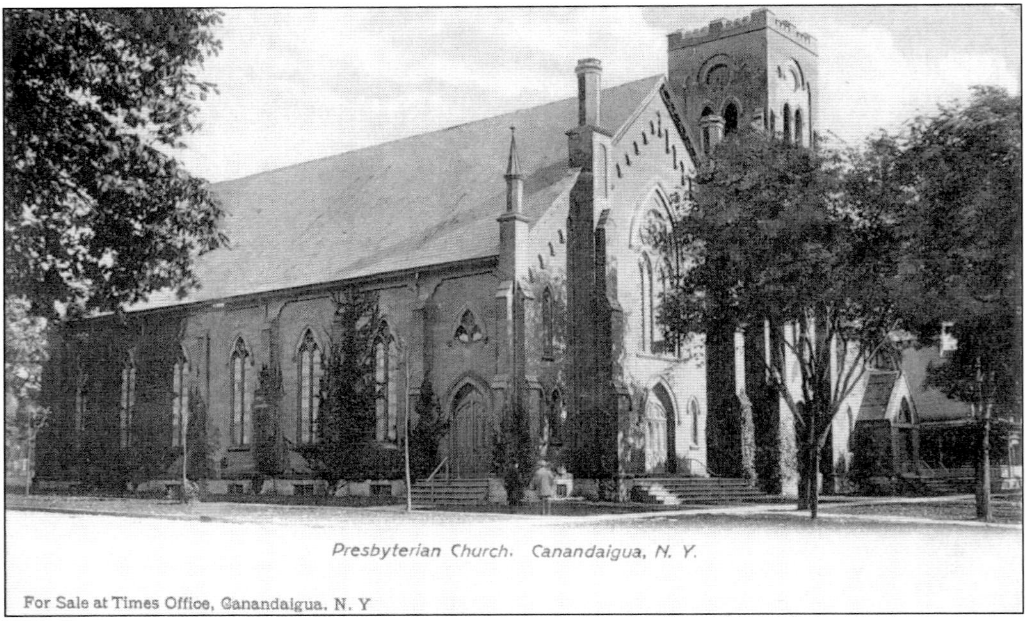

The Canandaigua Presbyterian Church was established in 1870. This building was completed in 1872. A connected chapel was built next door in 1875 to accommodate the rapidly growing congregation. A local Baptist congregation, whose church burned in 1943, joined with the Presbyterians to form the Federated Church (Presbyterian/American Baptist) in 1955. The name was changed to United Church in 1960.

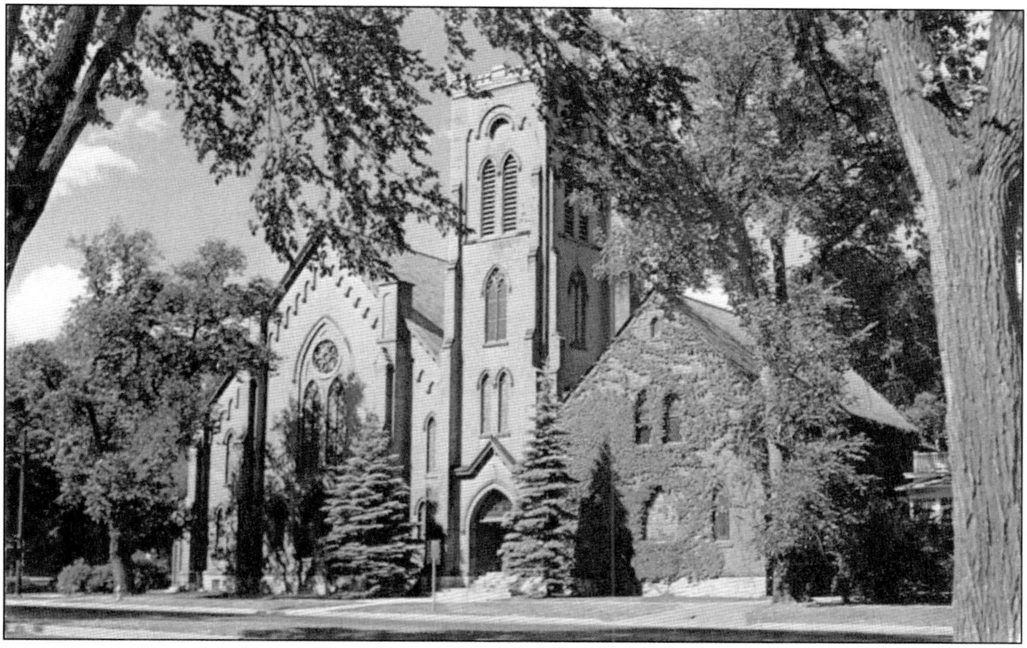

This modern-era postcard was postmarked in 1965. The information on the back calls the church the Federated Church, indicating that it was published between 1955 and 1960. This postcard provides a full view of the chapel that was demolished in 1972. An addition to the rear of the original church took the place of the old chapel building. (Photograph by Charles E. Cooksey.)

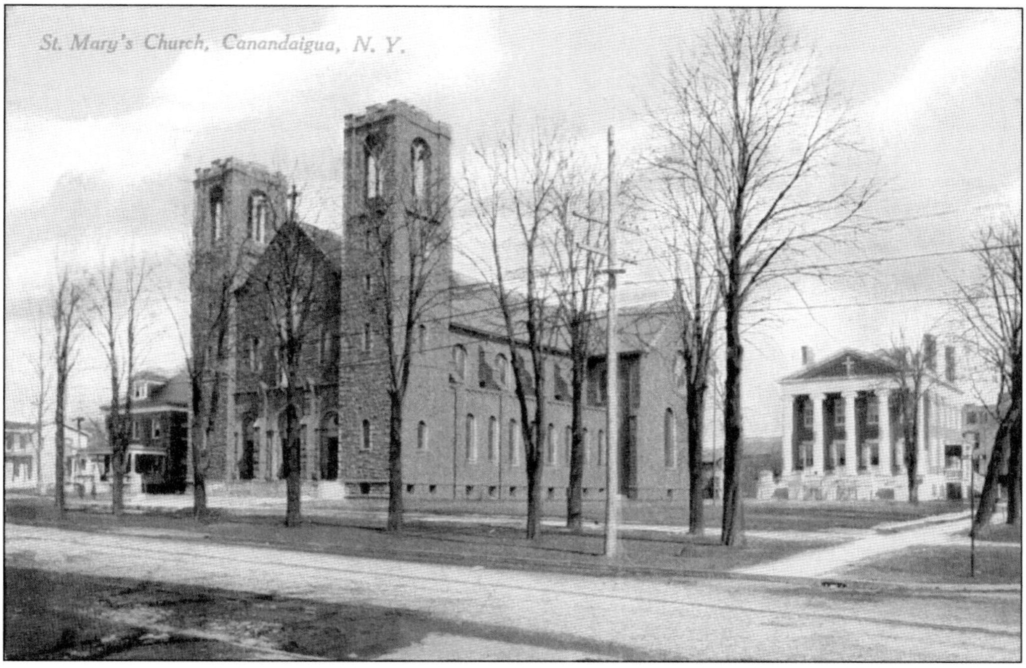

St. Mary's parish was established in 1844. In 1854, nuns came from Carondelet, Missouri, to open St. Mary's School. The first church, convent, and rectory were located around the intersection of Main and Saltonstall Streets. The school moved to this site in 1880. A new church was built in front of the school in 1904. This postcard was mailed in 1920.

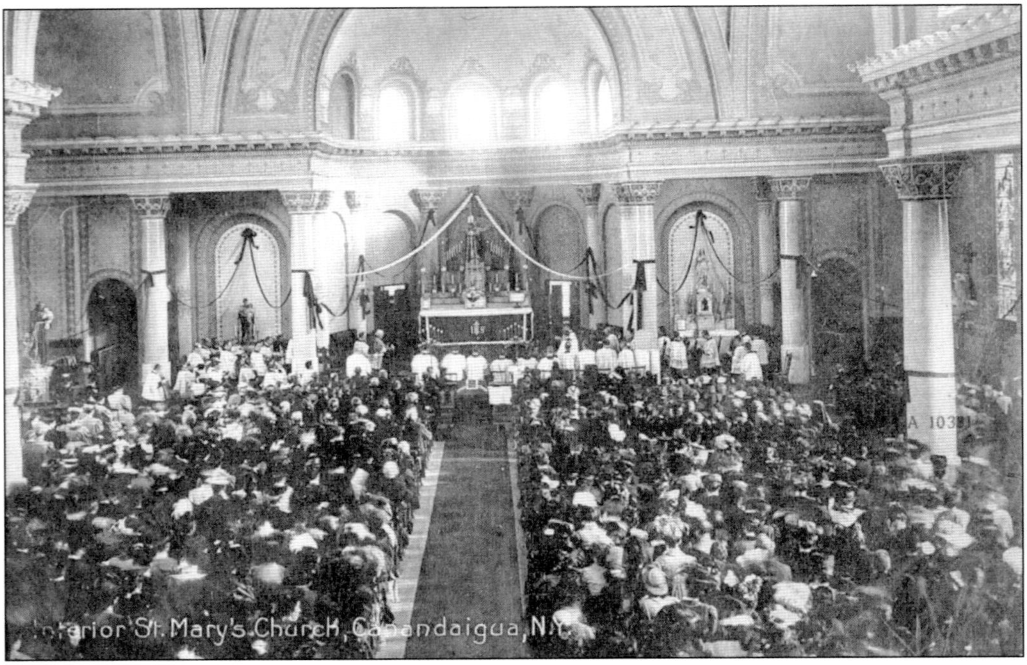

This postcard presents a rare interior image. Film speeds and camera technology at the turn of the 20th century did not permit many interior pictures. This view inside St. Mary's Roman Catholic Church was probably made soon after the new building opened in 1904. A century later, it looks little different.

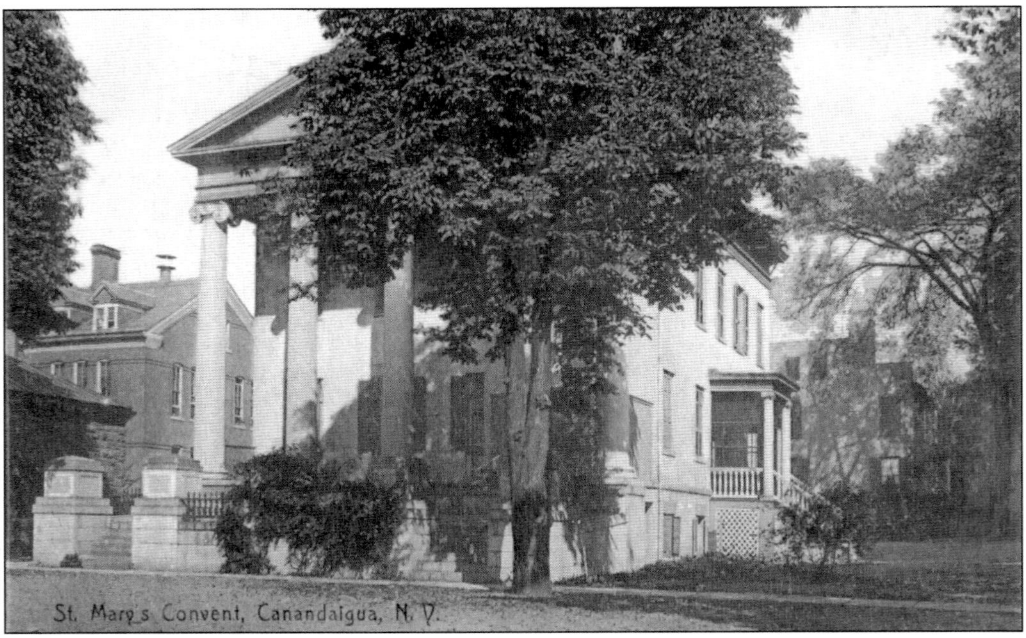

The building that became St. Mary's Convent was constructed about 1834 for militia general John A. Granger. It became St. Mary's Convent in 1873. From 1873 to 1901, the sisters operated a Catholic orphanage here. The house is now a community center. The front steps and gardens have been removed. General Granger entertained Henry Clay, Gen. Winfield Scott, Pres. Martin Van Buren, and Pres. Millard Fillmore in this home.

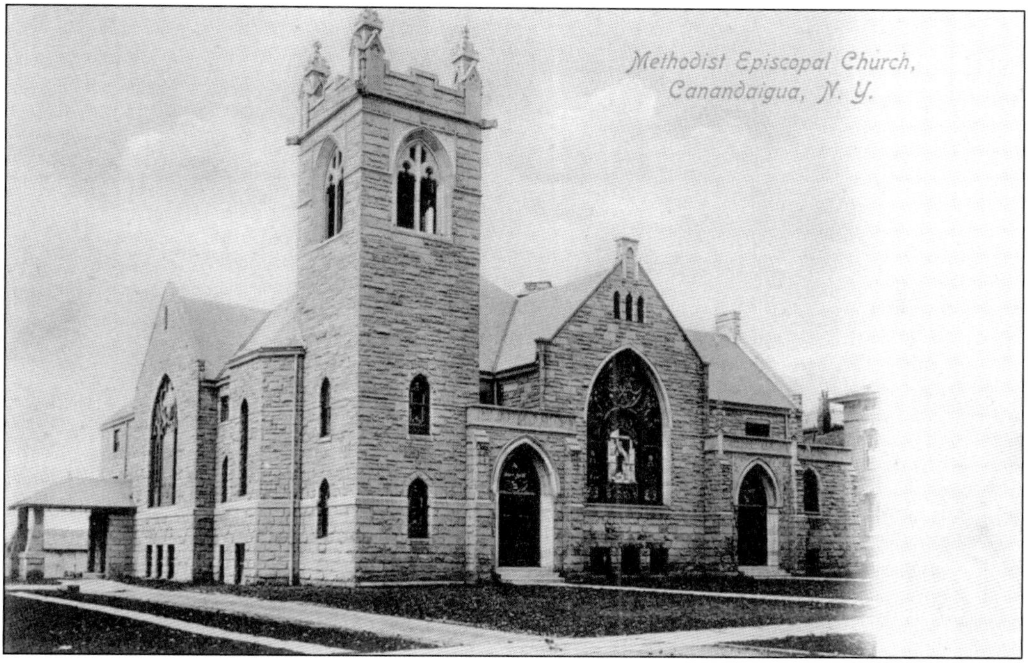

The First Methodist Church was originally located on Chapel Street, giving the street its name. The congregation moved to this location on North Main Street in 1835. This building replaced the original building moved to the site and was dedicated in 1903. An education wing and Memorial Chapel were added in 1957.

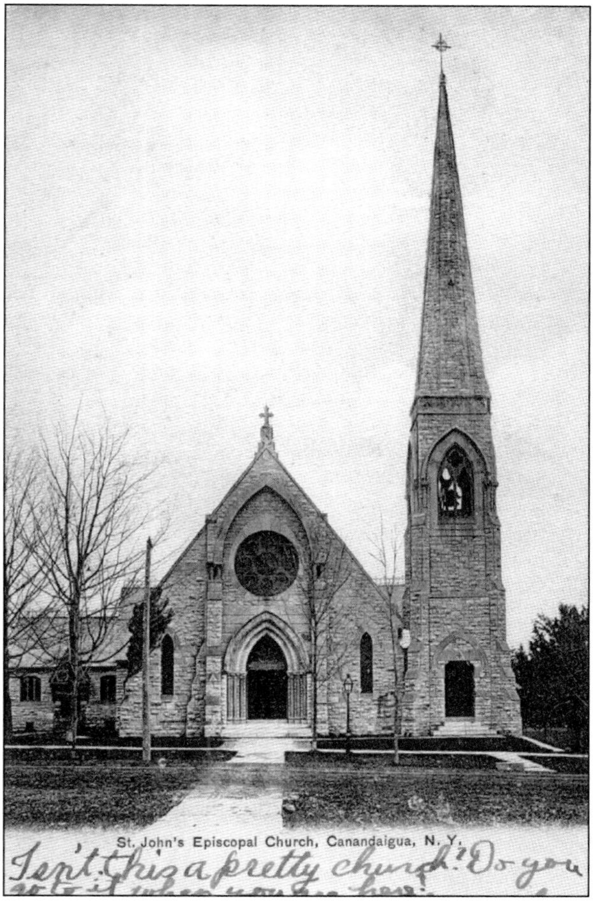

The present St. John's Episcopal Church was built in 1872. The architect was Emlyn T. Little, of New York. Several windows from the original church were installed in this building. The spire was removed in 1928.

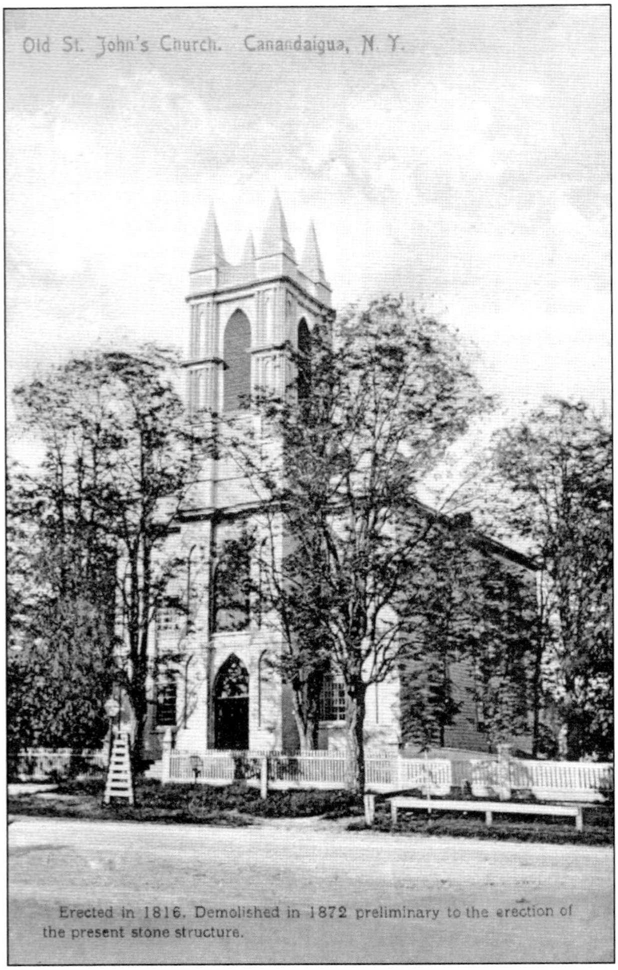

The original St. John's Episcopal Church, built in 1816, was a wood-frame structure, dedicated by Bishop John Henry Hobart. While St. John's parish was organized in 1814, a previous Episcopal congregation, known as St. Matthews, was organized in 1799. That congregation did not have its own building, so they met in the courthouse.

The oldest continuous church in Canandaigua, the First Congregational Church, United Church of Christ, was organized by Zadoc Hunn and John Rolph in 1799. This building was erected in 1812. Known for many years as "Old Brick," it is a visual reminder of the New England heritage of the area. The chapel to the right was built in 1872.

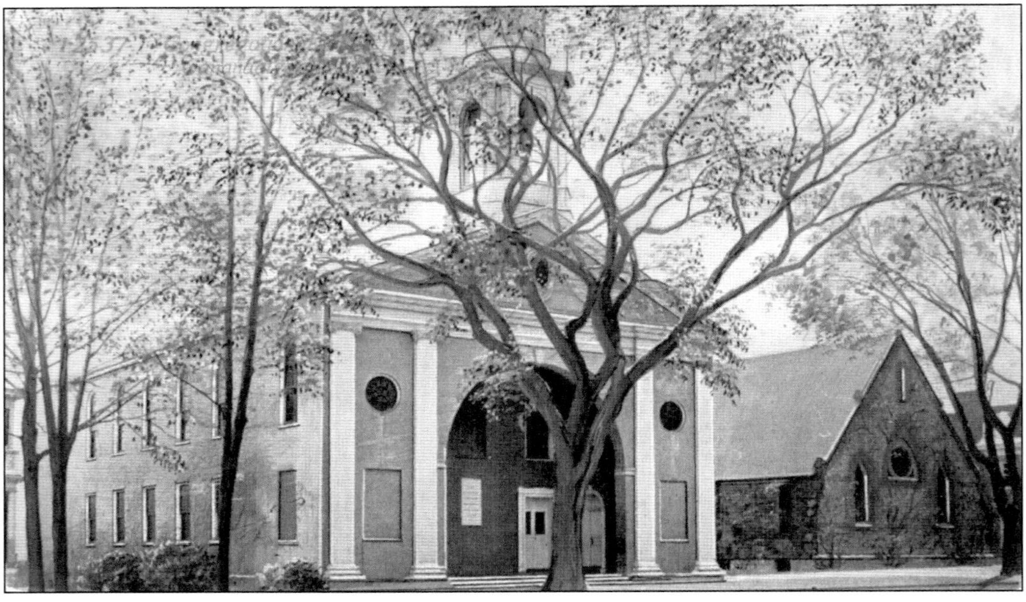

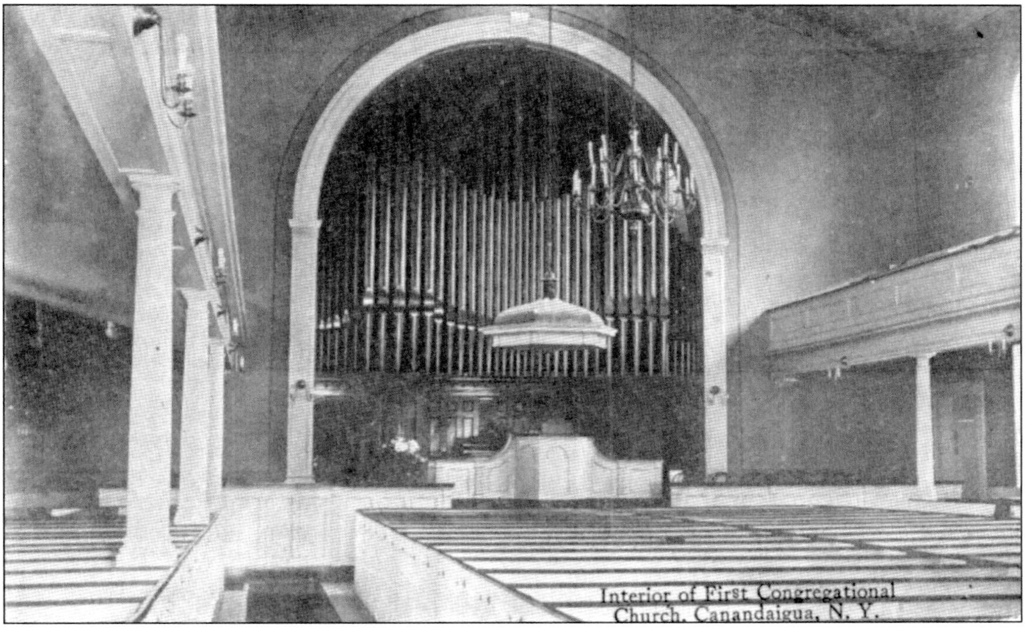

This postcard provides another rare look at the interior of an early church. The First Congregational Church has changed very little since this postcard was published a century ago. The pulpit canopy and the box pews are still in use, and the pipe organ is one of the oldest in Canandaigua. (Courtesy of the Ontario County Historical Society.)

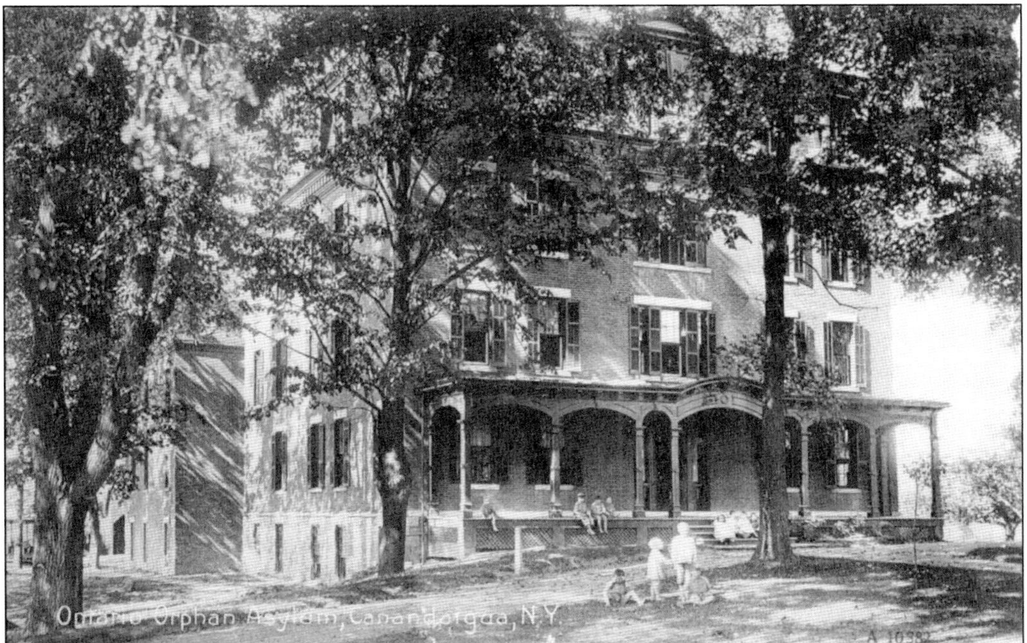

The Ontario Orphan Asylum was located at the intersection of North Road and North Main Street. Established in 1863 by the Young Ladies Aid Society, it was originally for the benefit of those orphaned by the Civil War. Closed after World War II, the building was sold to the Moose Club. It burned in 1961. The organization continues its work as the Ontario Children's Home Foundation, a charitable foundation managed by Canandaigua National Bank.

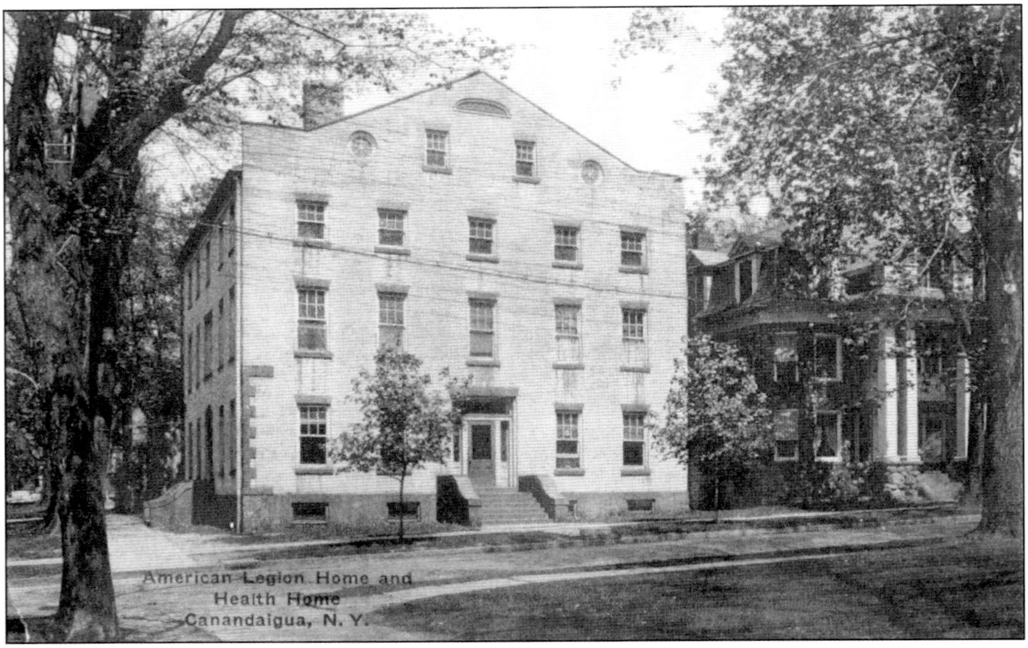

The Red Jacket Building was built about 1812. Originally a bank and office space for the Gorham family, it later became a doctor's office. The Red Jacket Club, an exclusive men's group, used the building from 1889 to 1910. The building was the home of American Legion Post No. 256 from 1926 to 1947. Today, the building is an apartment complex.

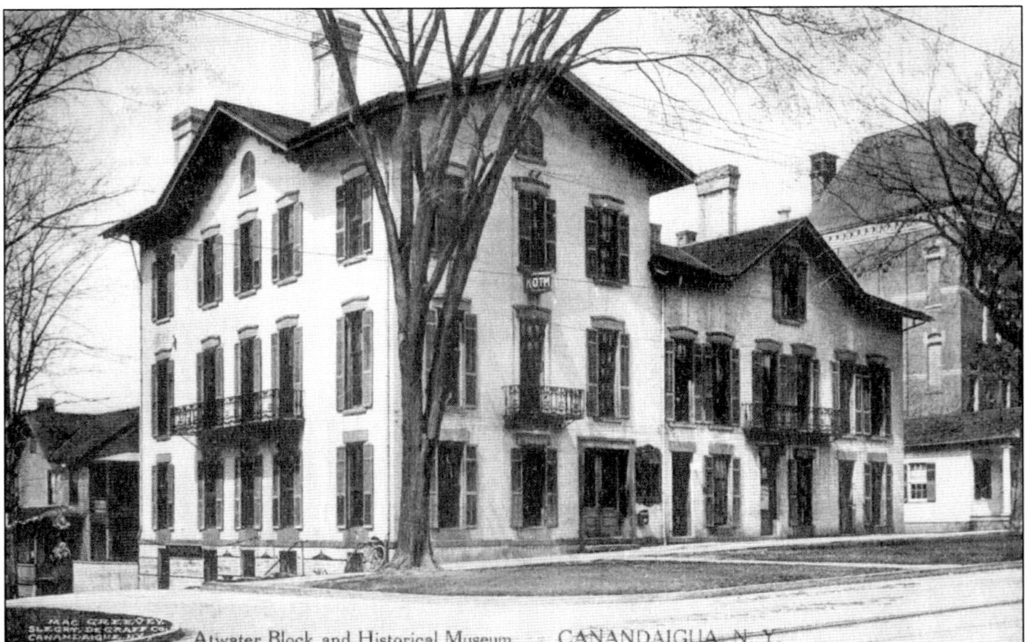

The Atwater Block was built in 1850 and served as offices for attorneys and others. For a brief time after its founding, the Ontario County Historical Society was located in the small office just visible at the far right. The Atwater Block was torn down in 1910, clearing the way for the construction of the new Canandaigua Post Office on the site.

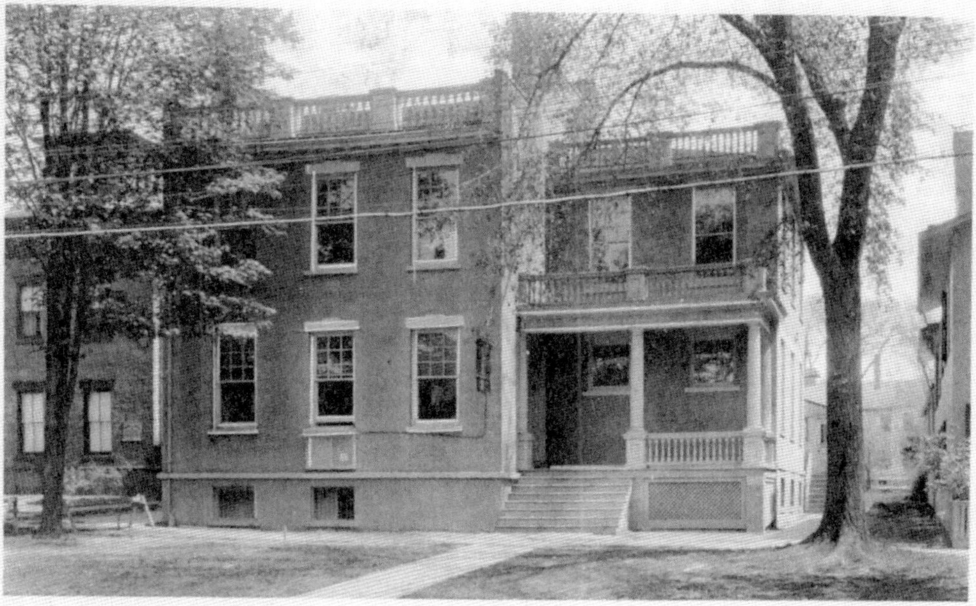

Y. M. C. A. COMMUNITY BUILDING. CANANDAIGUA, N. Y.

The Canandaigua YMCA grew out of a Congregational Sunday school class that was organized by Samuel Cole Fairley in the 1890s. After raising $15,000, the former Theodore Crosby house was purchased and opened with a gymnasium; game, meeting, and locker rooms; and a bowling alley in 1905. The YMCA moved across Main Street to the site of the former Union School in 1959.

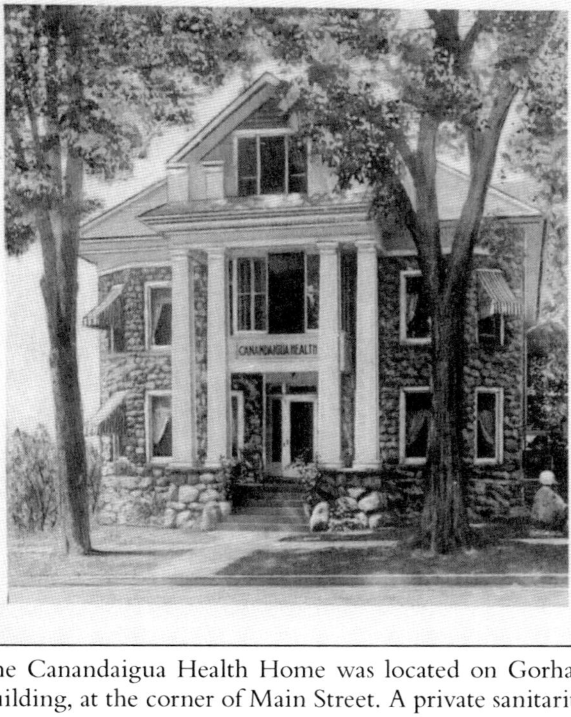

CANANDAIGUA HEALTH-HOME

Canandaigua, N. Y.

A Sanitarium devoted to the treatment of bed patients, convalescents, nervous and chronic ailments, giving special attention to the care of old people. Nurses on duty all hours day and night. Rates fifteen to thirty-five dollars per week.

The Canandaigua Health Home was located on Gorham Street, right behind the Red Jacket Building, at the corner of Main Street. A private sanitarium, it was a pioneer nursing home with very low rates by today's standards. The unique stone-faced building is now used for law offices.

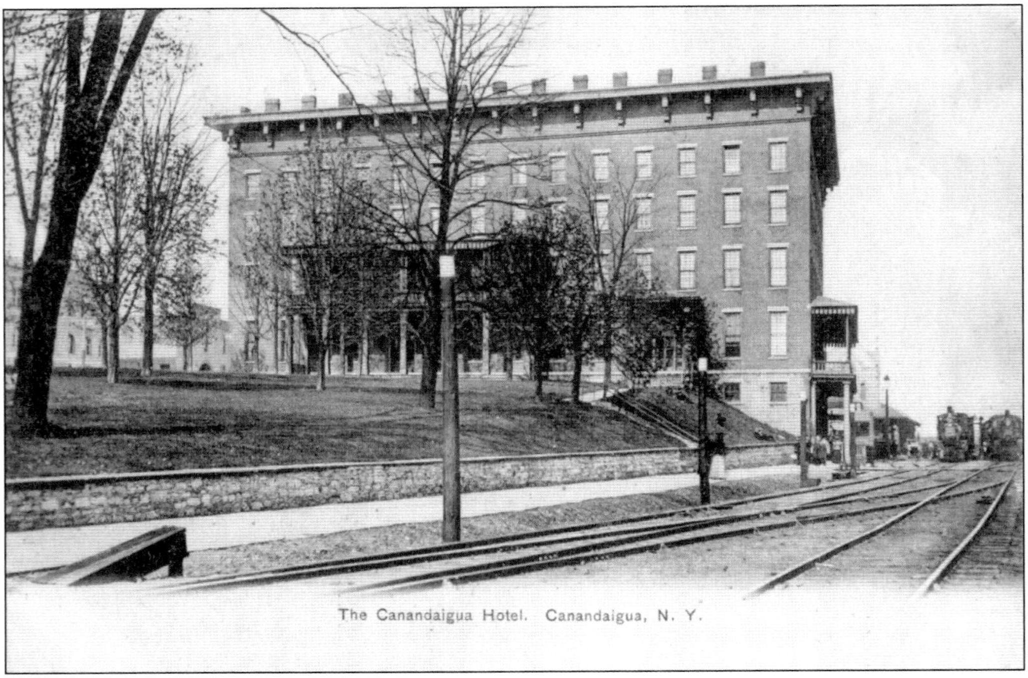

The Canandaigua Hotel burned in 1971. It had been one of the oldest hotels in town, built in 1853 to replace Blossom's Hotel, and was a transportation junction in the 19th century. For a while, Canandaigua's railroad station was located in the basement, although the 1890 station is visible.

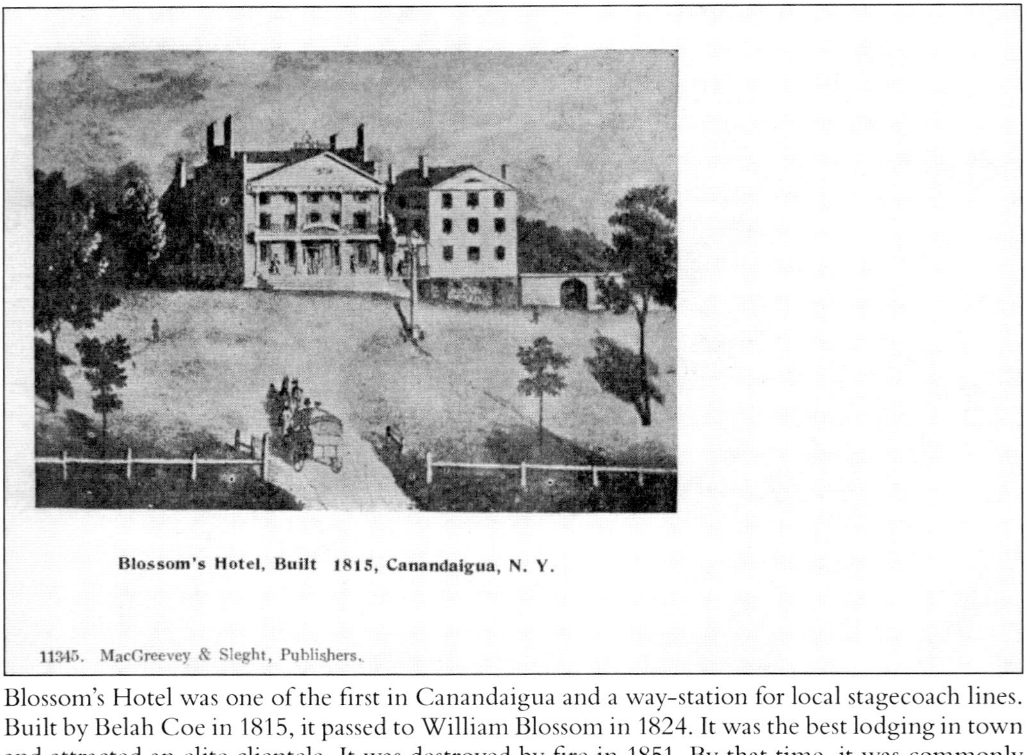

Blossom's Hotel was one of the first in Canandaigua and a way-station for local stagecoach lines. Built by Belah Coe in 1815, it passed to William Blossom in 1824. It was the best lodging in town and attracted an elite clientele. It was destroyed by fire in 1851. By that time, it was commonly referred to as the Canandaigua Hotel. This historical postcard view was produced prior to 1907.

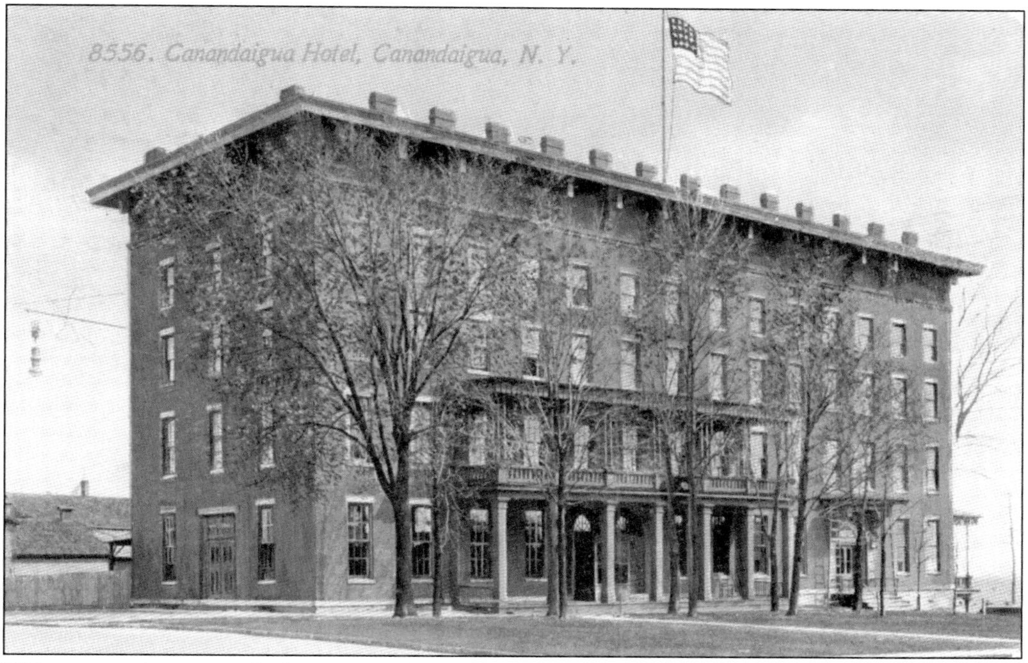

This postcard, postmarked in 1914, shows the timeless facade of the Canandaigua Hotel as it turned 60 years old. At the time of World War I, the old hotel looked much like it did before the Civil War. Stately, but tired, the hotel became another civic project of Mary Thompson in 1921.

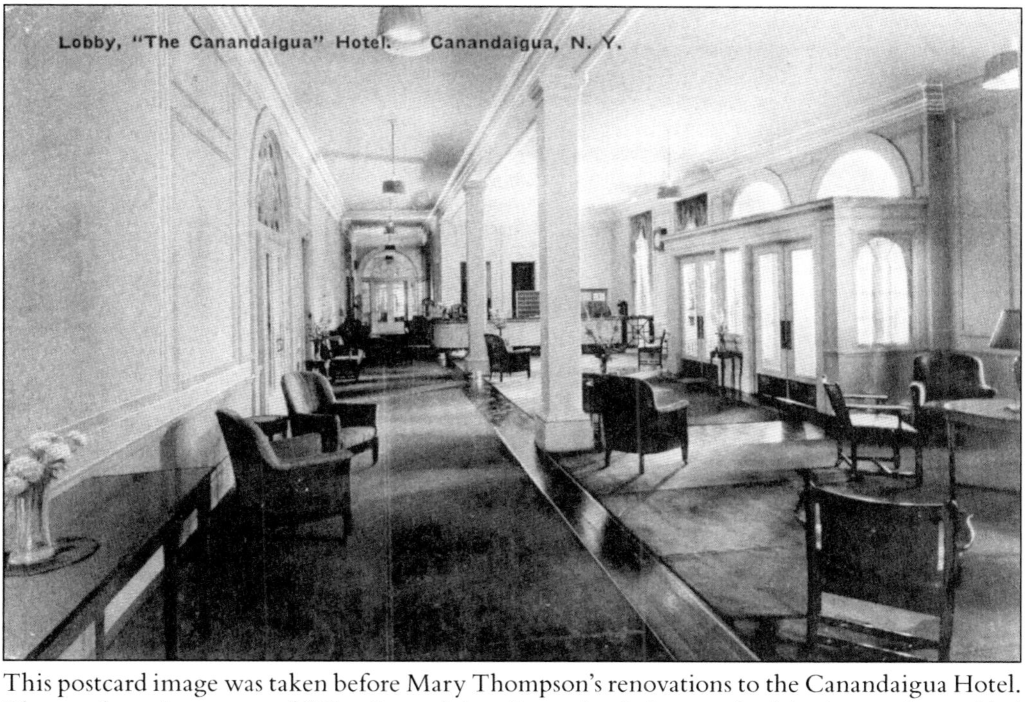

This postcard image was taken before Mary Thompson's renovations to the Canandaigua Hotel. The stately, quiet nature of "The Canandaigua" can clearly be seen in this picture. It provided a panoramic view of much of the town from its front porch.

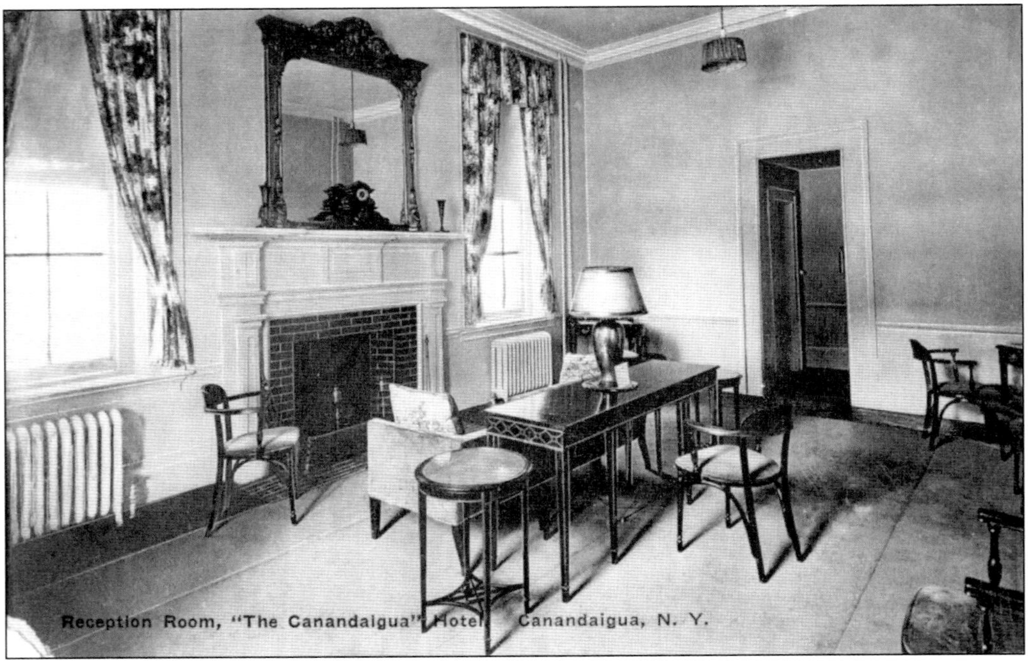

Floyd Gunnison produced postcards showing the different rooms at the Canandaigua Hotel. This postcard shows one of the reception rooms. There were many working fireplaces at the hotel.

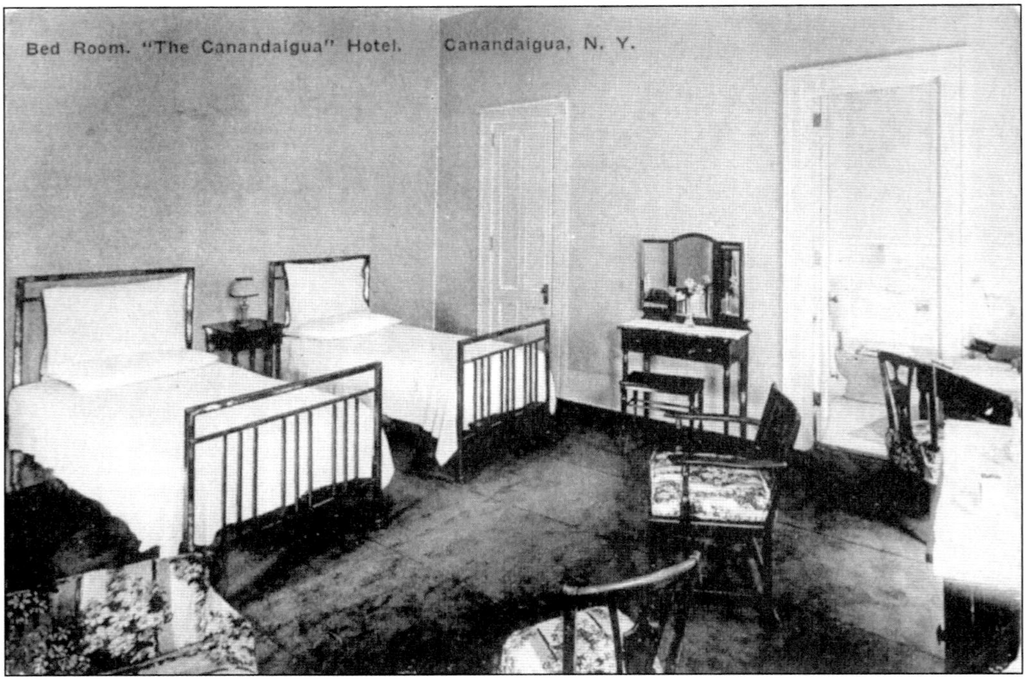

This Gunnison postcard was postmarked in 1924. Notice that the bathroom door was left open to show off the modern plumbing in the hotel. Sparse by today's standards, this was considered a very nice modern room. (Courtesy of the Ontario County Historical Society.)

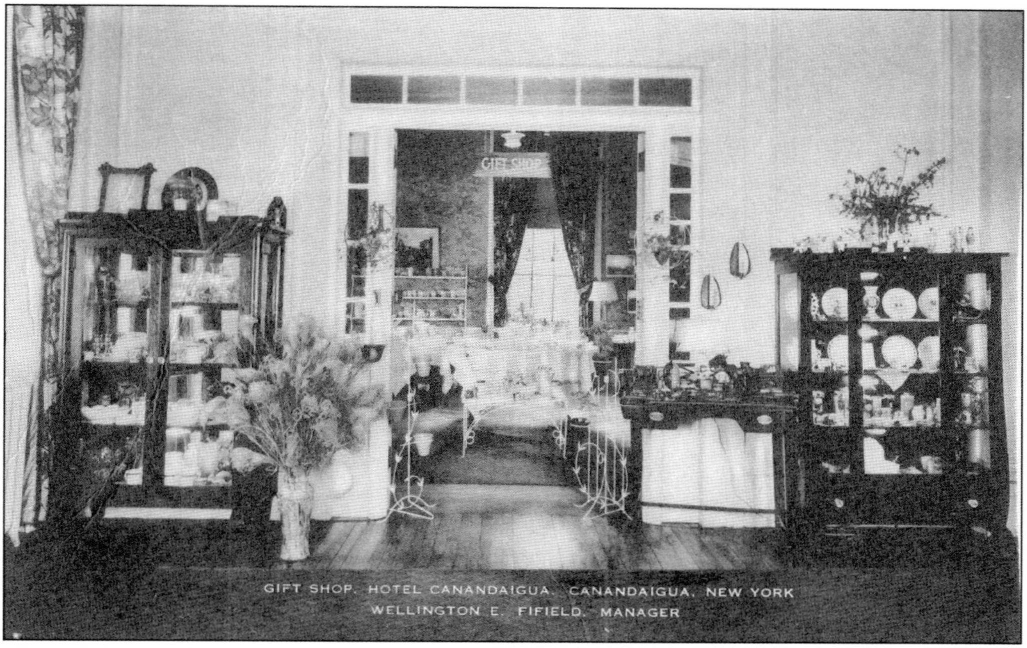

The gift shop at the Canandaigua Hotel offered many popular items of the time. Many of them can be found in antique shops today. (Courtesy of the Ontario County Historical Society.)

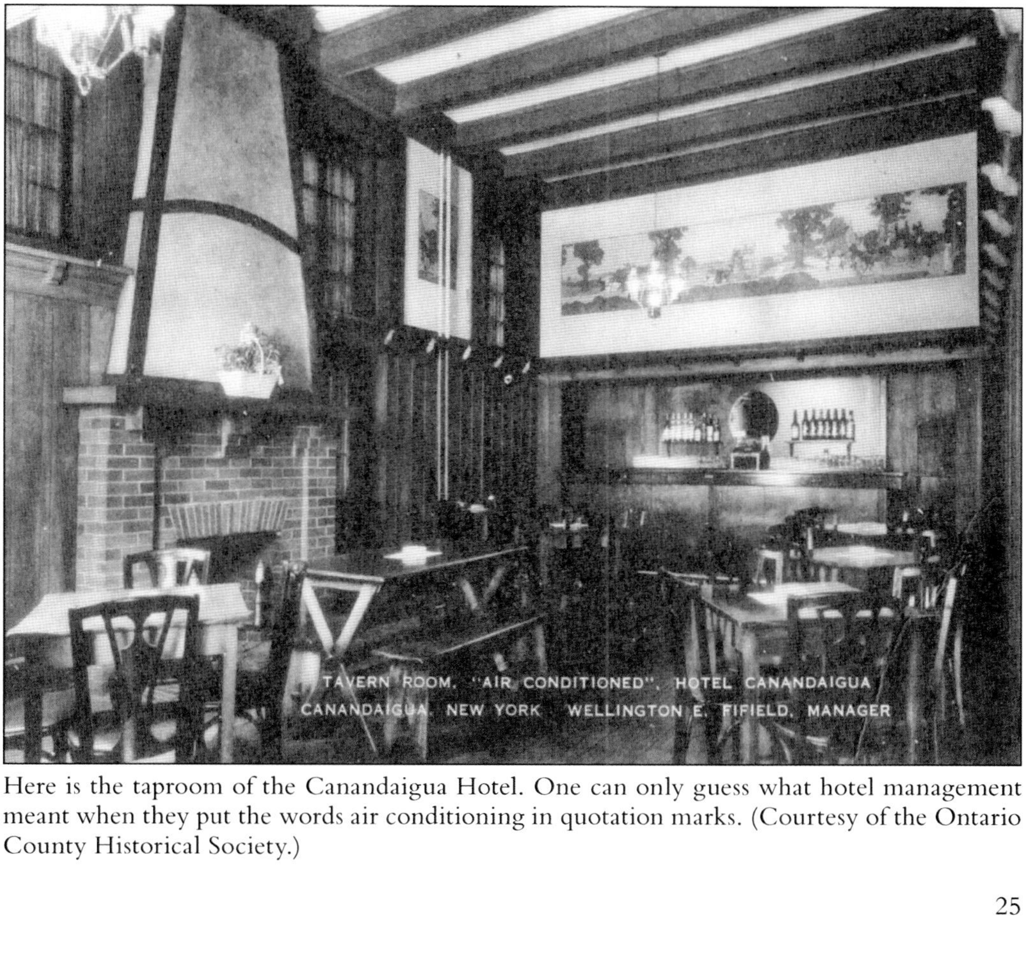

Here is the taproom of the Canandaigua Hotel. One can only guess what hotel management meant when they put the words air conditioning in quotation marks. (Courtesy of the Ontario County Historical Society.)

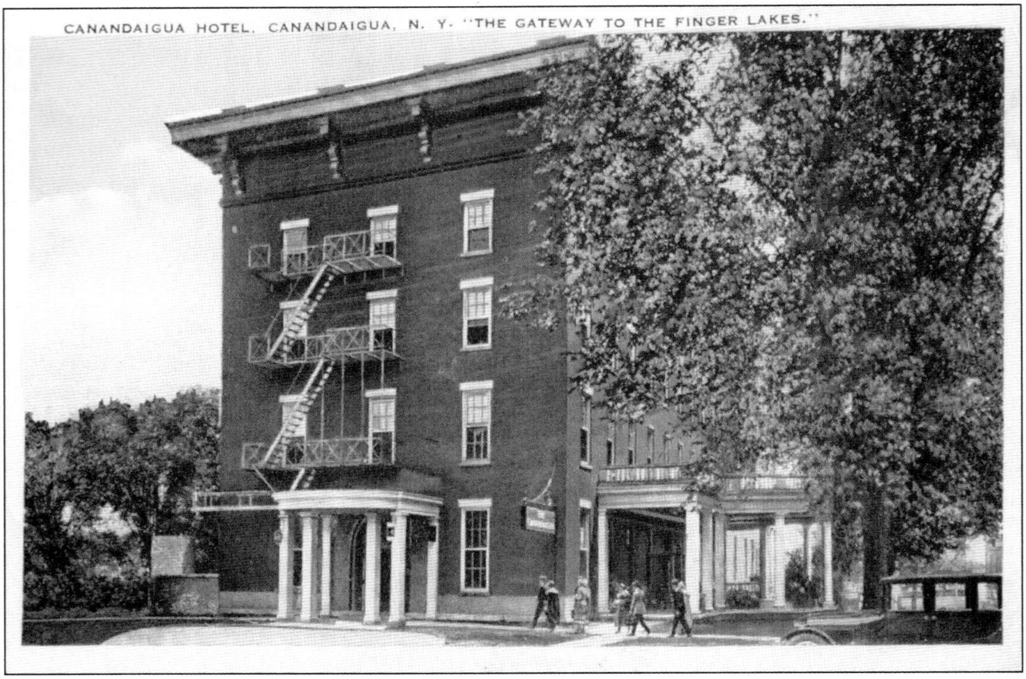

This north side view of the Canandaigua Hotel was made in the late 1920s, judging from the automobile visible in the lower right corner and the expanded porch and portico just to the left of the vehicle. Mary Thompson purchased the building in 1921 and gave it a face-lift. It continued to be a center of Canandaigua's social life for nearly half a century.

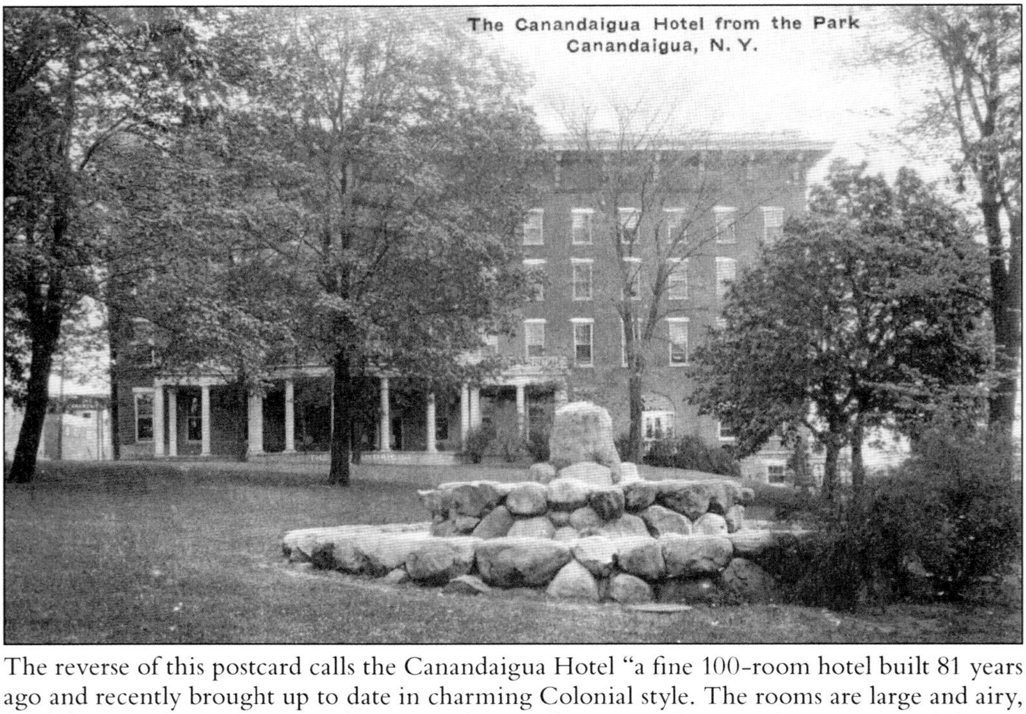

The reverse of this postcard calls the Canandaigua Hotel "a fine 100-room hotel built 81 years ago and recently brought up to date in charming Colonial style. The rooms are large and airy, food the finest." The finest hotel in Canandaigua after Mary Thompson's renovations, it is seen here with a stone fountain, built by John Handrahan, located on the public square.

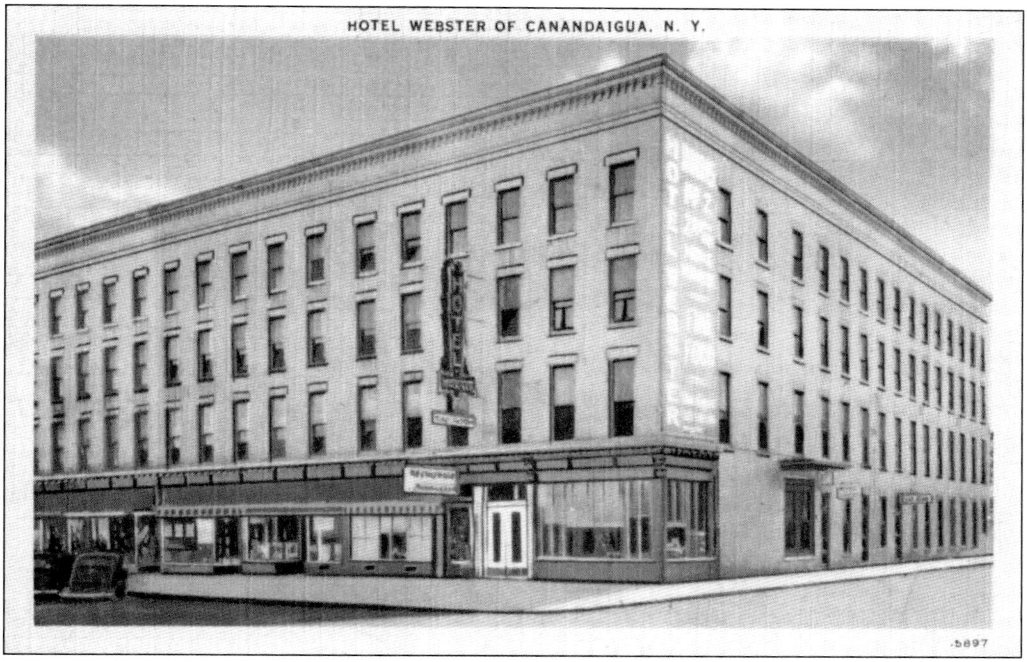

The Hotel Webster, built in 1860, was located at the corner of Coach and Main Streets. Later known as the Pickering Hotel, it burned in 1967 and is now the site of Commons Park. John Surratt, one of the Lincoln assassins, stayed in the hotel in 1865 as he fled from Washington.

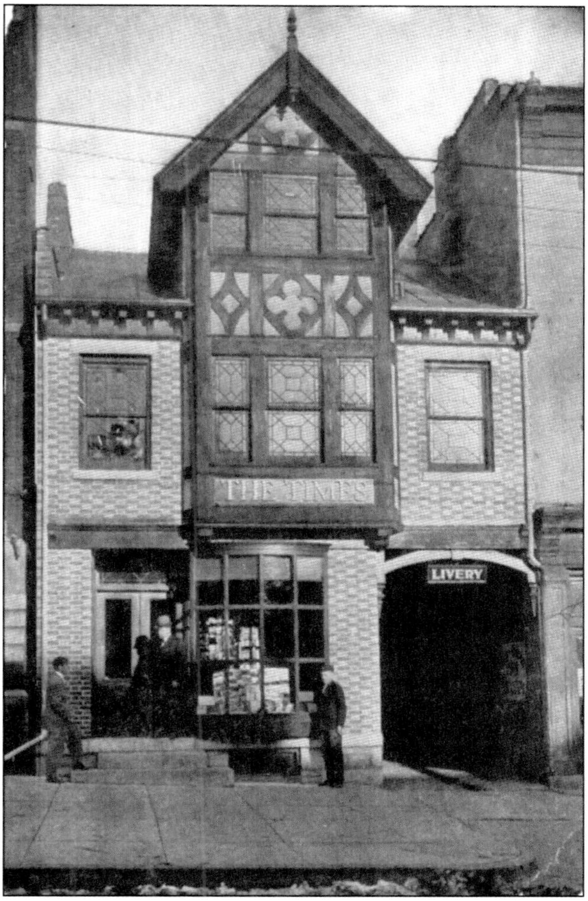

Nathan Milliken established the Times Publishing Company when he came to Canandaigua from Seneca Falls to publish the *Ontario County Republican Times* in 1854. The paper later became the *Ontario County Times-Journal* and ceased publication in 1976. The Times Company published many local history articles, pamphlets, and postcards. Charles Milliken, Nathan's son, founded the Ontario County Historical Society in 1902. This Tudor-style building still stands in the business district.

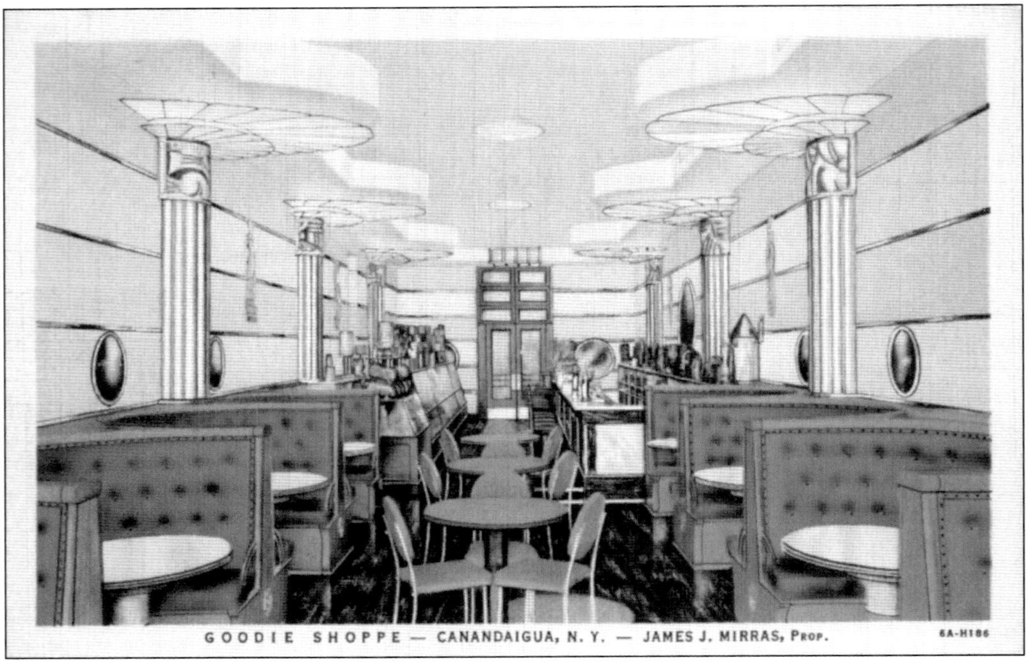

GOODIE SHOPPE — CANANDAIGUA, N. Y. — JAMES J. MIRRAS, PROP. 6A-H186

Known to generations of young people simply as "The Greeks," James Mirras's Goodie Shoppe was a favorite soda fountain at the corner of South Main and Bristol Streets. It was just around the corner from the Playhouse Theatre. "Modern decoration" and air conditioning added to the attraction of homemade candy and ice cream. The store lives on as the Goodie II gift shop.

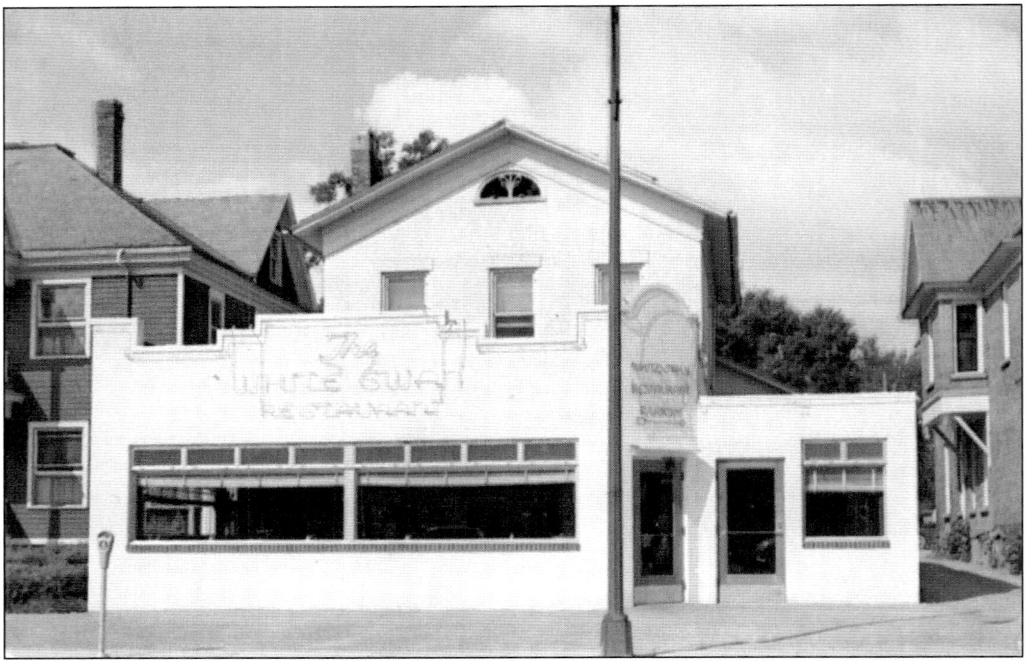

The White Swan Restaurant was located at 254 South Main Street, near Antis Street, on the site of present-day Byrne Dairy. Proprietor George St. Angelo noted that he specialized in turkey and chicken dinners. The restaurant was built in front of two older houses, was remodeled in the 1960s, and finally demolished about 1979. (Photograph by Margery M. Elling.)

Canandaigua National Bank and Trust Company was chartered in 1887. An advertising piece, there is no provision for mailing or message on the reverse of this card.

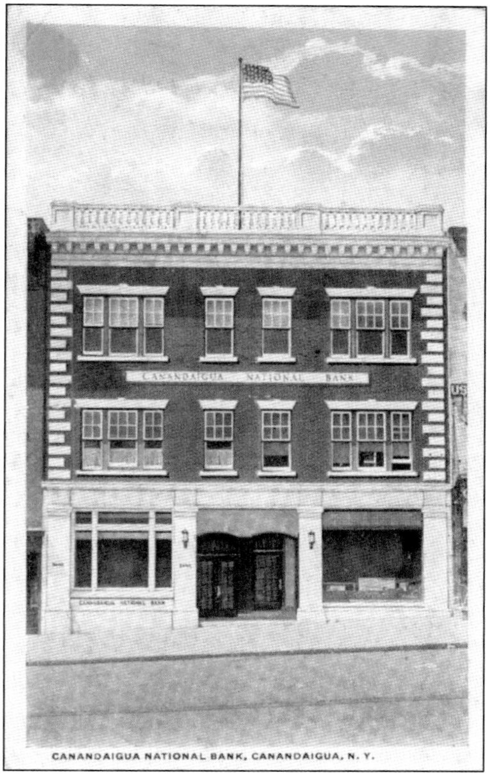

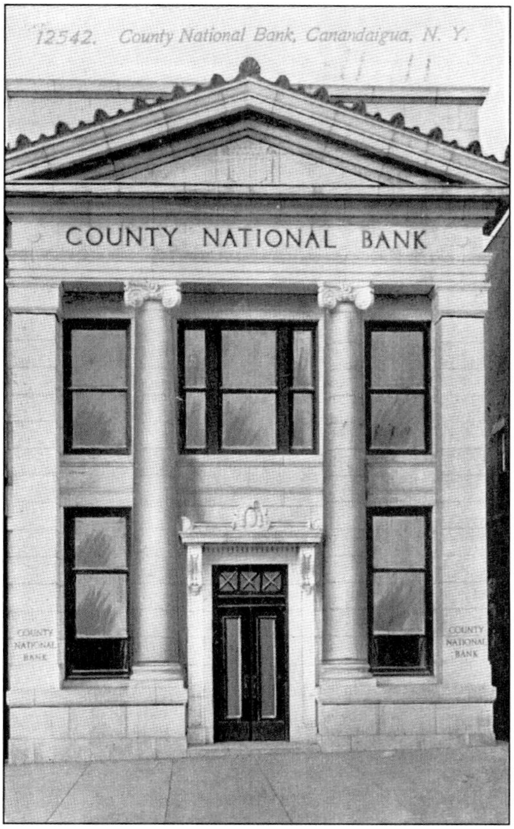

The County National Bank Building was built in 1910 by Ontario County Trust Company. That bank failed during the Great Depression. The building, however, has been used by a succession of banks since that time. Today, J.P. Morgan/Chase Bank occupies the historic structure. Postmarked in 1914, this postcard shows the building as it originally looked.

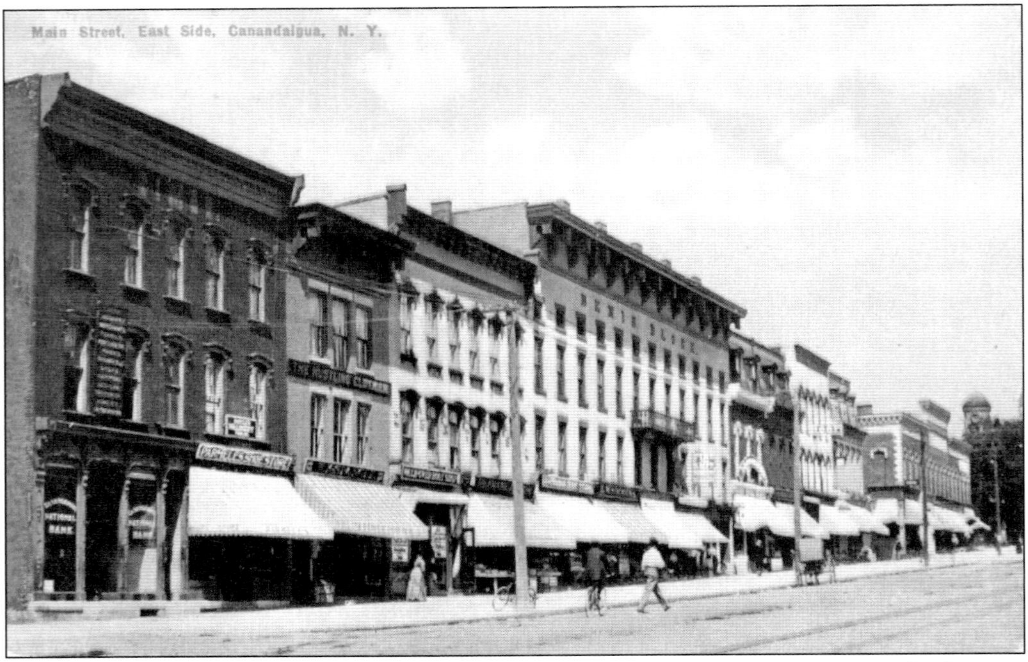

This view of the west side of Main Street was published about 1910 and shows the historic Bemis Block. Built in 1850 by William Bemis, it included a large auditorium and ballroom on the upper floor. Speakers here included Susan B. Anthony, Frederick Douglass, and abolitionist crusader Parker Pillsbury. The Bemis Block survives today, looking much like it has always looked. The building at left is the original location of Canandaigua National Bank.

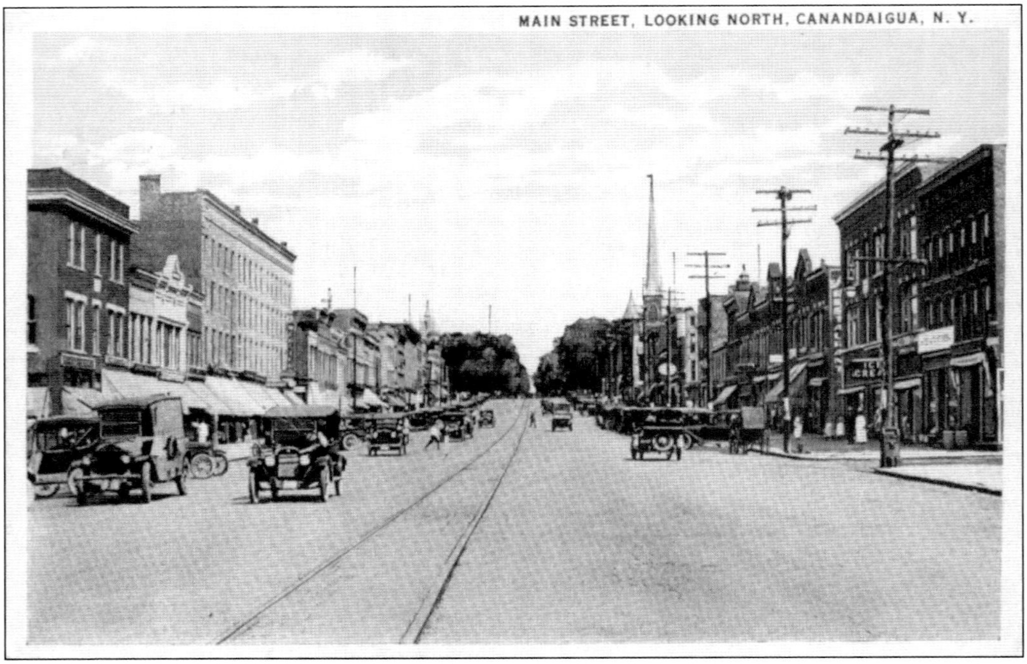

The first electric streetlights were installed in Canandaigua in 1886. The first telephone lines were strung on lower Main Street in 1883. Postmarked in 1910, this postcard clearly shows the poles that were starting to line the streets. The trolley line can be seen over the center of Main Street.

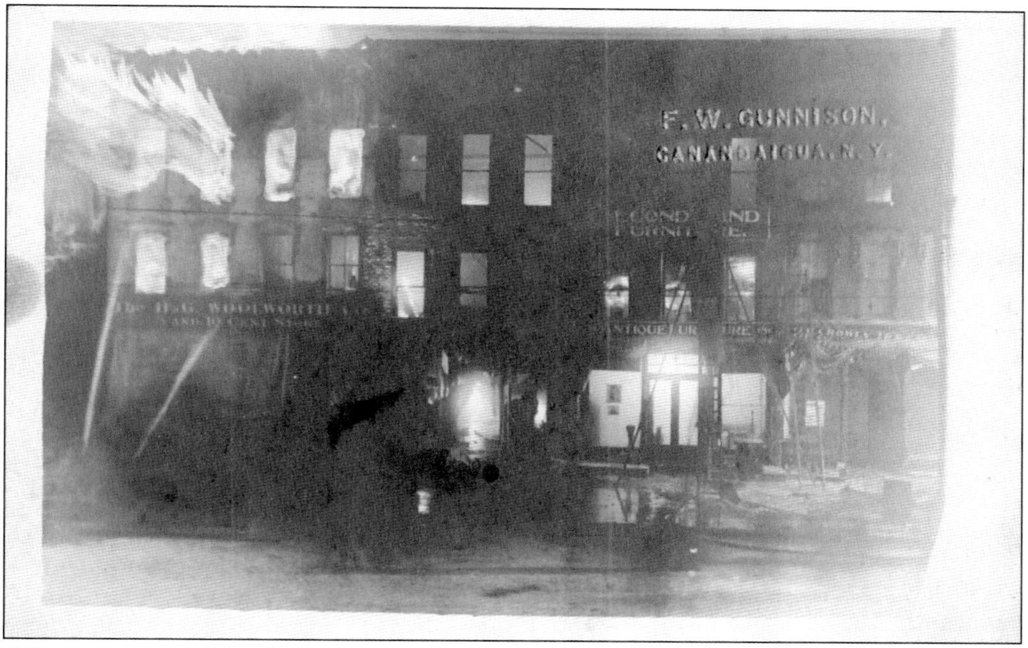

This postcard is a difficult night scene. The photographer took this at a time when film speeds were slow. Several fires devastated the Canandaigua's business district in the late 19th and early 20th centuries. This conflagration raged through the building at the corner of South Main and Beeman Streets in March 1915.

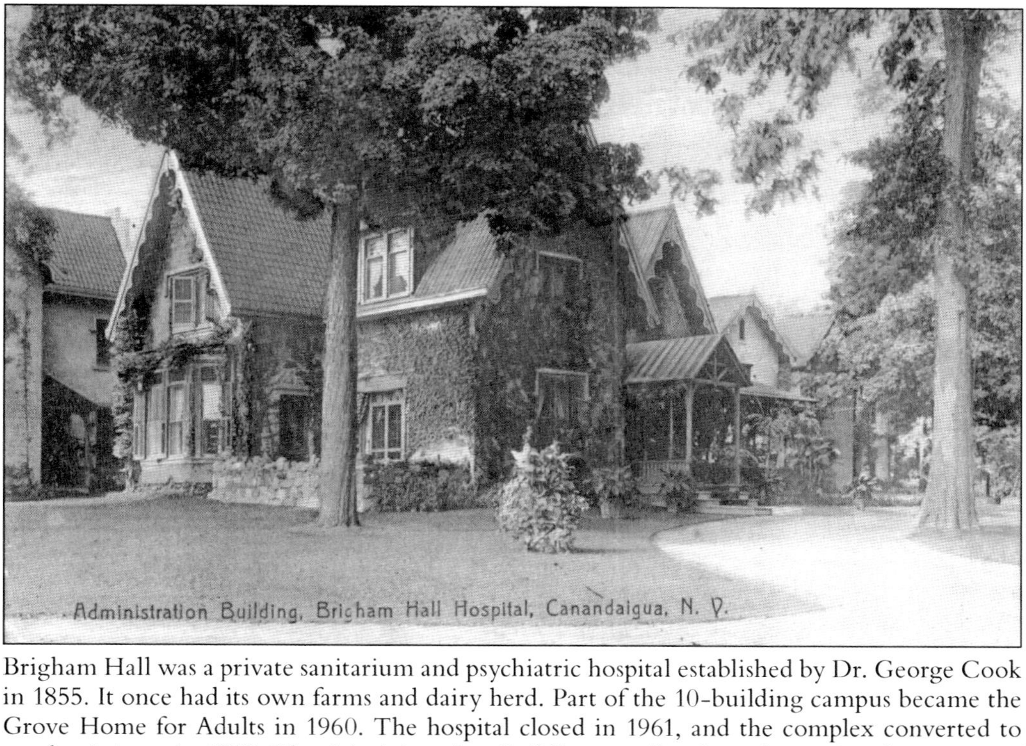

Brigham Hall was a private sanitarium and psychiatric hospital established by Dr. George Cook in 1855. It once had its own farms and dairy herd. Part of the 10-building campus became the Grove Home for Adults in 1960. The hospital closed in 1961, and the complex converted to condominiums in 1979. The Administration Building was listed on the National Register of Historic Places in 1884.

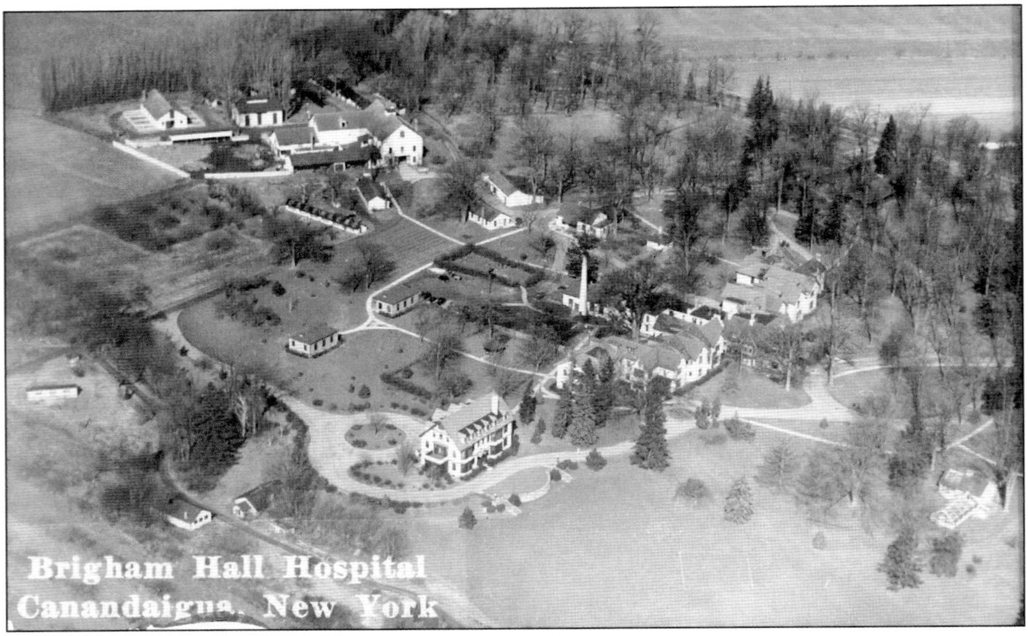

This postcard was certainly produced prior to the closing of Brigham Hall in 1961. It provides a view of the entire complex on upper Bristol Street (top right corner). (Courtesy of the Ontario County Historical Society.)

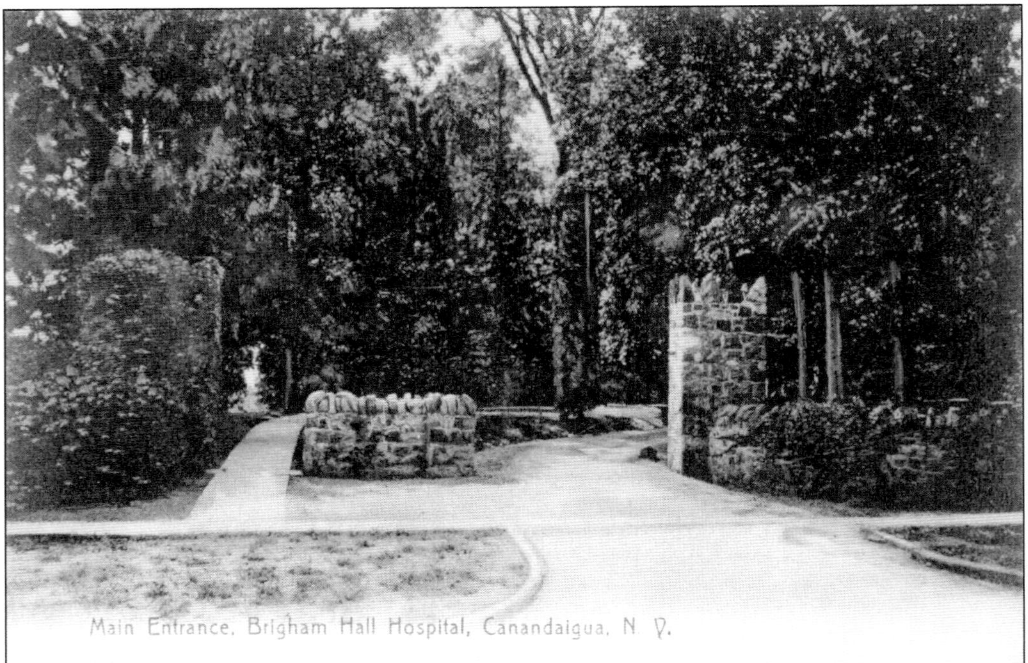

The main entrance to the Brigham Hall grounds has not changed substantially since it was built. Only the low stone structure between the taller pillars flanking the entrance has been removed. Today, this stone passageway provides access to the condominiums and houses in the grove that once housed the sanitarium. This image probably dates from about 1910.

Two

Schools and Public Spaces

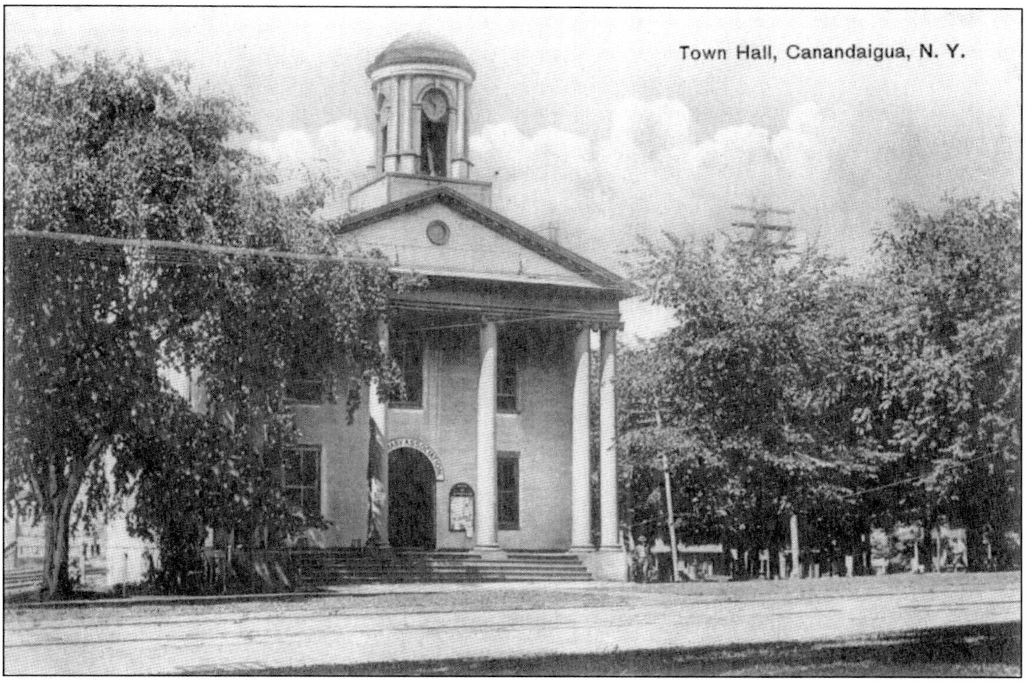

The former Canandaigua Town Hall served as the county courthouse from 1824 to 1858. It was the scene of the first trial of the William Morgan kidnappers in 1826. That crime resulted in the organization of the Anti-Masonic Party. Morgan, a renegade Mason, was kidnapped from the Ontario County jail and never seen alive again. This building serves as city hall today. At the time this image was made, the Wood Library occupied a room on the ground floor.

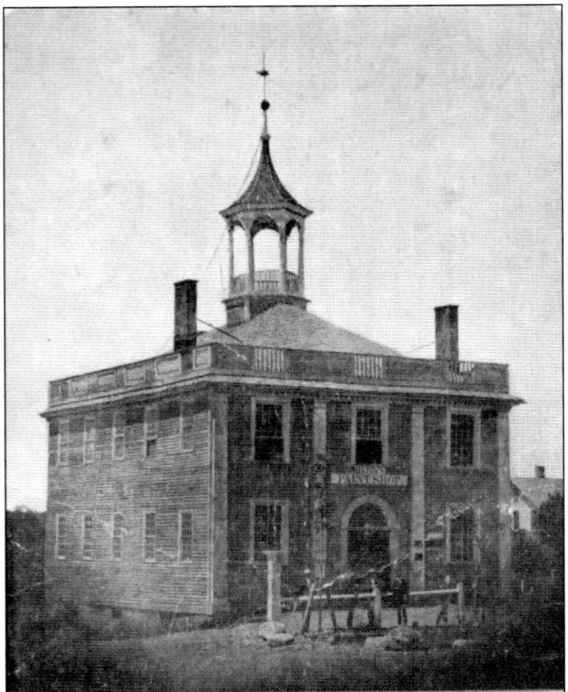

First Court House, Canandaigua, N. Y.

Erected in 1794, on public square, immediately south of present Court House. Was moved in 1825 to N. W. corner of Main and Cross Streets, where it stood when this picture was made and was used as a postoffice; was moved to Coach Street in 1859, used as a store house and was demolished in 1899. Scene of the trial of many famous cases, including that of "Stiff Armed George" whom Redjacket, the Indian orator, defended against the charge of murder.

By the time this postcard was printed, the old 1794 courthouse had been gone for several years. The first courthouse for Ontario County, it stood on the site of the present building. Moved across the street in 1824, it was sawed in half and rolled down to Coach Street in 1859. Known as the Star Building for many years, it was heavily damaged by fire and demolished in 1899.

This view of the courthouse shows the building as it looked in 1857. It was in this original building that the Susan B. Anthony trial took place in June 1873. Anthony was tried by the US government. She voted in the 1872 election because she felt the newly passed 14th Amendment gave her that right. In exchange for federal assistance in building construction, the US government used the north courtroom and located the Canandaigua Post Office here.

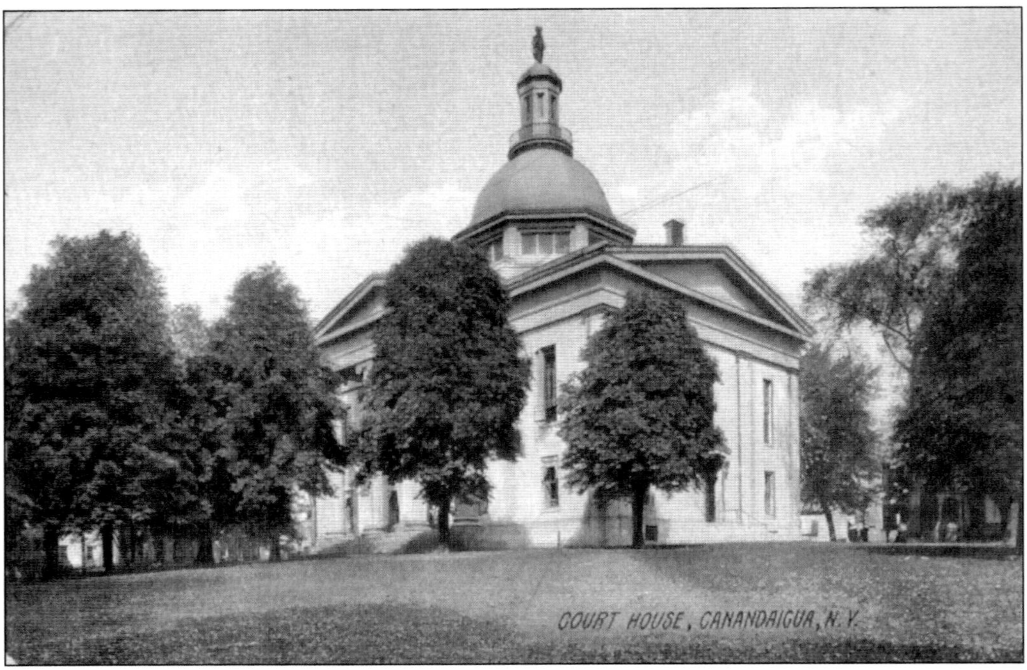

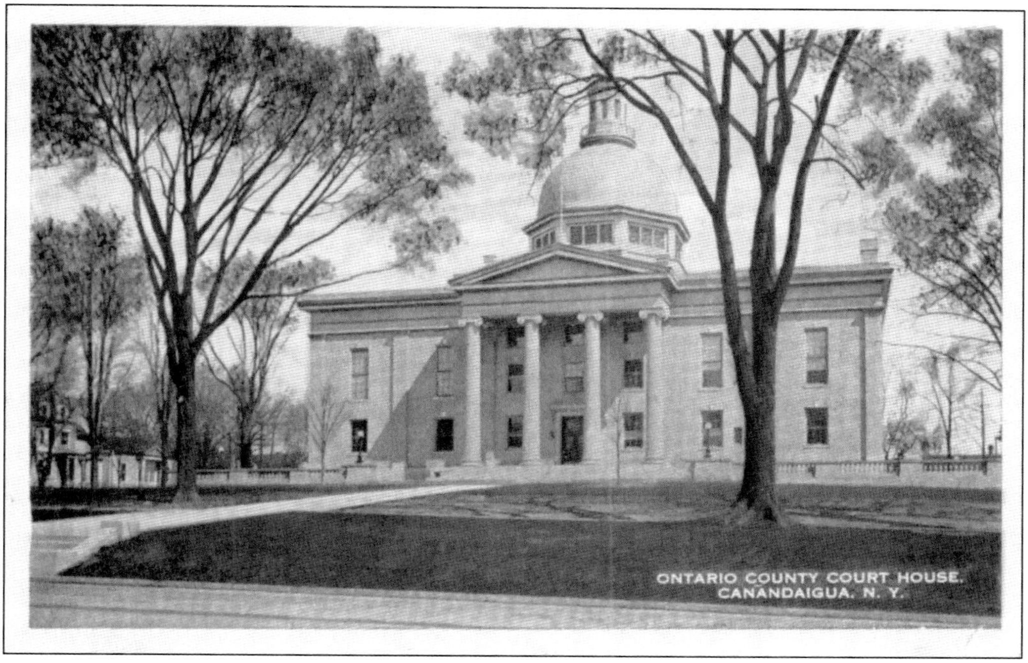

By 1908, the Ontario County Courthouse was in need of repair and too small for the caseload of the courts. That year, the supervisors authorized the enlargement of the building by 50 percent. It was lengthened one bay on each end, and a third floor was inserted. This image was made shortly after the building reopened in 1909.

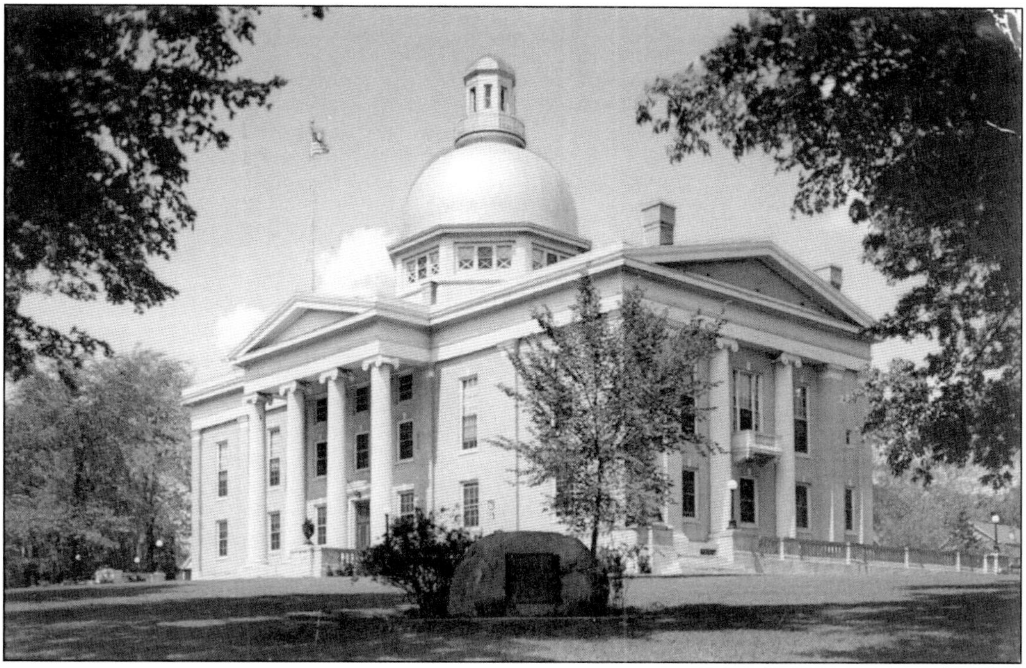

In 1951, the original wooden *Statue of Justice* atop the county courthouse had rotted beyond repair. That year, it was removed. For a decade, there was no statue over the dome. This postcard was produced during that time. (Photograph by Margery M. Elling.)

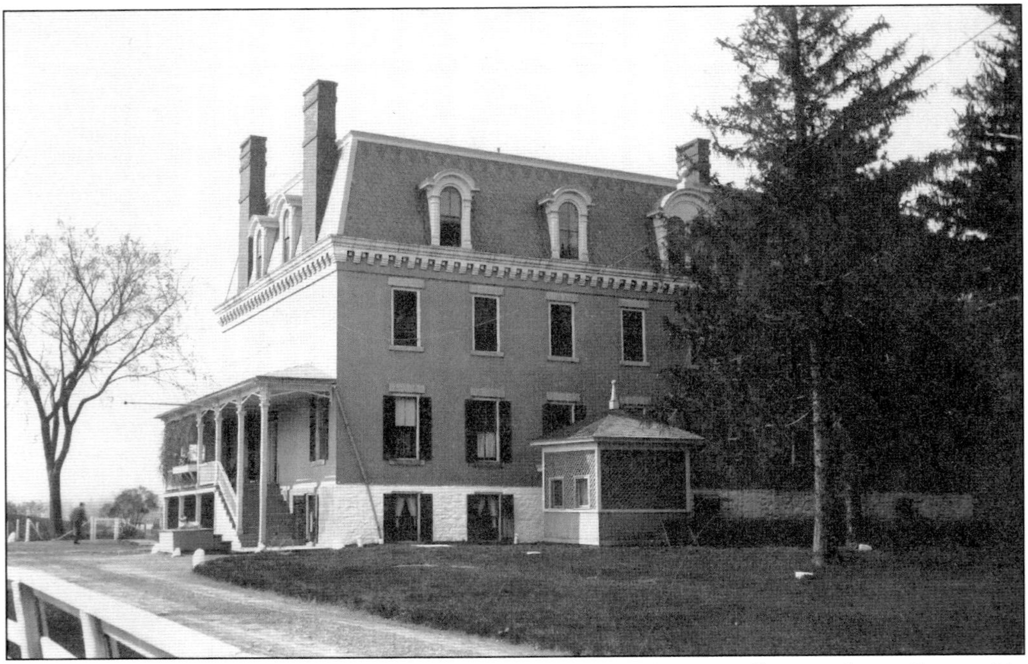

The Ontario County Poor House was opened in the town of Hopewell, just a few miles outside Canandaigua, after Ontario County established a "poor farm" in 1825. The farm supported those receiving "indoor relief" here, as well as the inmates of the county jail. This building was finally replaced in 1926, long after it was first condemned by the state.

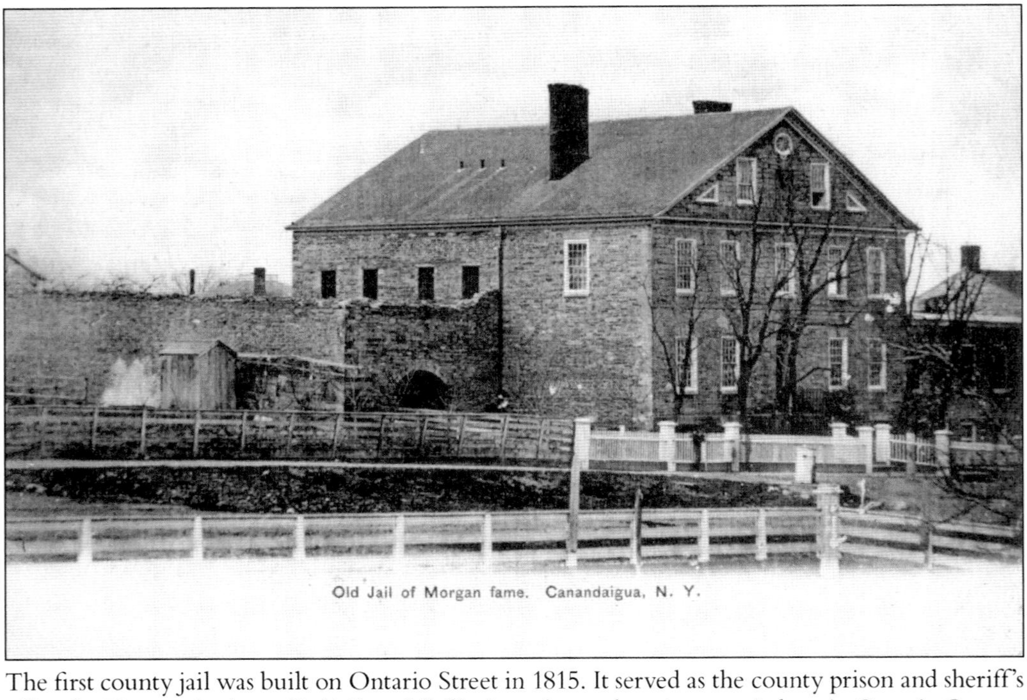

The first county jail was built on Ontario Street in 1815. It served as the county prison and sheriff's office for 79 years. In the walled jail yard (left), the only two hangings carried out in Ontario County took place in 1876 and 1889. From this jail, renegade Mason William Morgan was kidnapped in 1826. The nationwide Anti-Masonic political movement grew out of that incident.

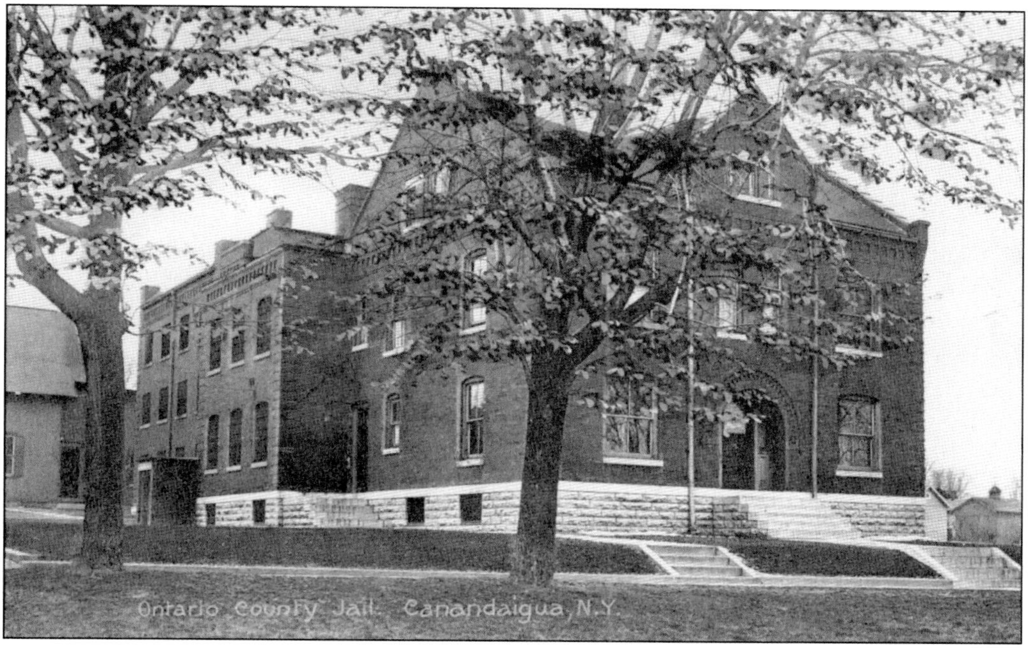

In 1894, Ontario County built a new jail just to the north of the 1815 building. This building served as the county jail until 1961, when a third was built to the right on the original site. The front part of the building continued to be used into the 1980s. The site of this building and the site of the 1815 jail are now occupied by the Ontario County Department of Information Services.

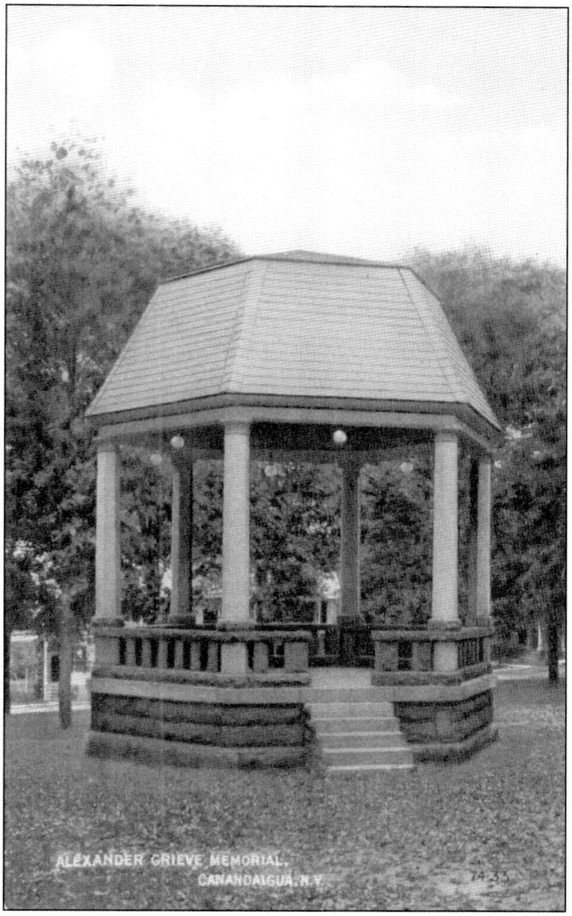

The bandstand on Public Square is really a memorial to local businessman Alexander Grieve. It replaced an earlier wooden bandstand on the same site and was erected in 1912. It continues to be the centerpiece for that part of the public square known as Atwater Park. This postcard was produced before 1925.

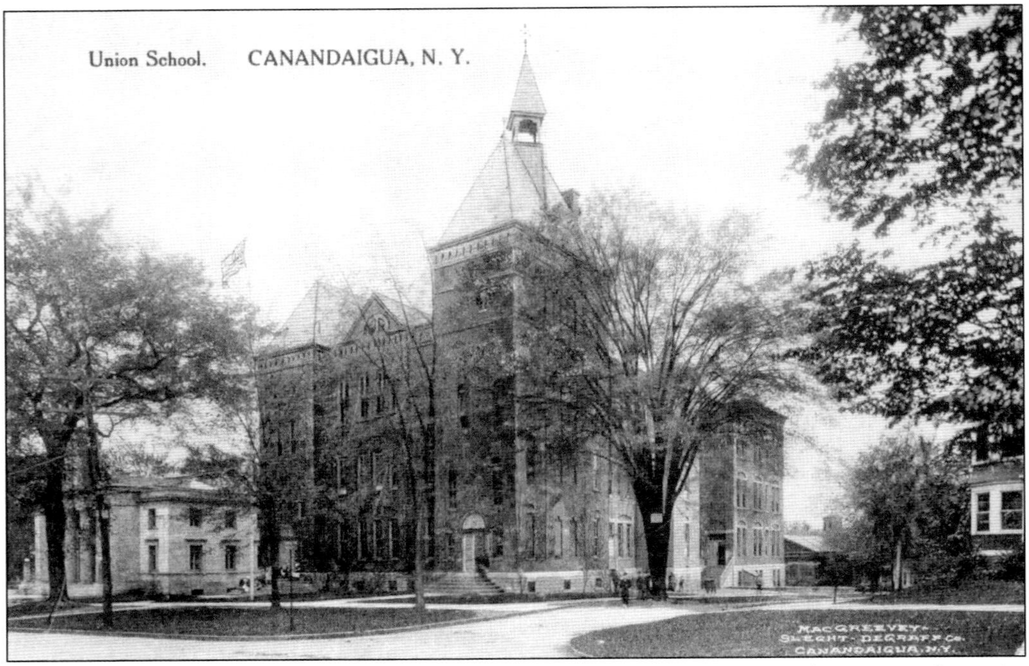

The Union School stood on North Main Street from 1876 to 1951. It took its name from the fact that the building housed upper elementary students from a union of several small village school districts. For a brief period prior to 1907, the old Union School provided the first few years of public high school instruction for Canandaigua. (Courtesy of the Ontario County Historical Society.)

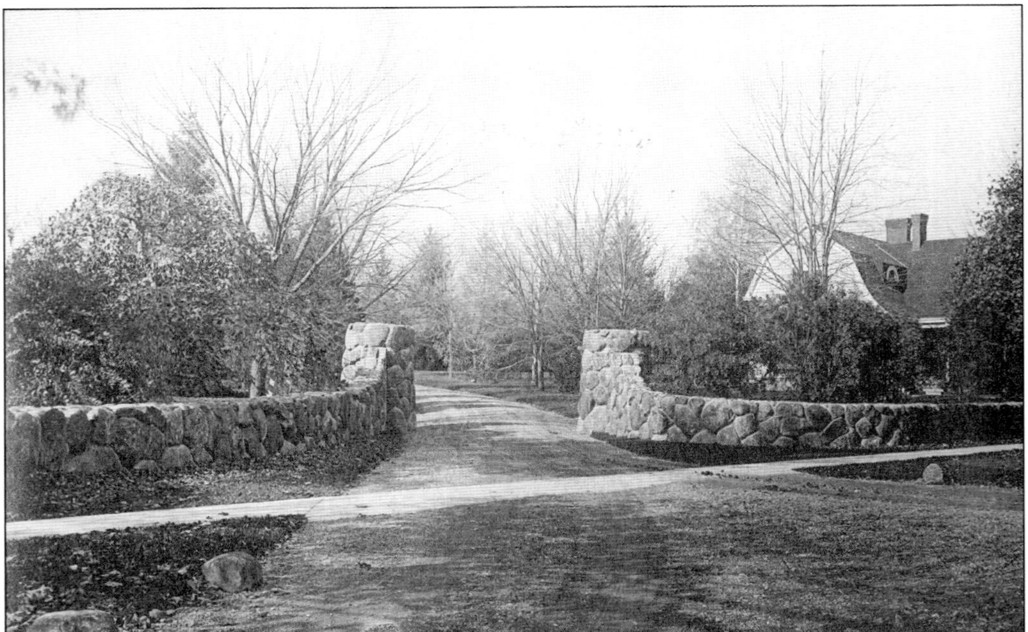

Landscape architect John Handrahan, working at Mary Thompson's direction, produced the stone wall across the entrance to Woodlawn Cemetery in 1909. Opened in 1887, Woodlawn was modeled on the landscaped, "rural" cemeteries that became popular by the mid-19th century.

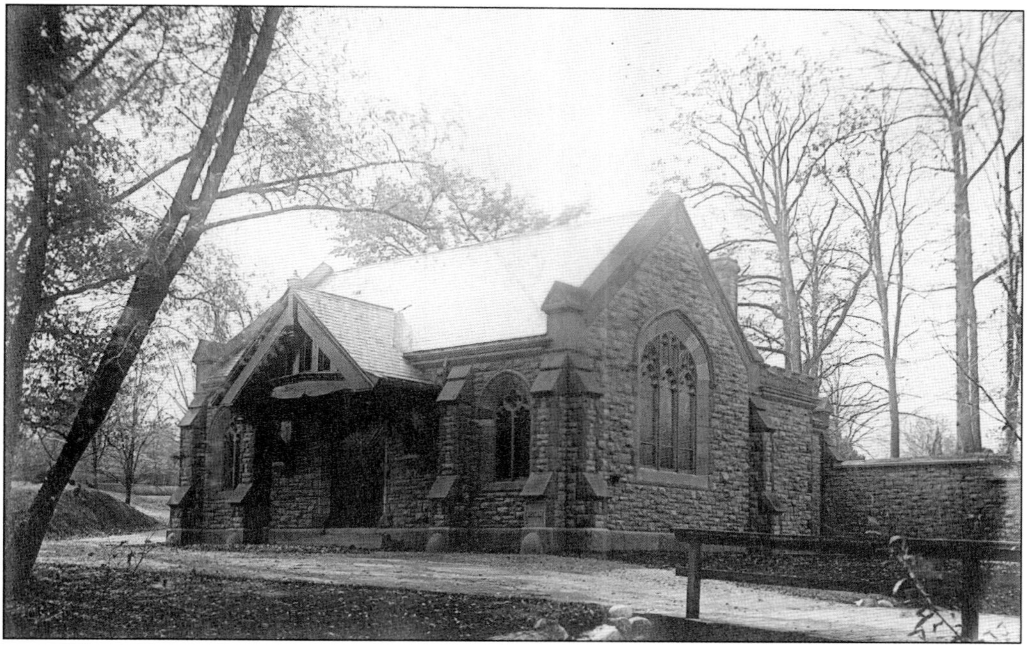

Mary Thompson paid for this chapel in Woodlawn Cemetery, dedicated in 1910. It replaced a small burial vault and provided space for funeral services. Constructed of limestone, it has a slate roof. Today, a covered portico extends out over the road.

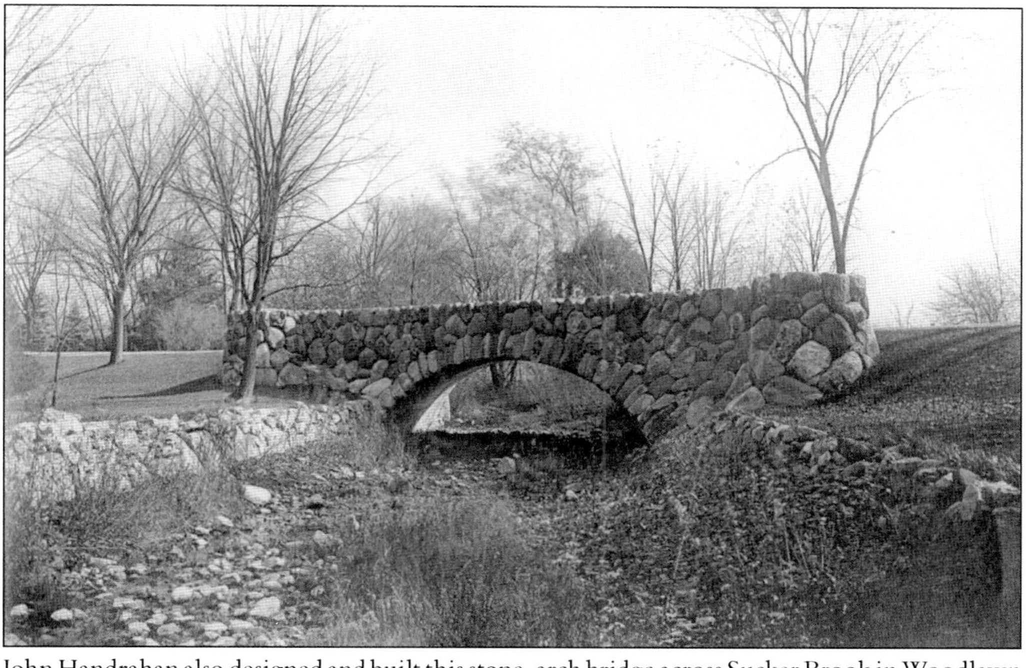

John Handrahan also designed and built this stone-arch bridge across Sucker Brook in Woodlawn Cemetery. Such architectural enhancements lent an air of serenity and permanence to the grounds. They also invited public visits and use of the cemetery as a kind of memorial park.

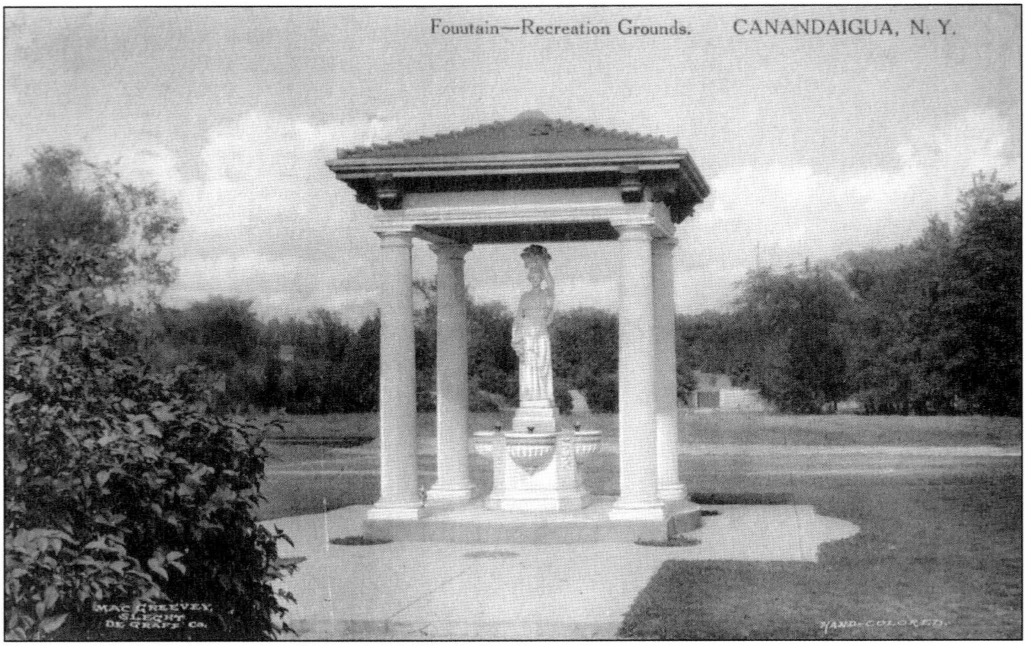

This fountain was the focal point of the recreation grounds, known as Sonnenberg Playground, donated to Canandaigua by Mary Thompson in 1901. Most of the fountain still stands on its original site in the center of the park on Howell Street. The statue itself has been frequently vandalized over the years. This postcard was postmarked in 1910. The sender reported being "through Sonnenberg at Canandaigua today. It is grand."

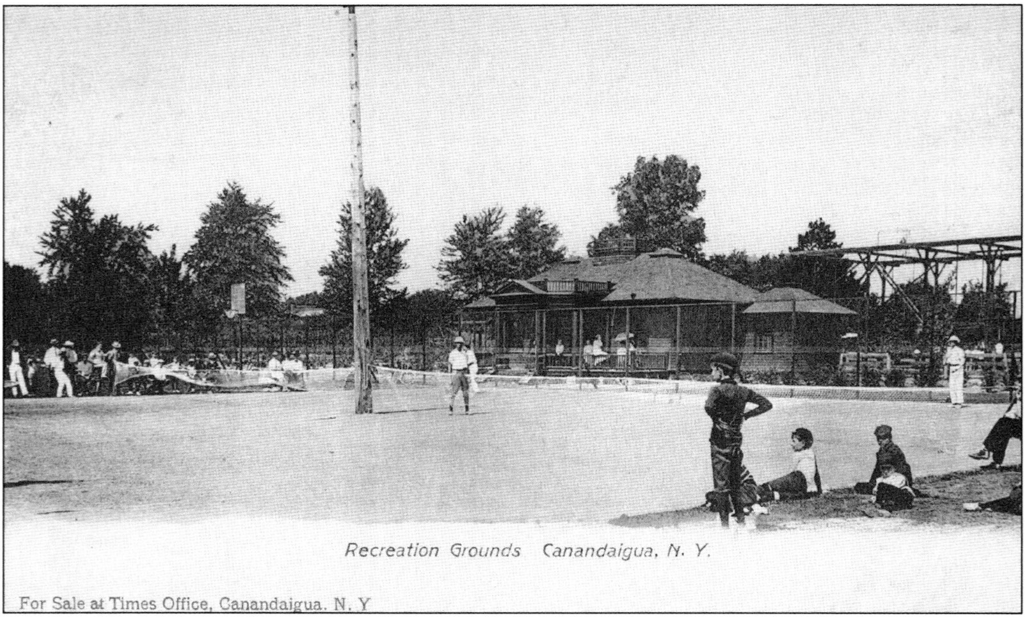

The Sonnenberg Recreation Grounds offered well-kept tennis courts, a baseball diamond, and a large and extensive wooden complex for gymnastics. Formal instruction, sponsored by the schools and the YMCA, provided some of the first true physical education classes in Canandaigua. Today, Sonnenberg Recreation Ground is one of Canandaigua's city parks. This postcard was produced prior to 1907. (Courtesy of the Ontario County Historical Society.)

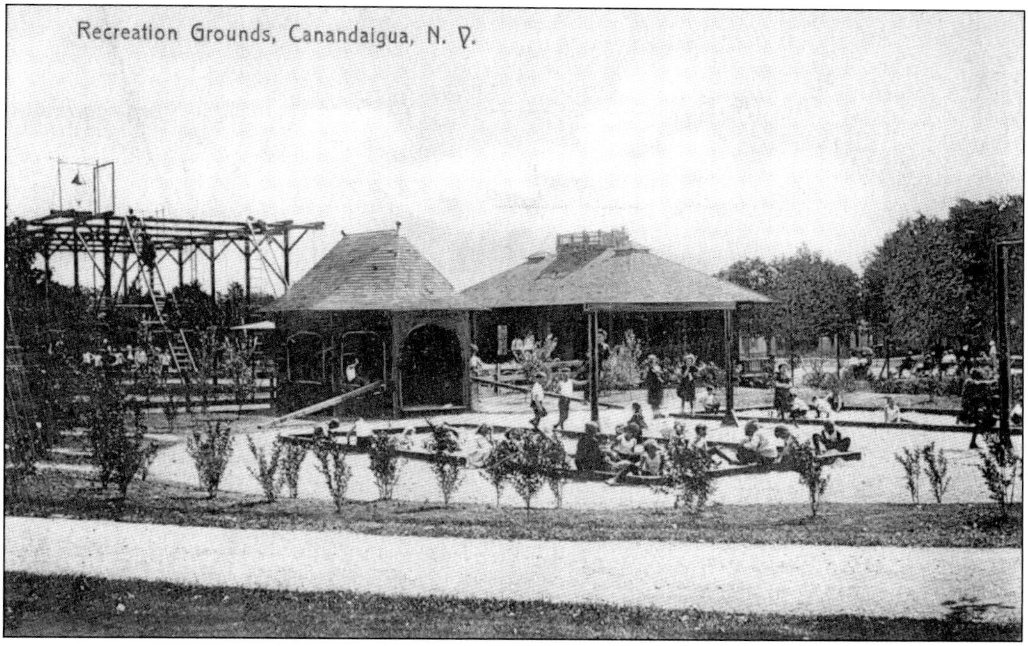

This image of the Sonnenberg Recreation Grounds gives a clear view of the large gymnastic apparatus, as well as the spacious and popular sand box. (Courtesy of the Ontario County Historical Society.)

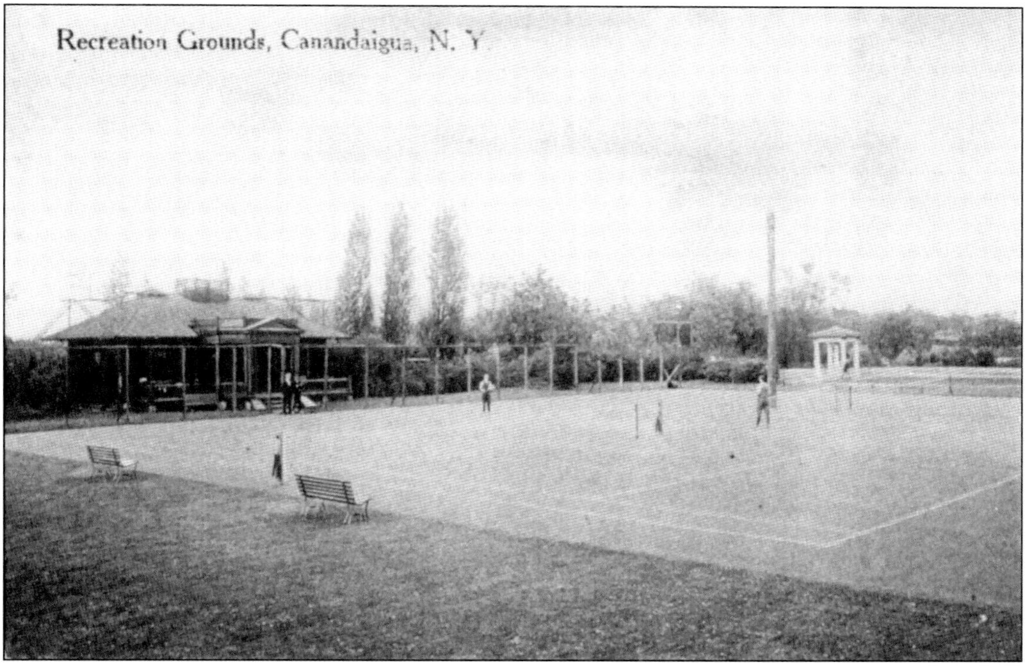

The elaborate fountain can be seen in the right center background, in view of the tennis courts. (Courtesy of the Ontario County Historical Society.)

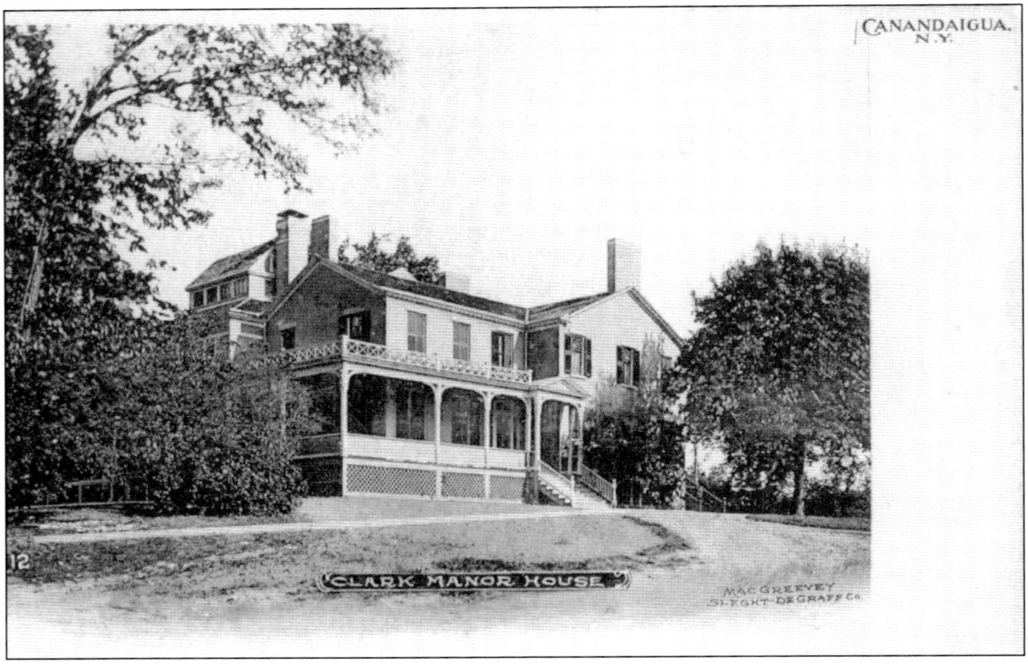

Another example of Mary Thompson's generosity was her endowment of the Clark Manor House, near the Sonnenberg Estate, on Fort Hill Avenue. Opened in 1900, she called it her least annoying charity. More than a century later, the Manor House is still serving elderly residents.

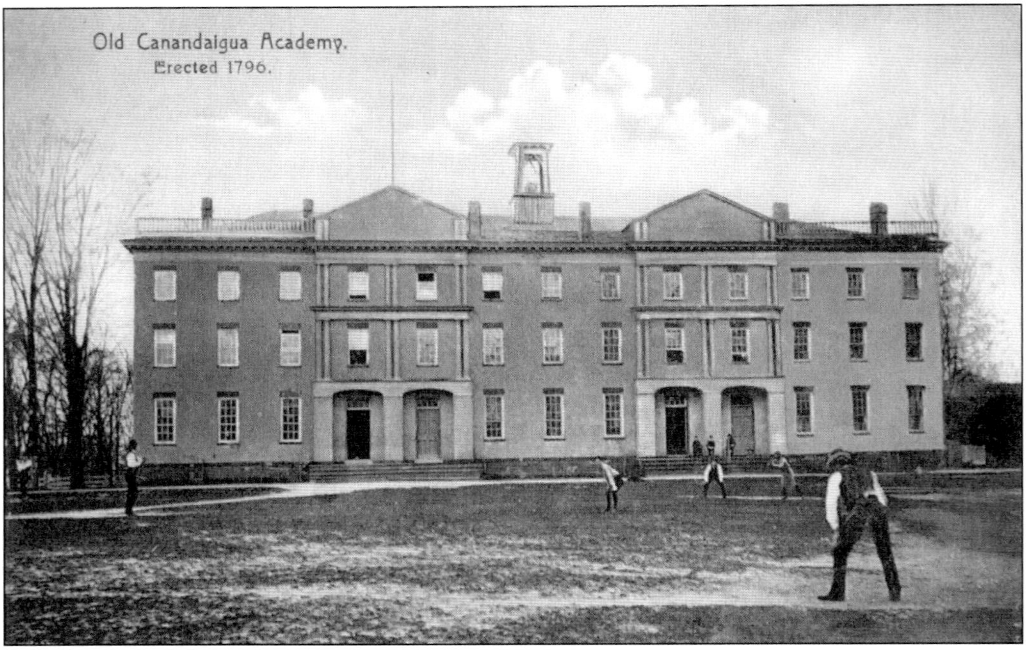

Oliver Phelps and Nathaniel Gorham endowed Canandaigua Academy with a gift of over 6,000 acres of land. Originally a private school for boys, its most famous graduate is Stephen A. Douglas. When the old school closed in 1899, its assets and name were given to the public school board. The original building was completed in 1804. It was enlarged in 1834 and finally demolished in 1905.

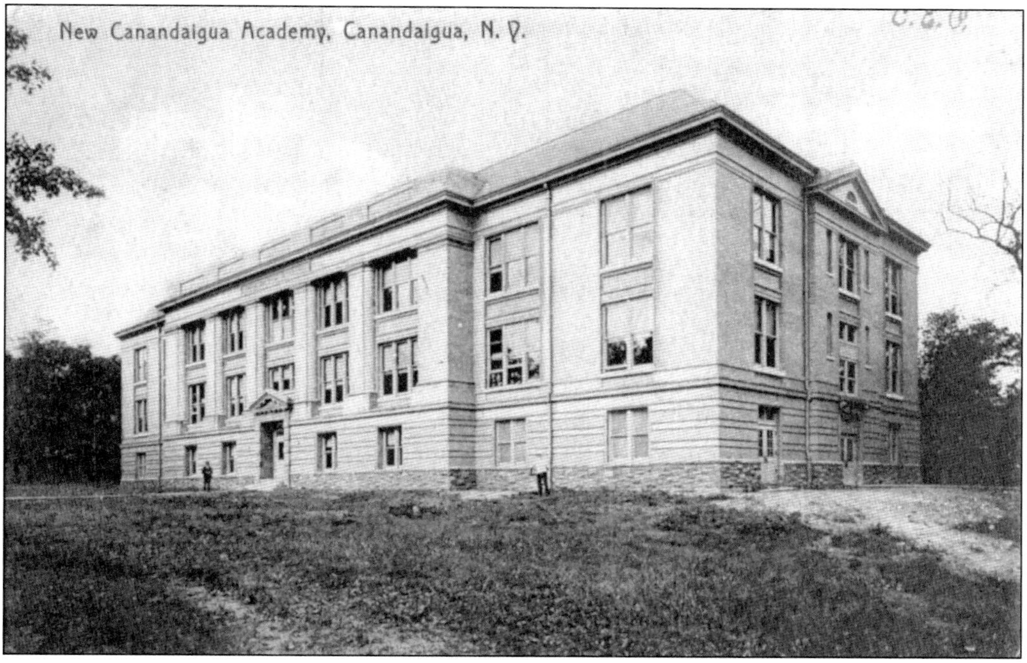

In 1907, this new public high school building, known by the traditional name of Canandaigua Academy, was opened at the corner of Fort Hill Avenue and North Main Street. In 1929, an annex was built in the rear of this building to contain an auditorium, swimming pool, gymnasium, classrooms, and an industrial arts shop.

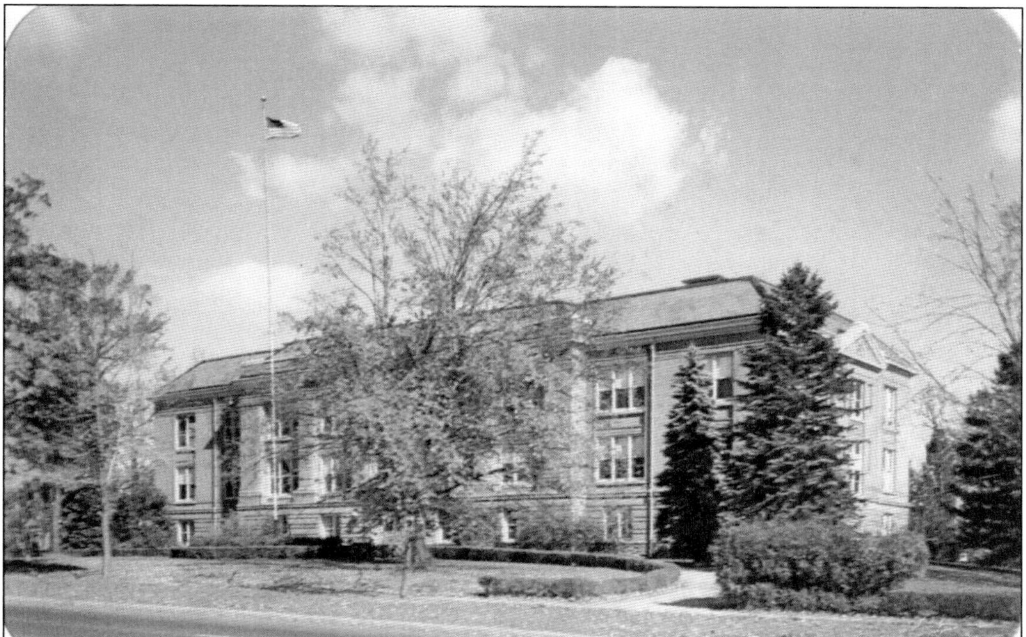

This postcard shows the academy's building, now an apartment building, as it looked in the 1950s. After many years of debate, a new building was opened at the end of Granger Street in 1963. This building served as a Junior Academy for the seventh and eighth grades until the current academy opened on East Street in 1992. (Photograph by Margery M. Elling.)

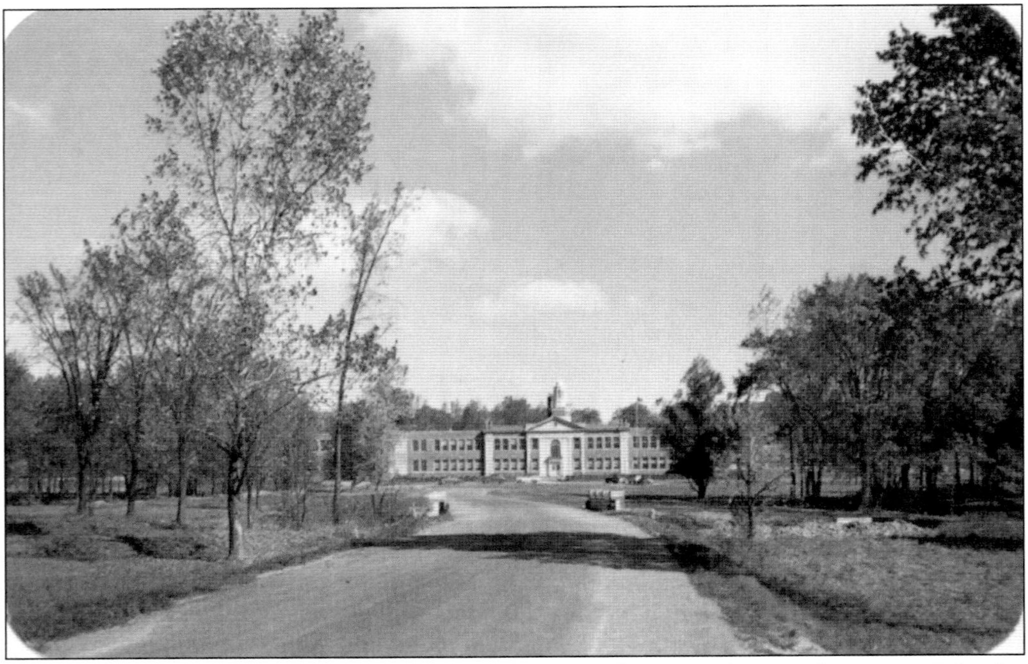

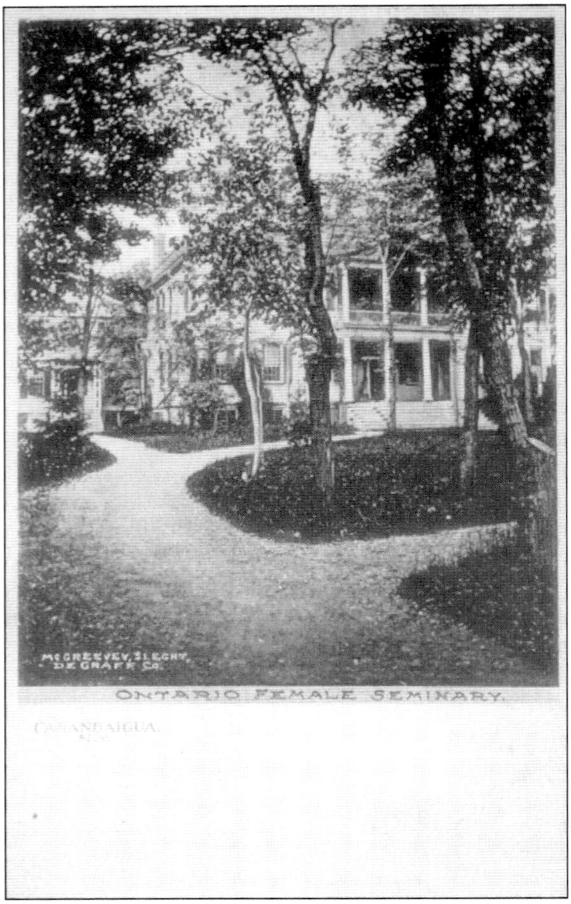

The Canandaigua Elementary School opened in 1950 and was located off North Pearl Street. It ended the need for ward schools and many of the rural schoolhouses. For the first time, elementary students would ride busses and eat in a cafeteria. This picture was made shortly after the elementary school opened. (Photograph by Margery M. Elling.)

The Ontario Female Seminary was a private school for girls, located on North Main Street, where Thompson Hospital was built in 1904. Among the distinguished graduates of this school was Caroline Cowles Richards, author of *Village Life in America*.

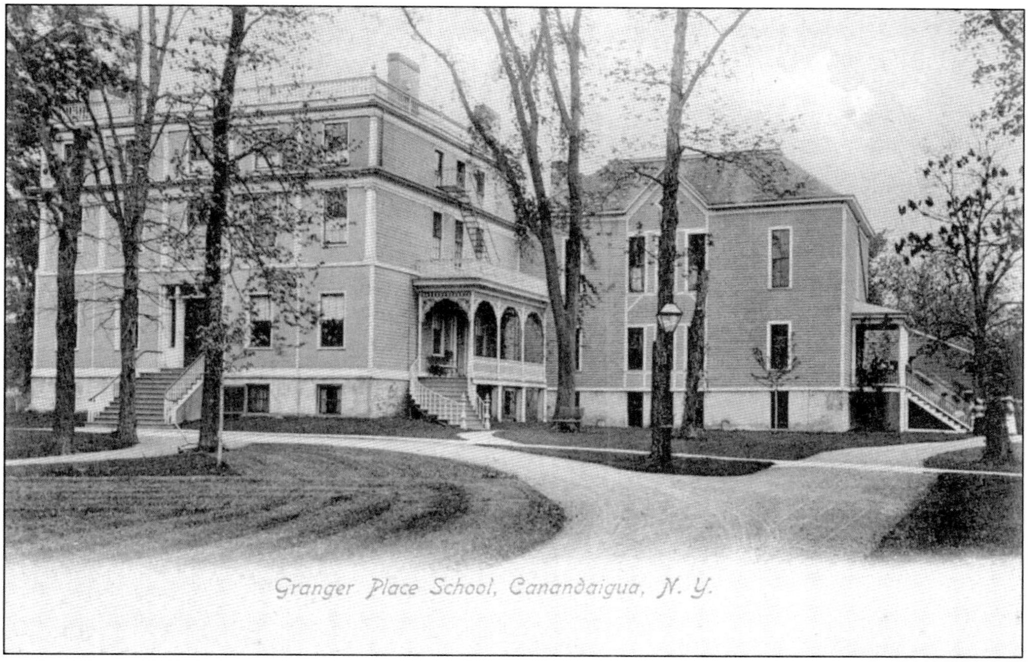

The Granger Place School opened in 1876. For 30 years, a private college preparatory school for girls occupied the old homestead and the classroom wing at the right rear. The wing was later moved to the rear of the property and houses the Carriage Museum today. This picture was probably made during the final year of the Granger Place School.

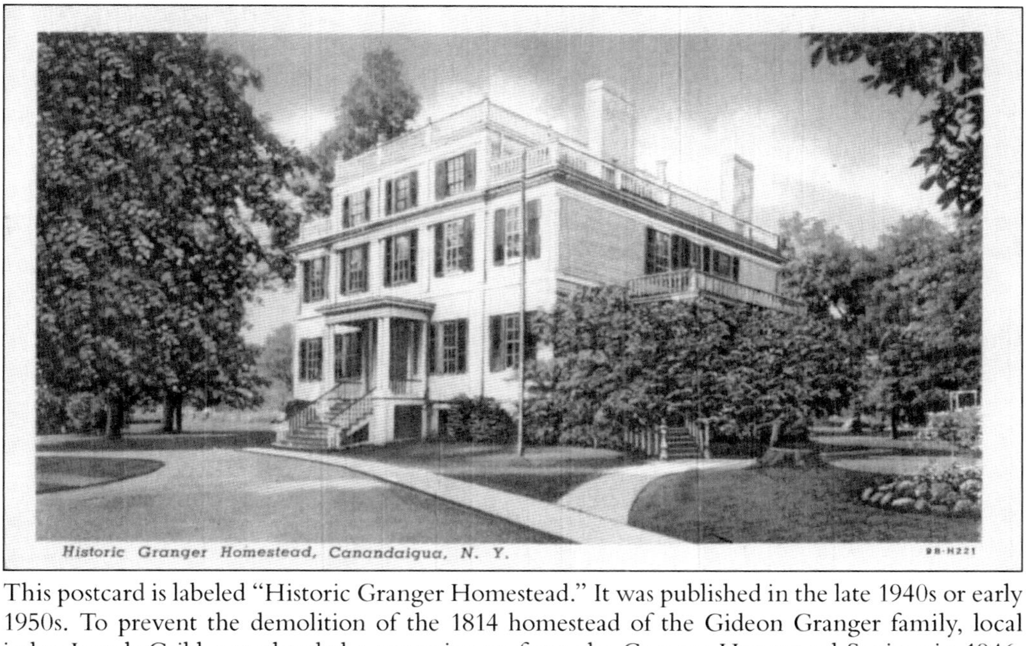

This postcard is labeled "Historic Granger Homestead." It was published in the late 1940s or early 1950s. To prevent the demolition of the 1814 homestead of the Gideon Granger family, local judge Joseph Cribb spearheaded a campaign to form the Granger Homestead Society in 1946. Today, that organization continues to operate the homestead as a historic house museum.

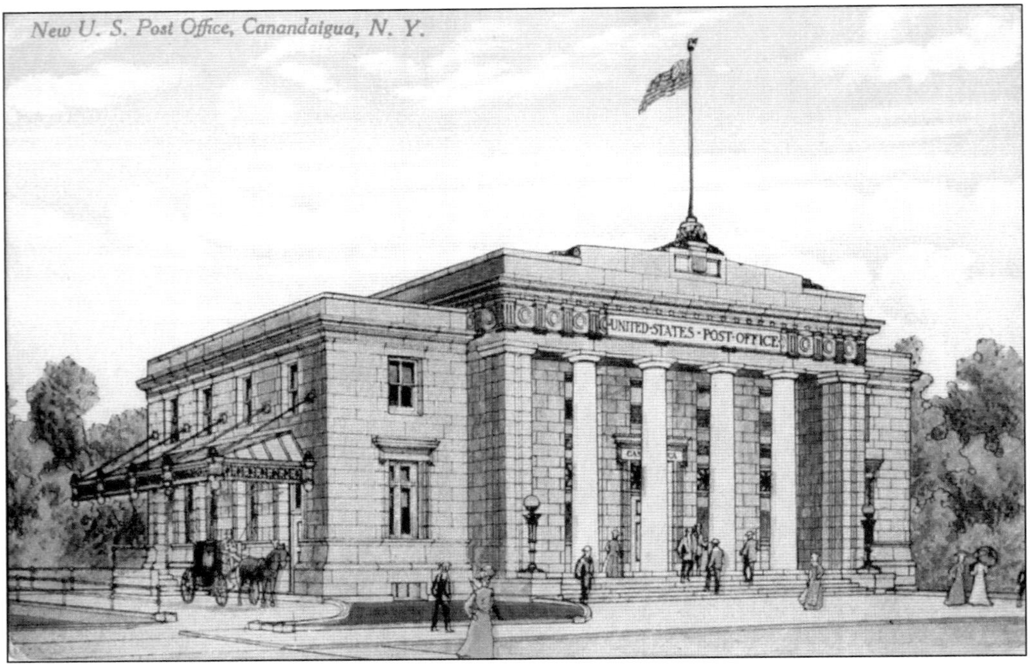

Deliberations over moving the post office moved slowly, as plans for courthouse expansion progressed. Finally, Mary Thompson paid for an architect to design the building and presented the plans to the postal service. This postcard was produced before the building was completed in 1911, demonstrating the excitement it generated.

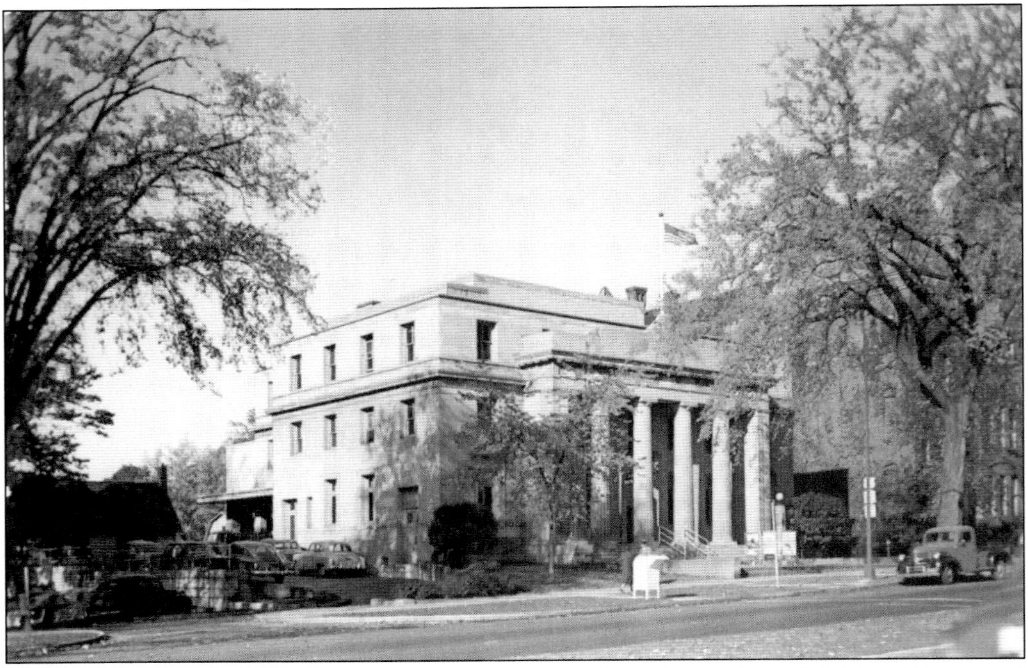

This mid-1950s postcard of the Canandaigua Post Office shows the old Union School still standing at right. The third-floor federal courtroom was added to the post office in 1935. Today, the Post Office Building is attached to an enlarged YMCA and is an integral part of that complex. (Photograph by Margery M. Elling.)

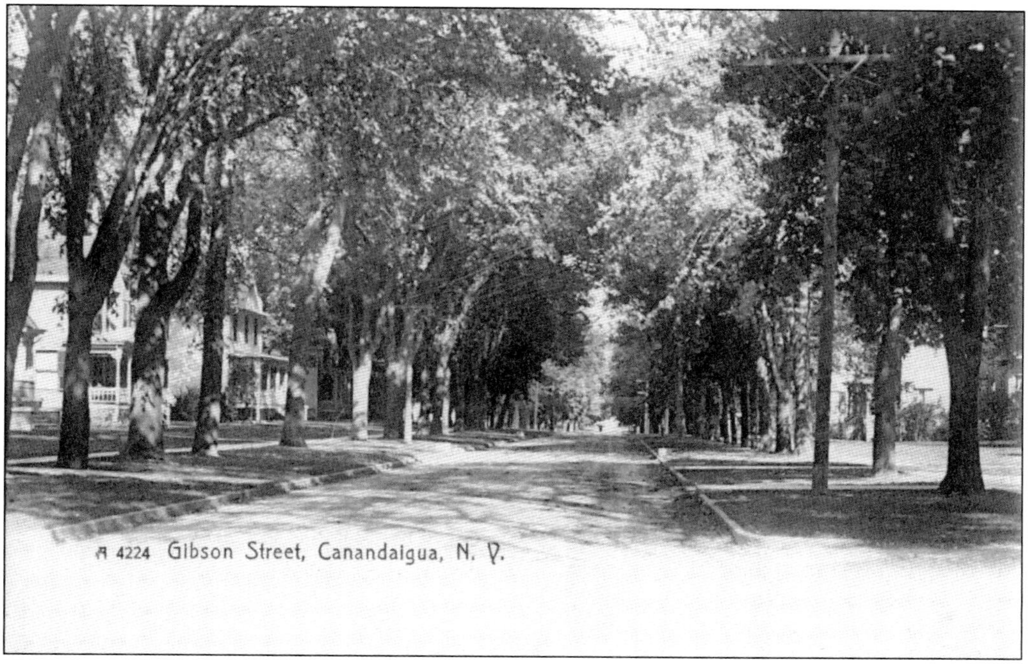

Henry B. Gibson, a prominent banker and businessman before the Civil War, opened Gibson Street in 1825. He bought the 1792 Abner Barlow house and farm and moved the house. Gibson Street led north to Chapin's Mills, Shortsville, Manchester, and the Erie Canal at Palmyra. Gibson developed Port Gibson on the canal, which opened in 1825.

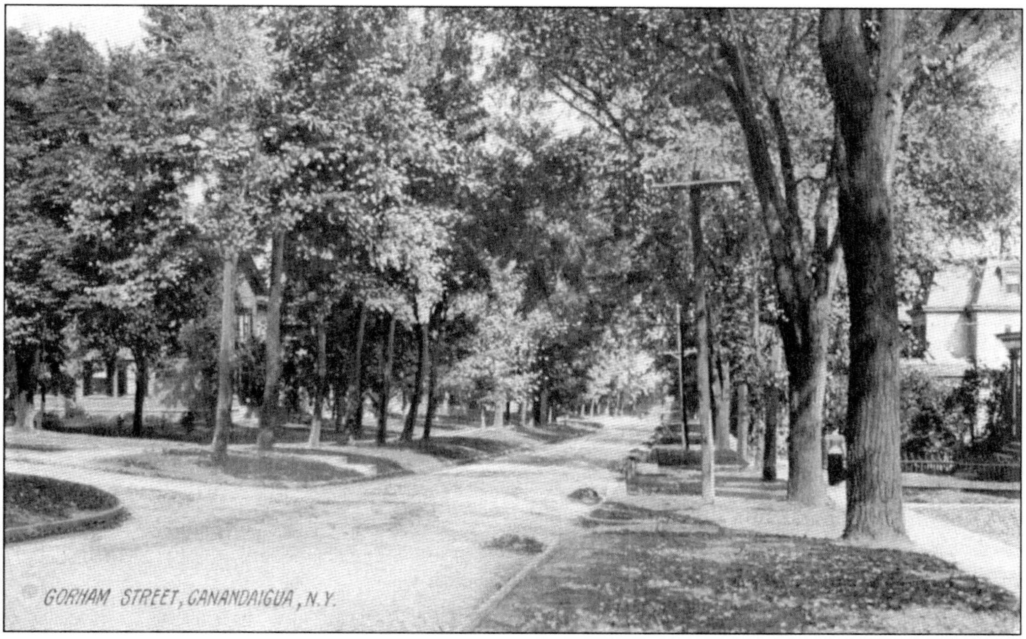

Gorham Street was opened through the land of Nathaniel Gorham III in 1849. The original Gorham house stood where the street is and sat back from Main Street. The house was moved to a lot on the north side of the street and is the fifth building on that side today. This is a divided postcard postmarked in 1907, which was soon after the new postal regulations took effect allowing messages to be written on the reverse.

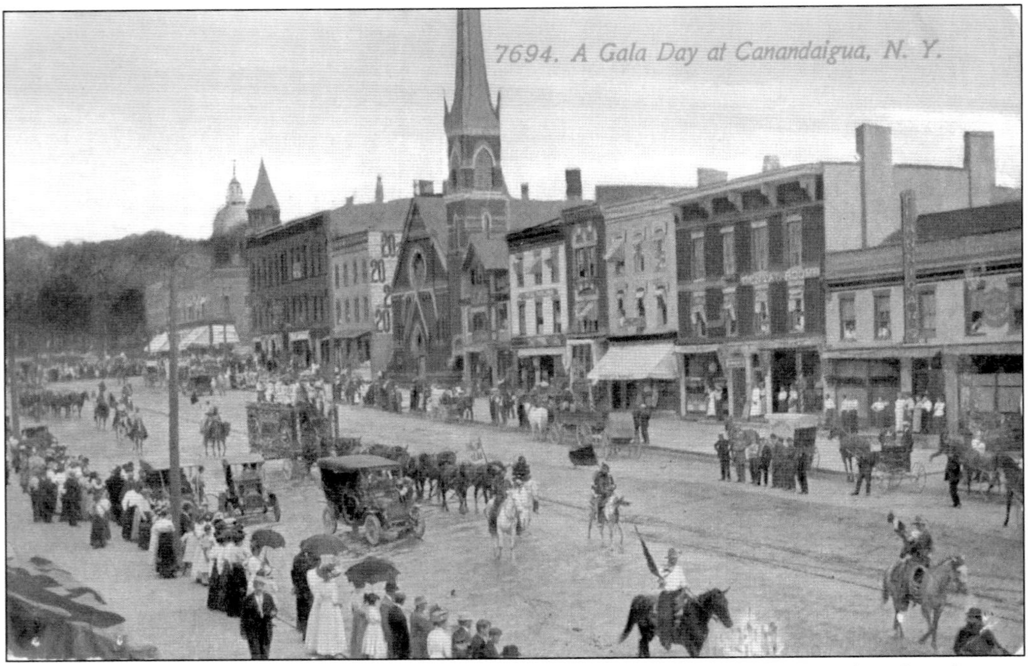

When the circus came to town a century ago, there was usually a parade as the animals and performers moved from the railroad yard to the circus grounds near the lake. It was a great form of advertising, and one of those parades prompted the publication of this postcard postmarked in 1913.

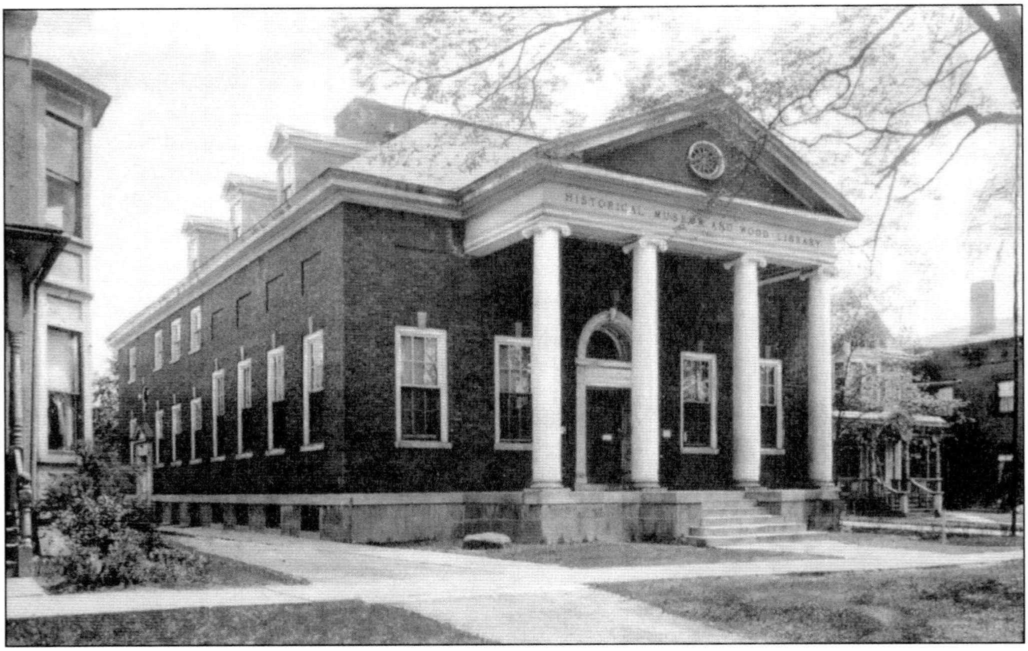

The Ontario County Historical Society was organized in 1902 with newspaper publisher Charles Milliken as its first president. In 1914, Claude Bragdon designed this building for the society. Until 1972, it was shared with the Wood Library. The society museum is renowned for its collection of artifacts and documents relating to all of Western New York.

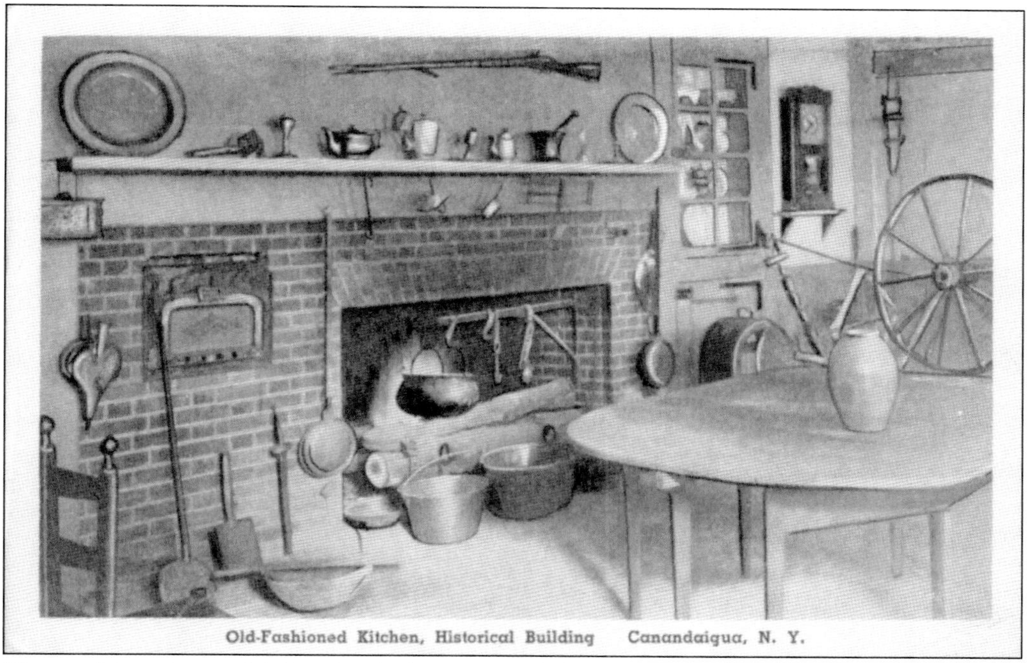

The working pioneer kitchen in the basement of the historical society's museum is a delight for the many young visitors who come to the museum for a school field trip or a personal visit. Here, children experience the trials and joys of open-hearth cooking.

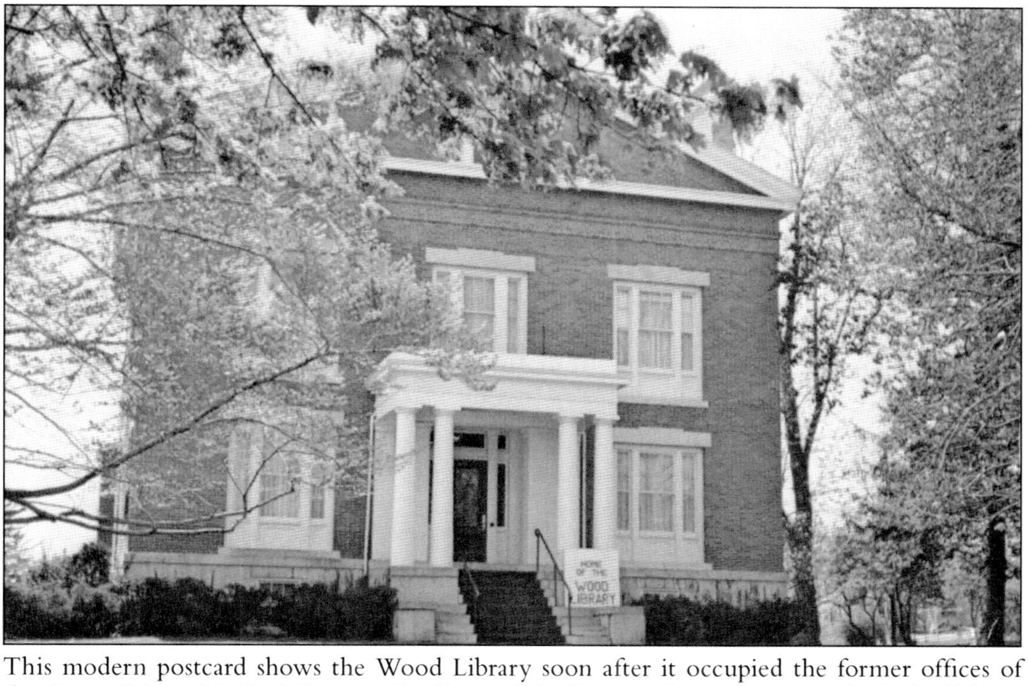

This modern postcard shows the Wood Library soon after it occupied the former offices of the Canandaigua Medical Group. The front of the library, shown here, was built in 1845 as the home of local attorney Mark H. Sibley. It served as the medical center from 1950 to 1972. (Photograph by John Guyette.)

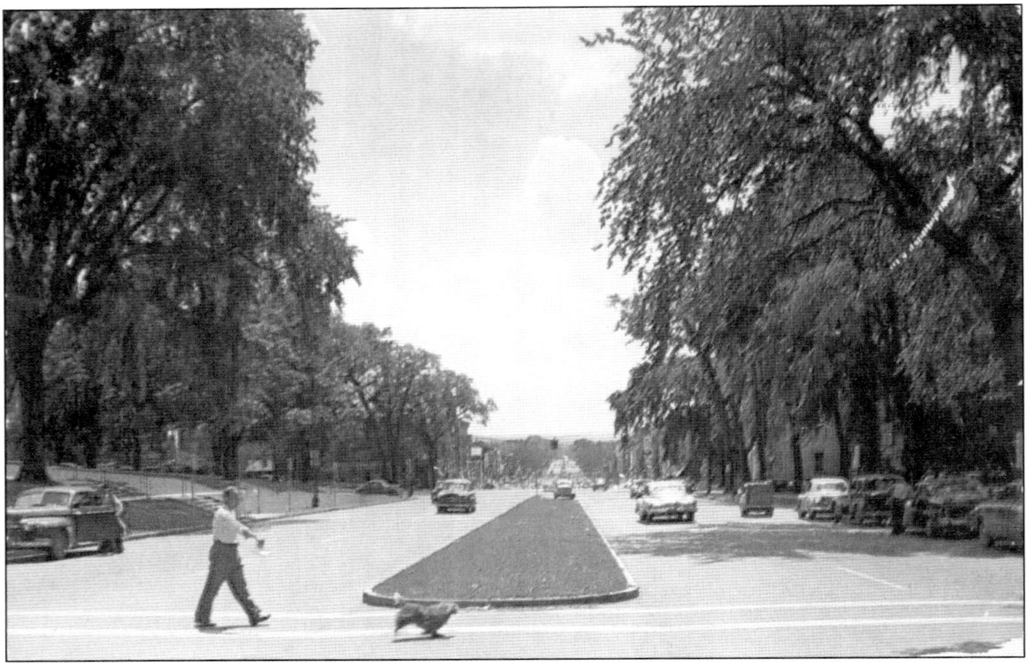

This view of Main Street, looking south from the courthouse, was photographed in the mid-1950s. Dutch elm disease later claimed many of the stately trees visible here. Main Street was completely rebuilt in 1950. (Photograph by Margery M. Elling.)

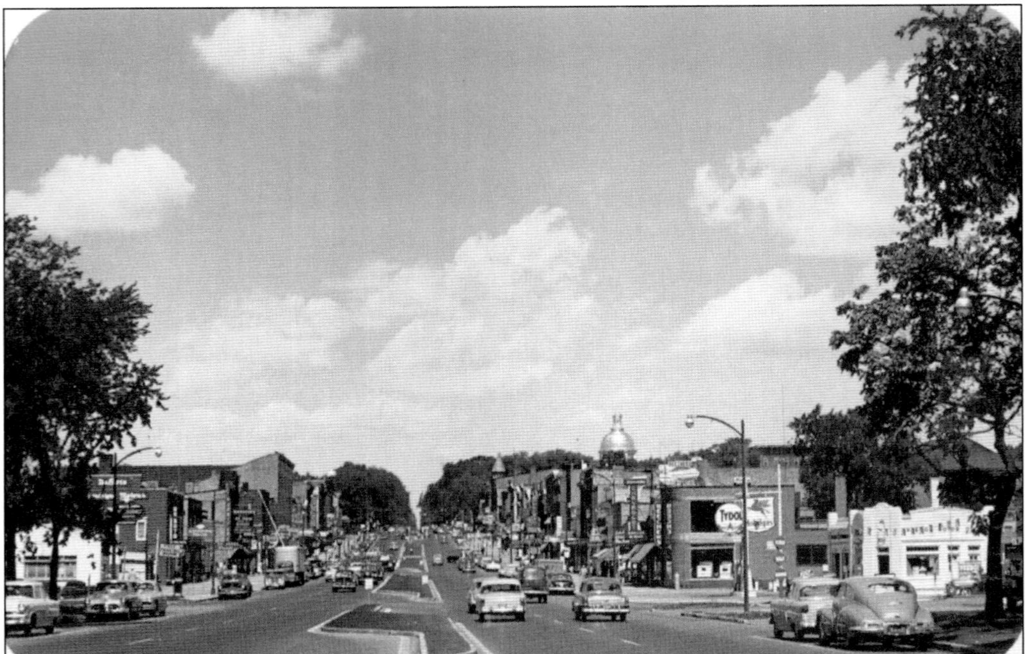

The first *Statue of Justice* was removed from the courthouse in 1951, and there was no replacement until 1961. The median on Main Street was part of the rebuilding that was completed in 1953. Those facts clearly date this postcard. There is no clearer statement of the impact of post–World War II prosperity on Main Street, Canandaigua. (Photograph by Margery M. Elling.)

Three

Sonnenberg and the VA Medical Center

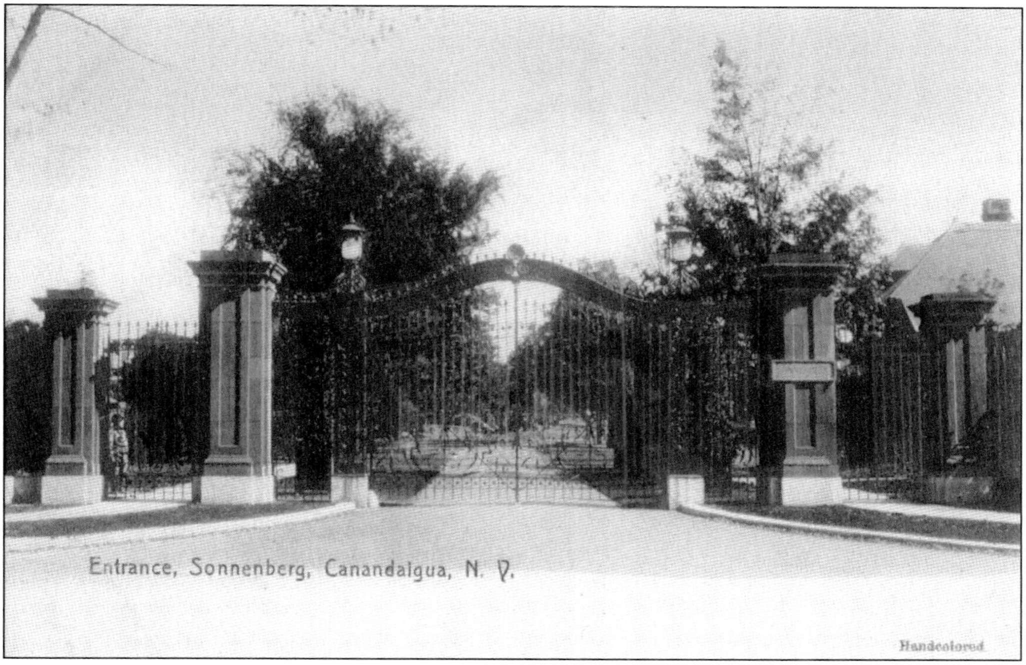

The main gate and the stone walls around Mary Thompson's Sonnenberg Estate were built between 1904 and 1906. It is said to be modeled after one of the gates belonging to Buckingham Palace in London. Today, this is the main entrance to Sonnenberg Gardens and Mansion State Historic Park.

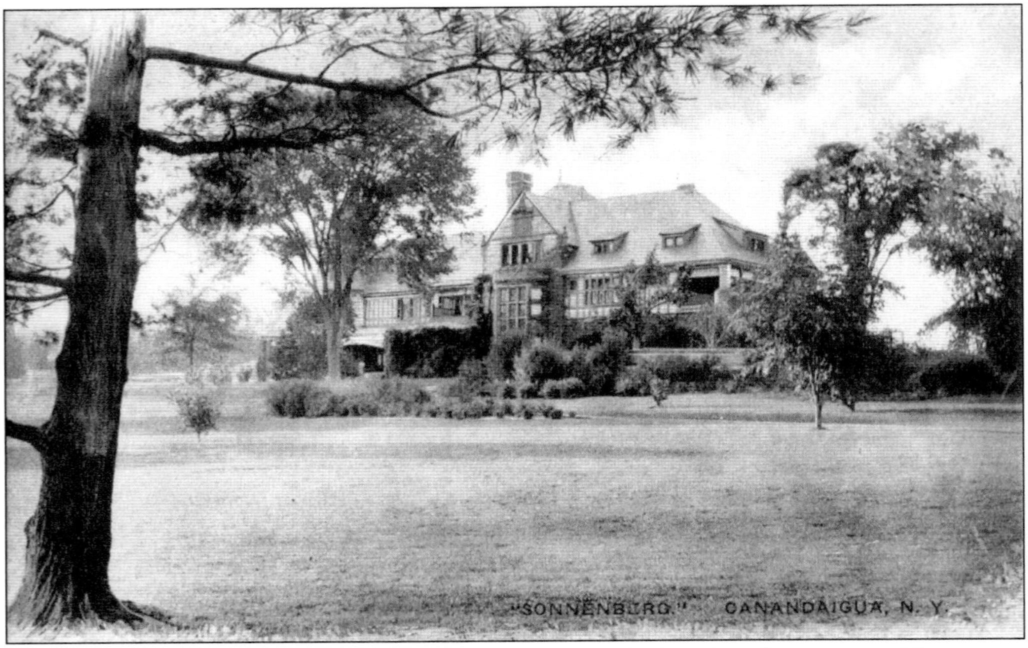

Sonnenberg was the estate, and summer home, of Mary Clark and Frederick Ferris Thompson. This lavish home replaced an early farmhouse. The Sonnenberg mansion house was built between 1885 and 1887. After the estate was purchased by the federal government as the site of a VA medical center in 1932, the house served as a nurses' residence. In 1973, Sonnenberg Gardens received 50 acres of the old estate property, including the mansion.

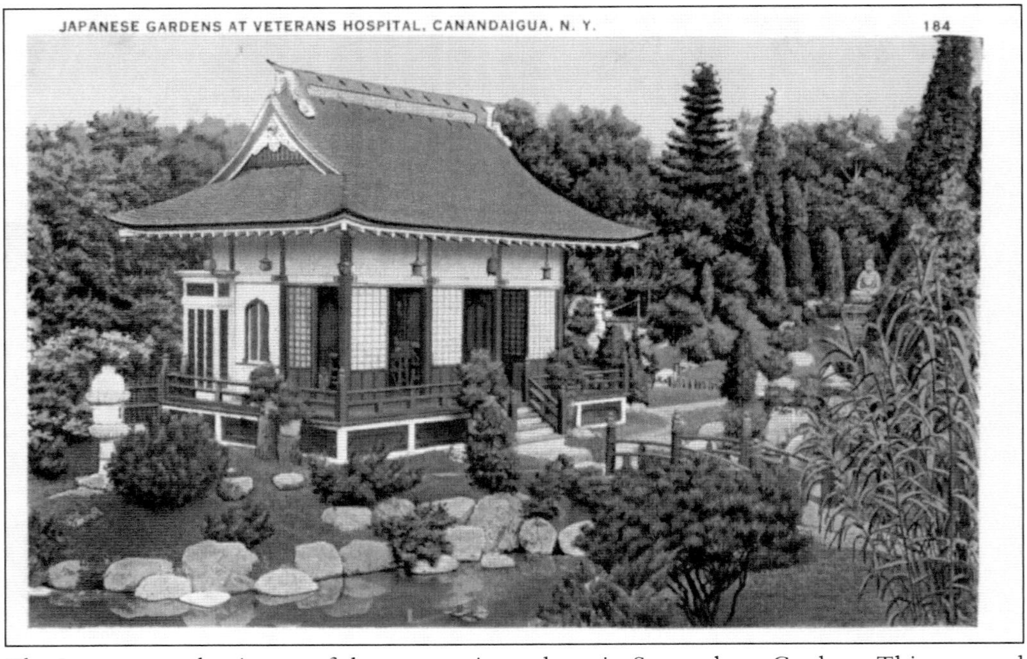

The Japanese garden is one of the most unique places in Sonnenberg Gardens. This postcard was produced during the time the gardens were still part of the VA medical center property, probably in the late 1940s or early 1950s. A force of Japanese carpenters and landscape artists began working on the garden and teahouse in 1904.

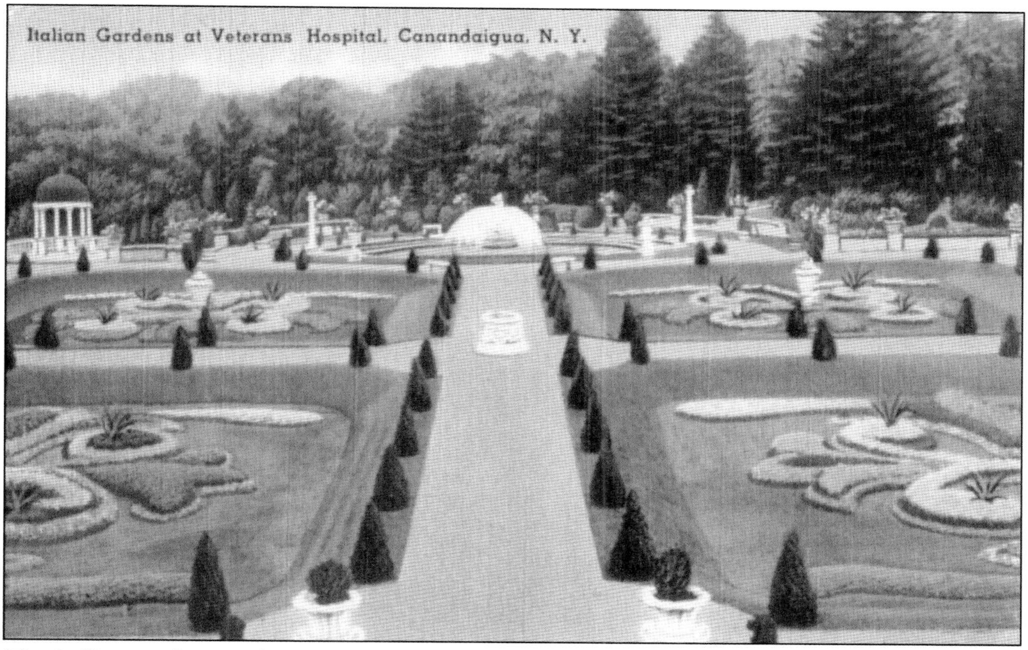

The Italian garden on the Sonnenberg Estate continues to be one of the high points of a visit to the site. Created in 1903 by landscape architect Ernest Bowditch, it is a favorite location for wedding photographs. This picture of the gardens was made after it became part of the VA medical center in 1932. Today, the garden has been restored to the way it looked when Mary Thompson planned it.

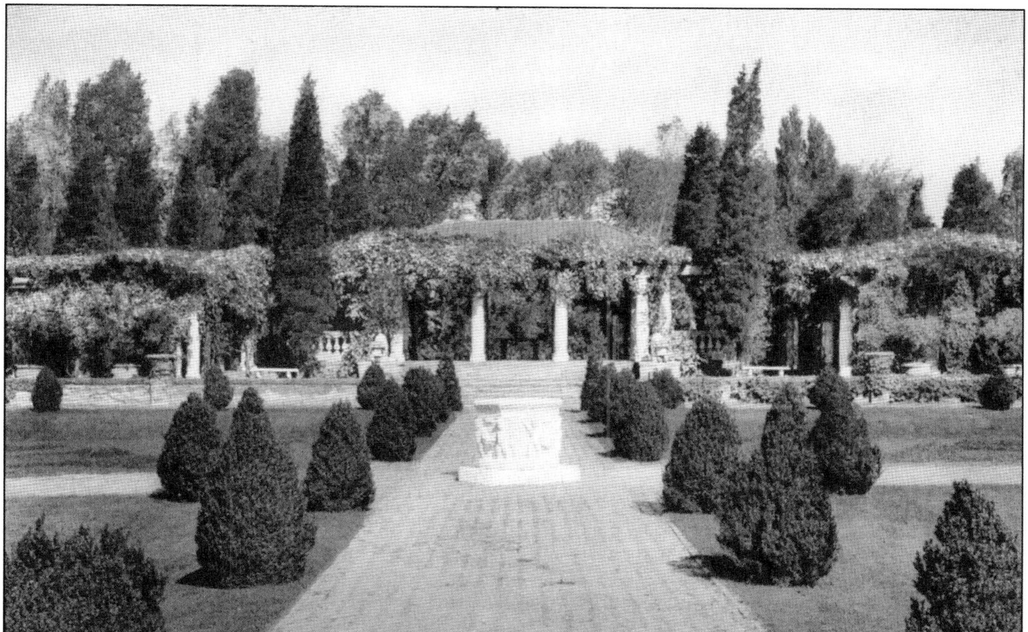

Dating from the late 1930s or early 1940s, this postcard provides a more detailed view of the gardens at Sonnenberg. As the caption indicates, this image dates from the early years of the VA medical center ownership of the gardens.

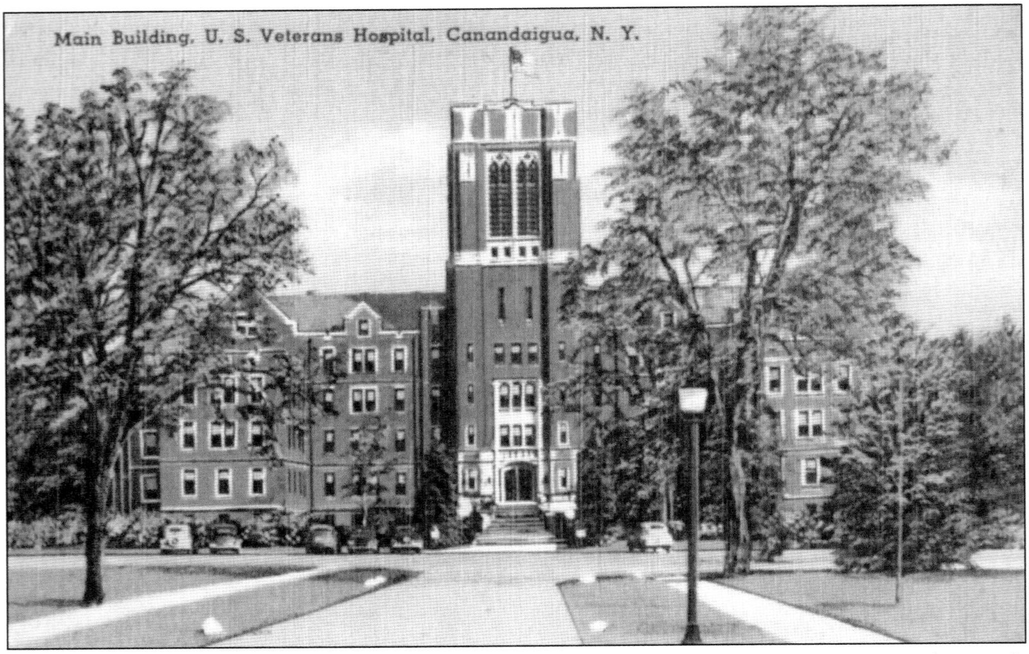

The main building of the VA medical center was built in 1934 along East Street on the north side of the Thompsons' Sonnenberg Estate. Based on the styles of the automobiles parked in front of the building, this linen postcard was probably published in the years right after World War II.

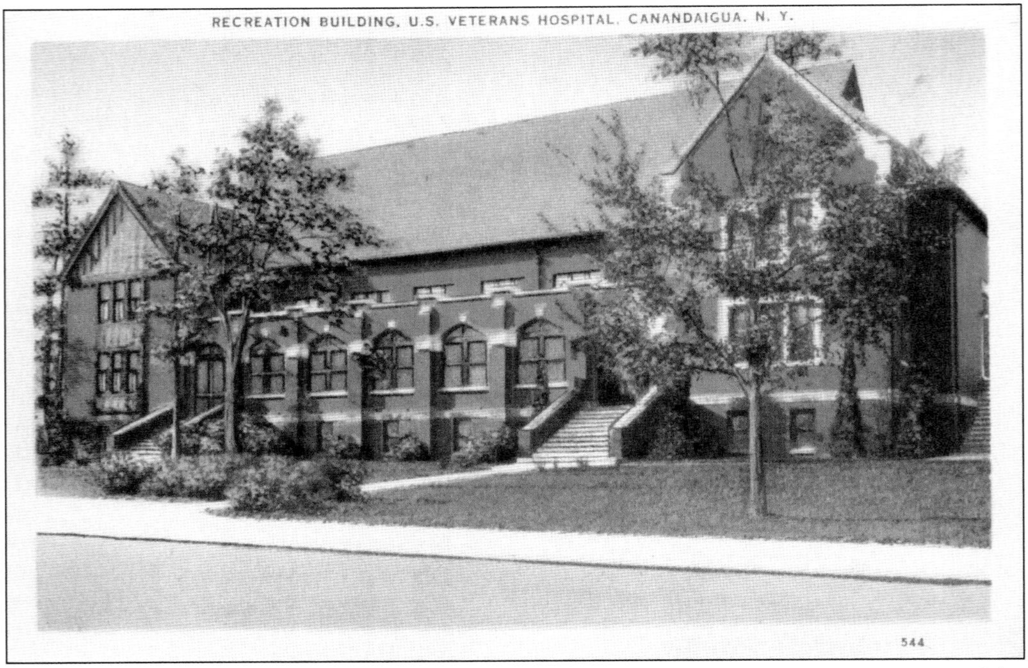

This recreation building is part of the original VA medical center campus. It is one of the few buildings not linked by an enclosed walkway connecting the main buildings on the hospital campus.

Four

Monuments

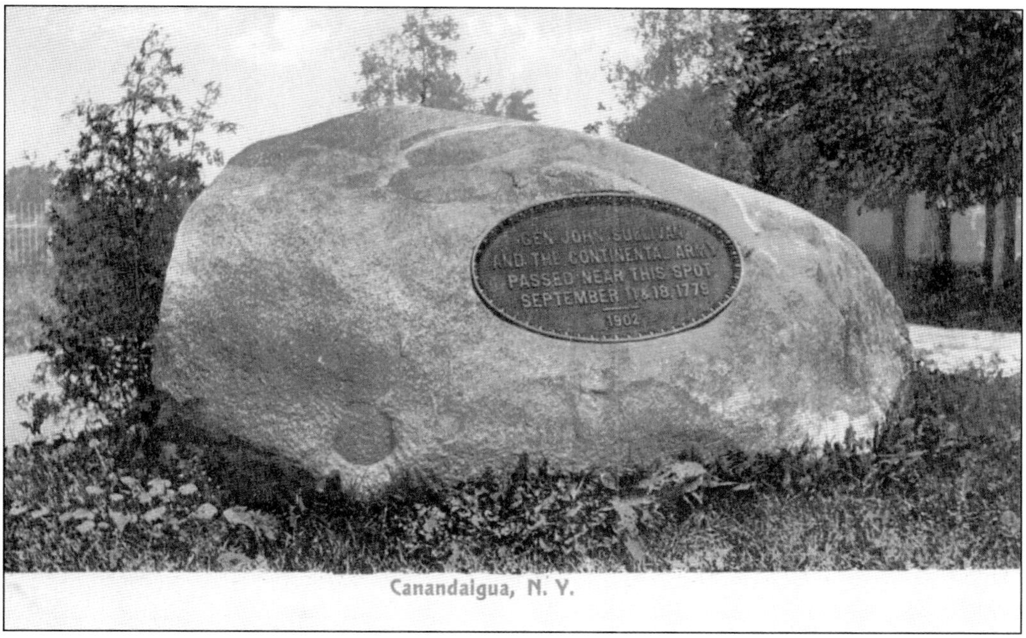

Dr. Dwight R. Burrell, the chief physician at Brigham Hall for many years, loved boulders. He was responsible for placing, directly opposite the entrance to his hospital, this monument commemorating the 1779 Sullivan Expedition. Given to the village in 1902, the boulder frightened horses and was considered a traffic hazard until it was broken up by the state in 1968. The bronze tablet is now affixed to one of the old gateposts across the street.

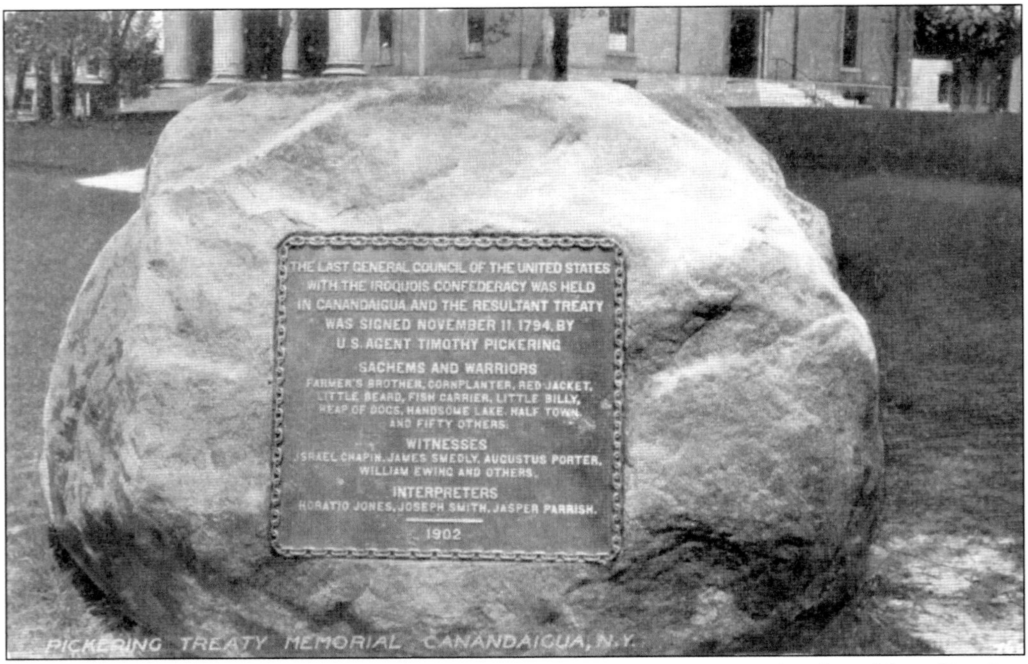

Dr. Burrell donated this boulder monument to Ontario County in 1902. The tablet affixed to the 30-ton granite boulder honors the 1794 Treaty of Canandaigua signed with the Iroquois people. It is sometimes called the Pickering Treaty after US commissioner Timothy Pickering.

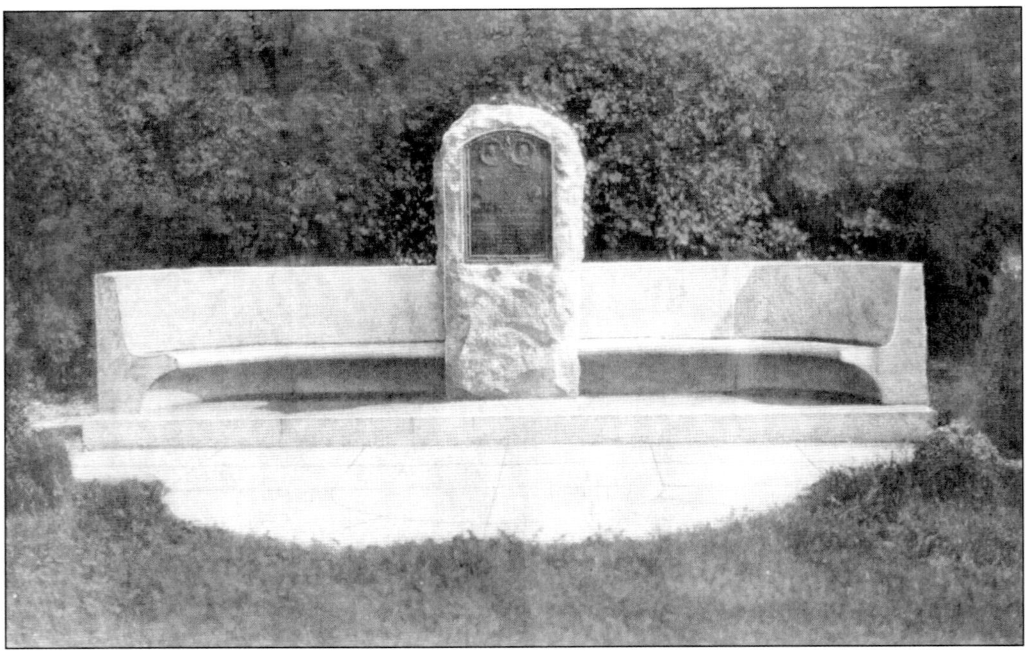

New York and Pennsylvania jointly celebrated Gen. John Sullivan's 1779 punitive expedition against the Iroquois people during the Revolutionary War. Canandaigua was one of dozens of Native American villages destroyed. In 1929, many of the village sites were marked by bronze tablets affixed to granite markers. This monument near the pier was dedicated on September 10, 1929, with a parade and speeches. The site was designed by John Handrahan.

Five

The Northern Lakeshore

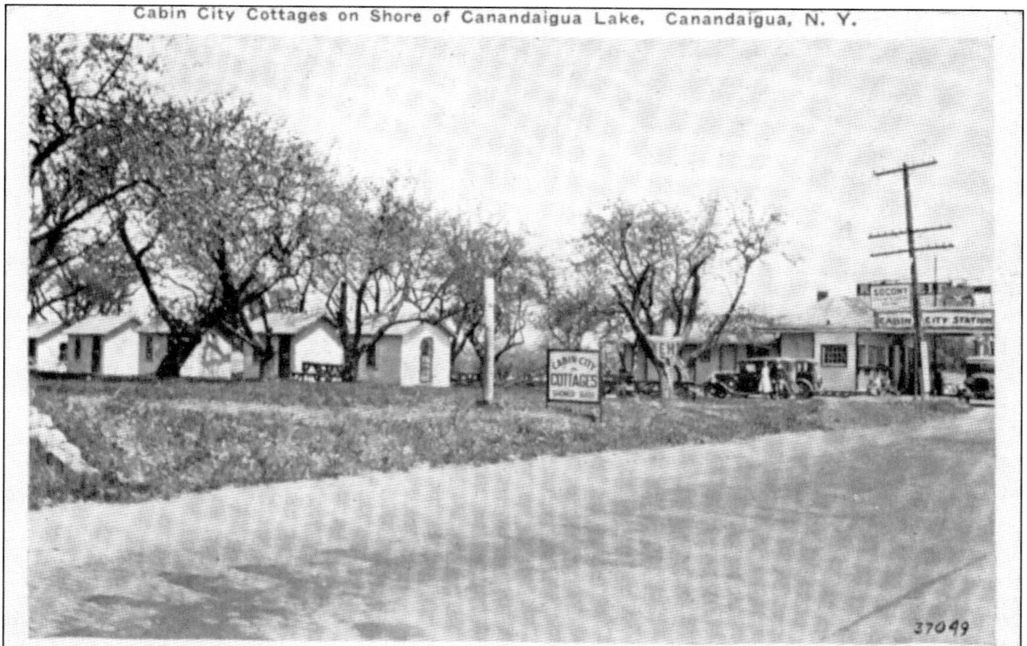

The Cabin City Cottages were established along Lakeshore Drive in the late 1920s. The Dibbles and Sissons opened the first permanent tourist facilities. This postcard shows the small filling station and cabins that became Sisson's cabin, motel, and tearoom complex in later years. Postmarked in 1932, the writer said, "Our first night in cabins. All O.K."

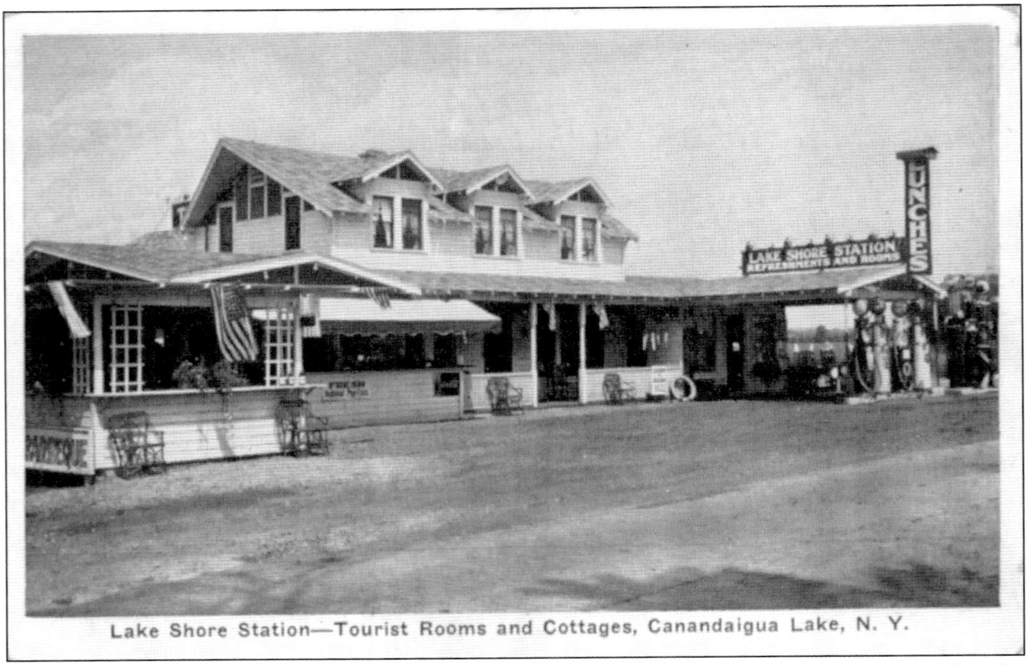

The Lakeshore Station, known as Dibbles, was typical of the burgeoning tourist trade after the 1920s. This restaurant–gas station–tourist home combination survived into the 1950s opposite Kershaw Park. The gas station burned in 1930.

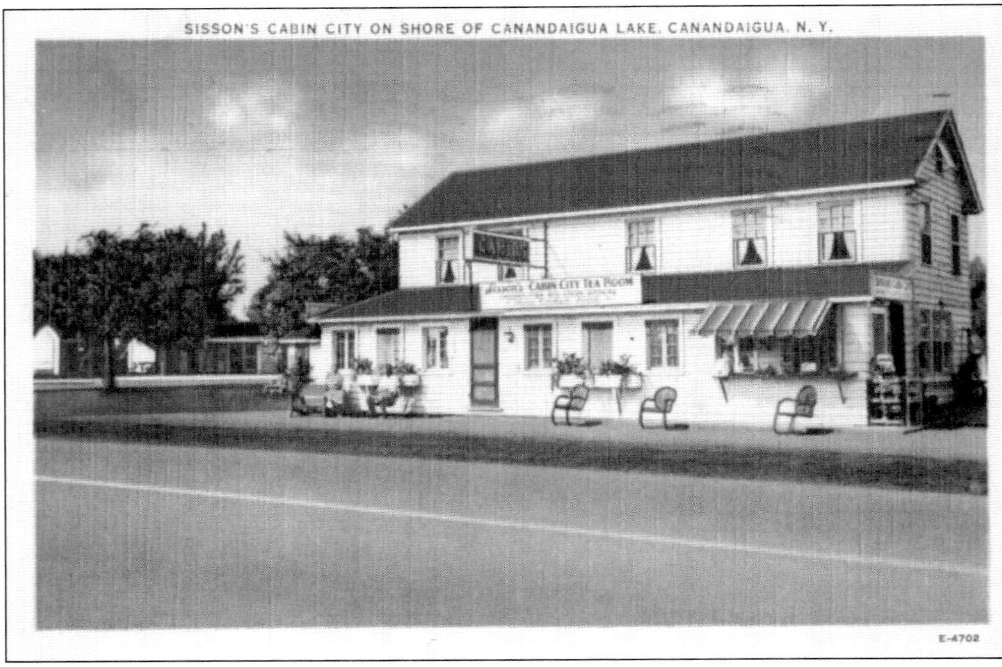

Sisson's Cabin City advertised private toilets and showers and hot and cold water on the reverse of this postcard from the mid–20th century. Postmarked 1941, this postcard reminds readers of how much expectations for overnight accommodations have changed.

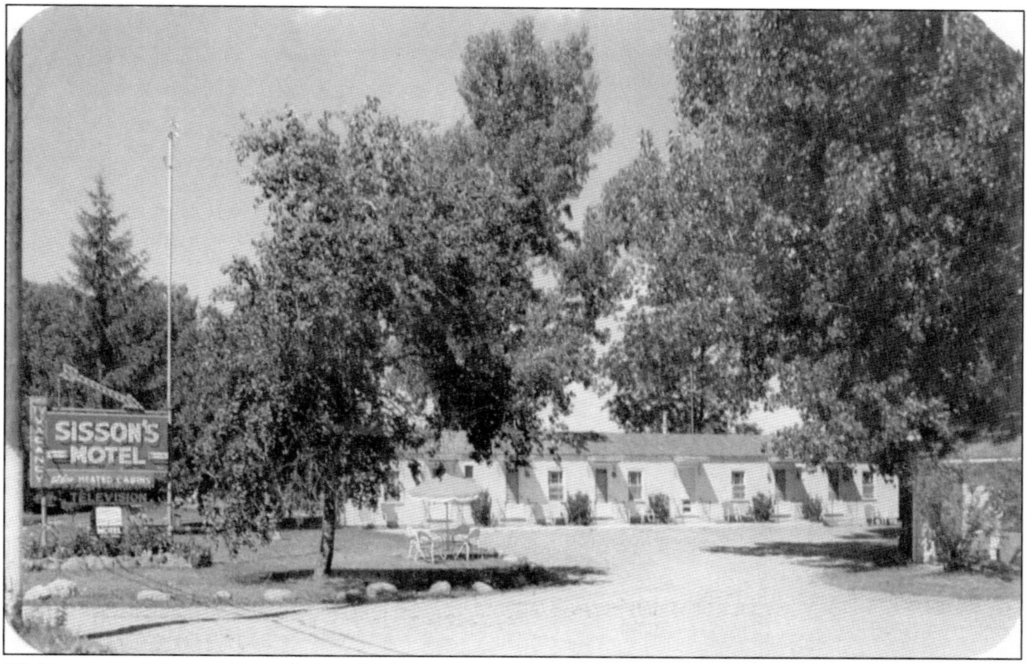

This postcard shows how this Lakeshore Drive motel changed over the years. Published about 1957, it shows Sisson's as a motel, complete with such amenities as heated cabins and television. The last of Sisson's motel was demolished in 1995. (Photograph by Margery M. Elling.)

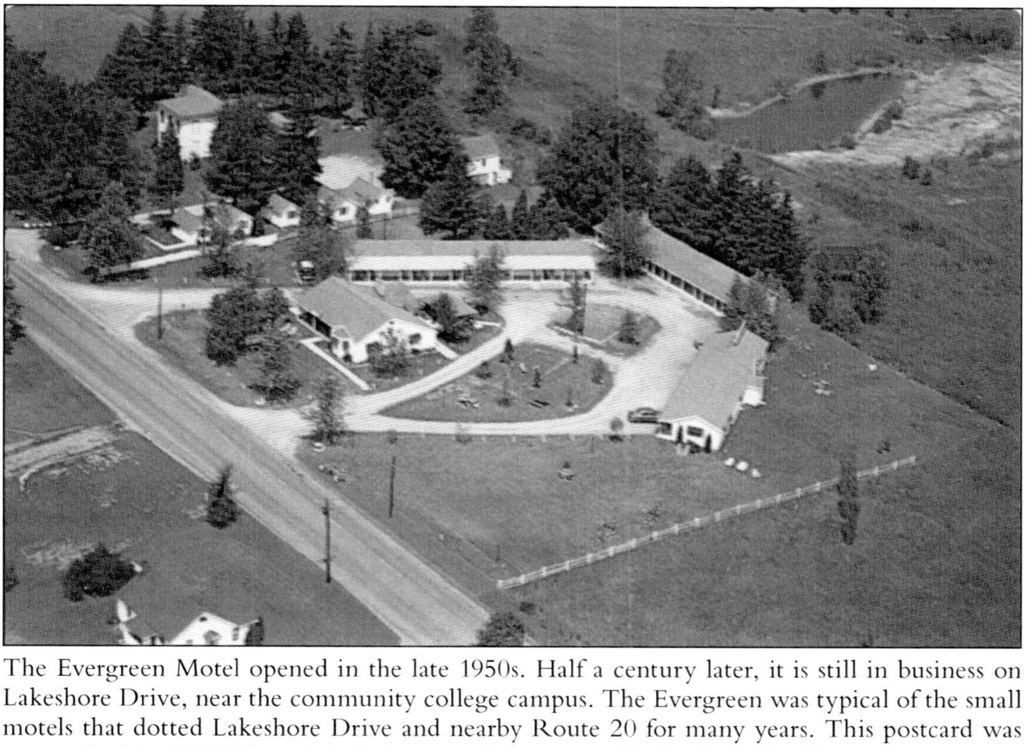

The Evergreen Motel opened in the late 1950s. Half a century later, it is still in business on Lakeshore Drive, near the community college campus. The Evergreen was typical of the small motels that dotted Lakeshore Drive and nearby Route 20 for many years. This postcard was postmarked in 1960. The original photograph was made for the Scott Studio.

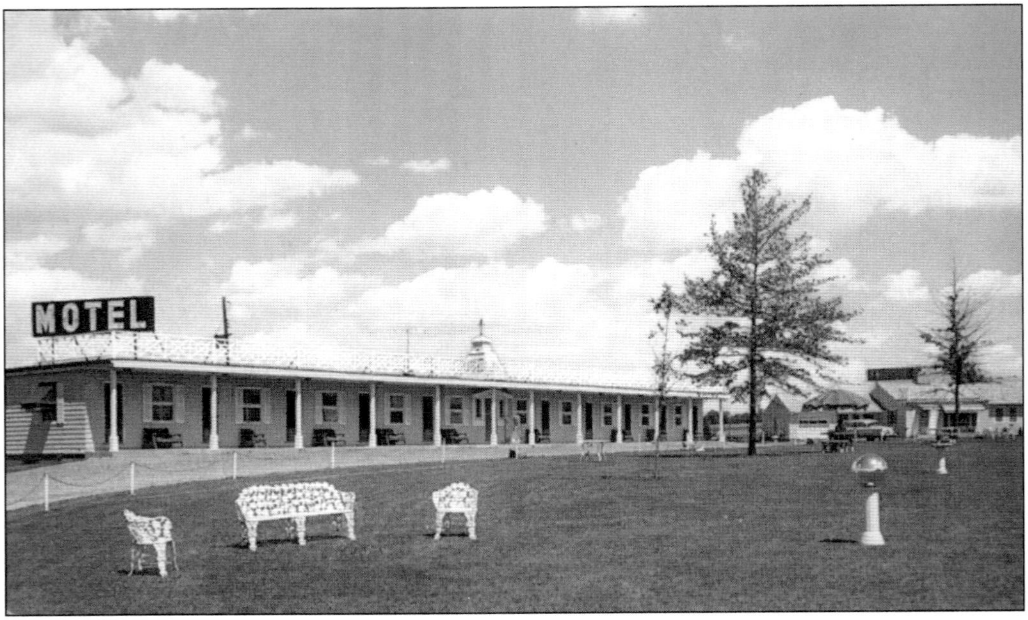

One of the motels farther out Routes 5 and 20 was the Mount Vernon Motel. It is still in business under another name. This early-1960s postcard listed all its neighboring attractions on the reverse. One of them was a heated swimming pool, rare at the time. Other attractions included a golf course, drive-in theater, restaurants, and free television in every room. (Photograph by Charles E. Cooksey.)

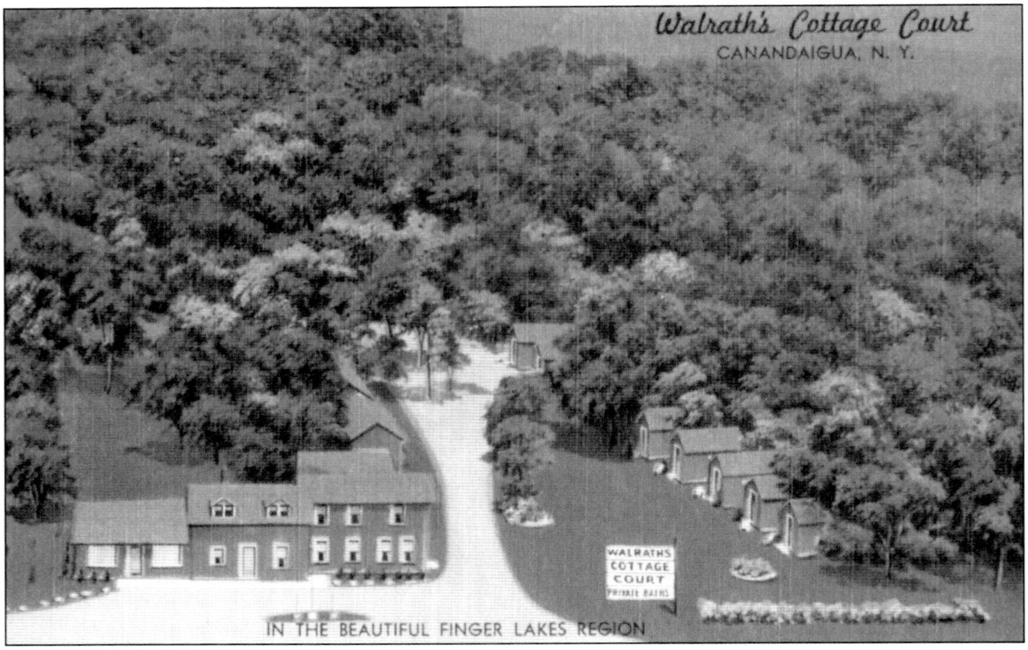

Three miles farther east was Walrath's Cottage Court at the intersection of Freshour Road and Routes 5 and 20. The main building and a few of the old cabins still stand in the town of Hopewell. Postmarked in 1952, the message on the reverse said that the cabins all had private baths and heat, something of a novelty still. "We arrived here about 7:00 p.m. fine and dandy," the writer said.

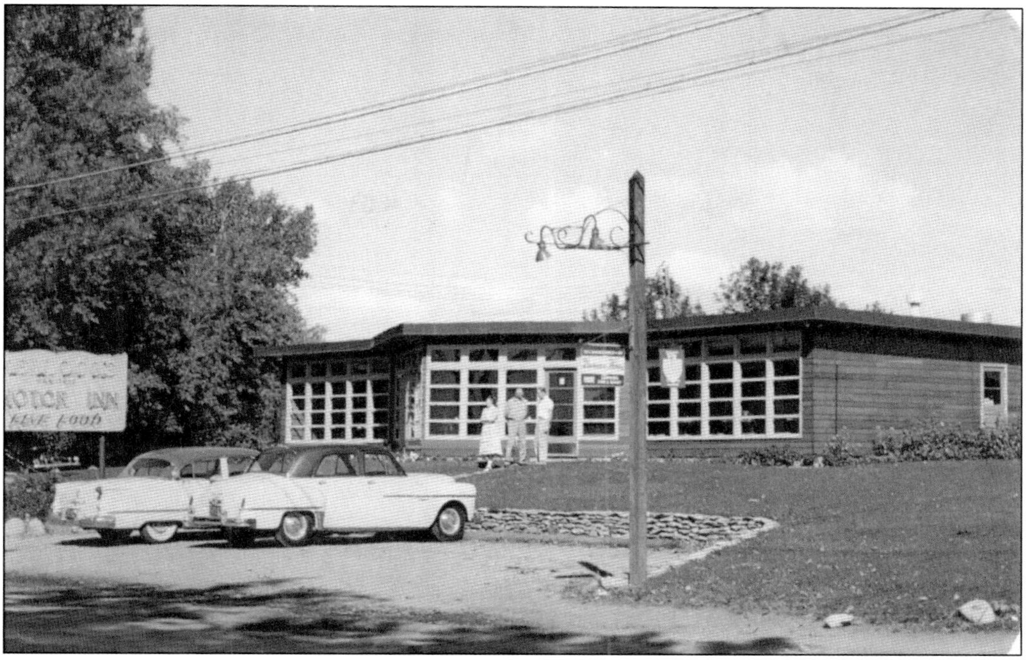

Kellogg's Pan-Tree Restaurant and Motor Inn was a popular establishment along Lakeshore Drive. Moved from the business district in 1948, it was operated by two generations of the Kellogg family. It was famous for its sticky buns. The restaurant survives today as the Lakeshore Grille. (Photograph by Margery M. Elling.)

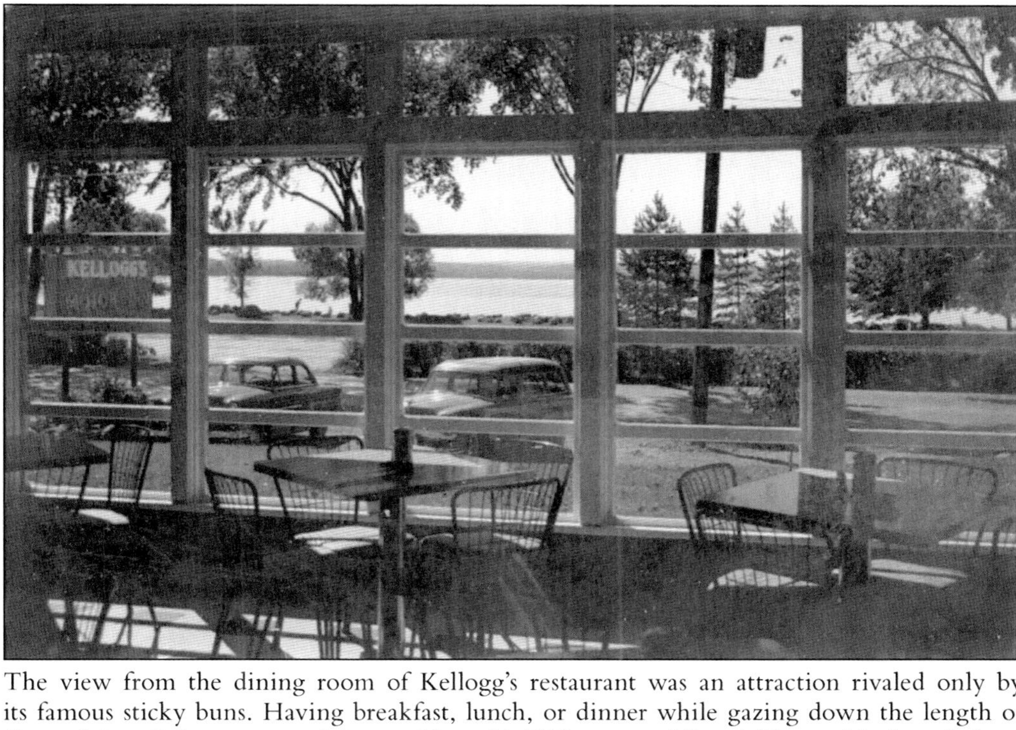

The view from the dining room of Kellogg's restaurant was an attraction rivaled only by its famous sticky buns. Having breakfast, lunch, or dinner while gazing down the length of Canandaigua Lake was a special treat. The mid-1950s automobiles visible outside the windows date this image. (Photograph by Charles E. Cooksey.)

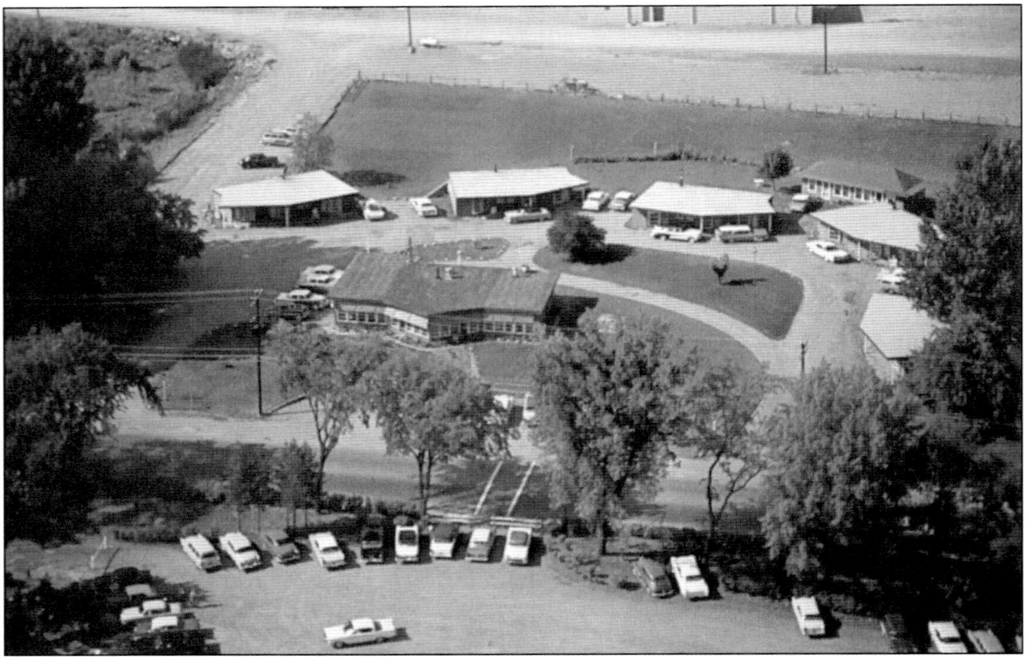

This aerial view of Kellogg's restaurant and motor inn dates from the mid-1960s. Note the parking lot inside Kershaw Park and the quiet, tree-lined Lakeshore Drive. Parkway Plaza, opened in 1958, shows along the top of the postcard.

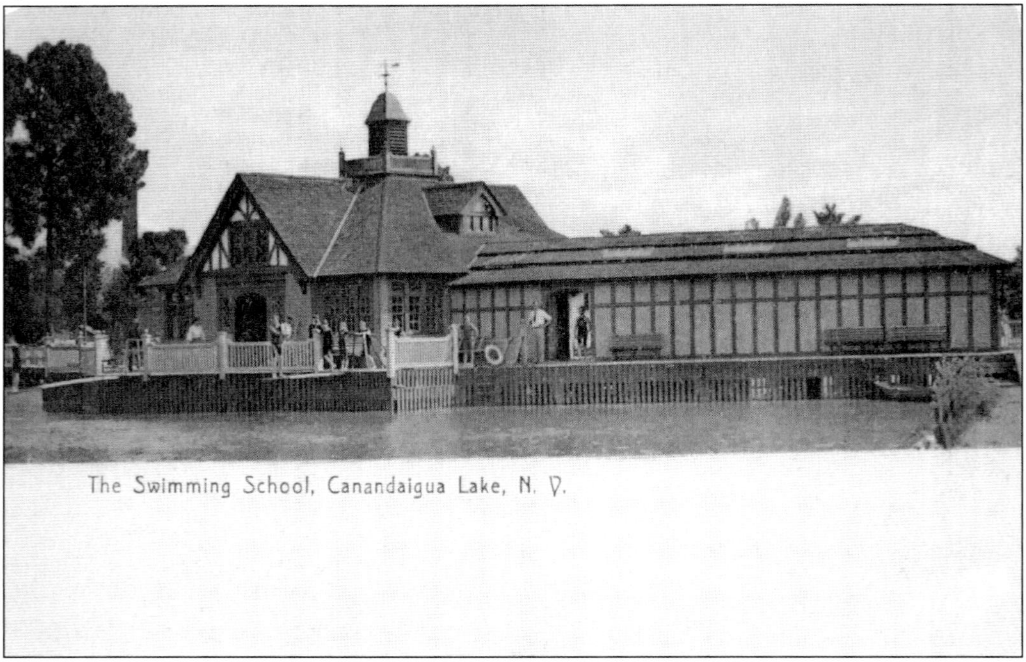

This close-up image of the 1906 Swimming School is printed on a postcard with a divided reverse. However, the blank area at the bottom is a reminder of the pre-1907 postal regulations prohibiting messages on the address side. This view of the building probably reflects its original appearance. The swimming pavilion now located at the opposite end of Kershaw Park was designed to look like the old Swimming School.

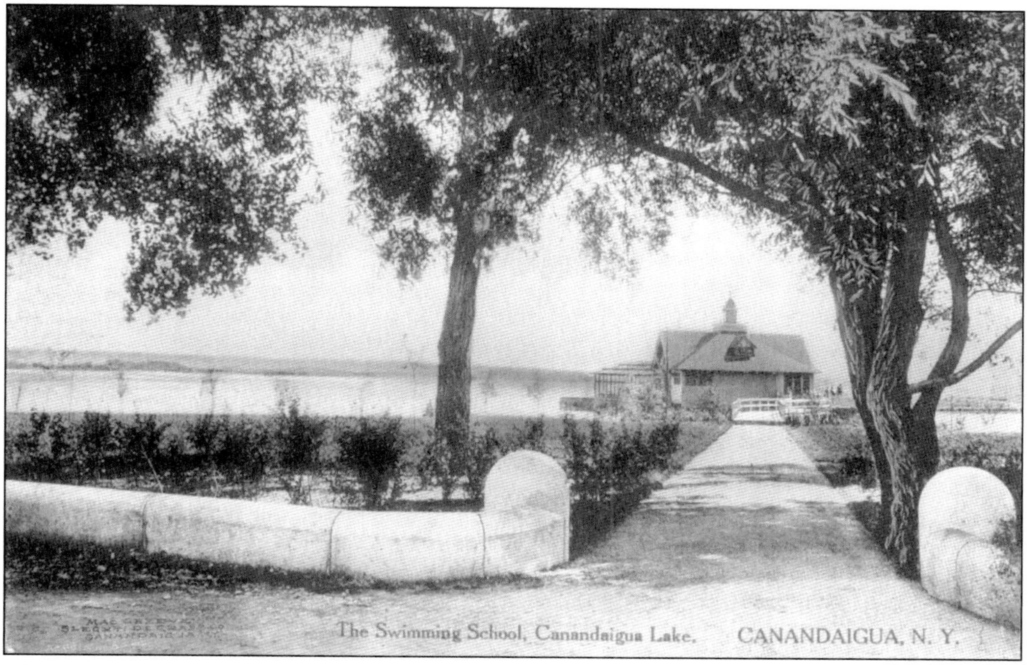

The Swimming School opened in 1906 and continued to be used until 1969. Its wooden platform was used for swimming instruction until 1983. The small park at the entrance to the Swimming School, also financed by Mrs. Thompson, was the first attempt to beautify the lakeshore. The short section of stone wall was later moved to the new bathhouse, modeled on the grounds of the Swimming School, in 1997.

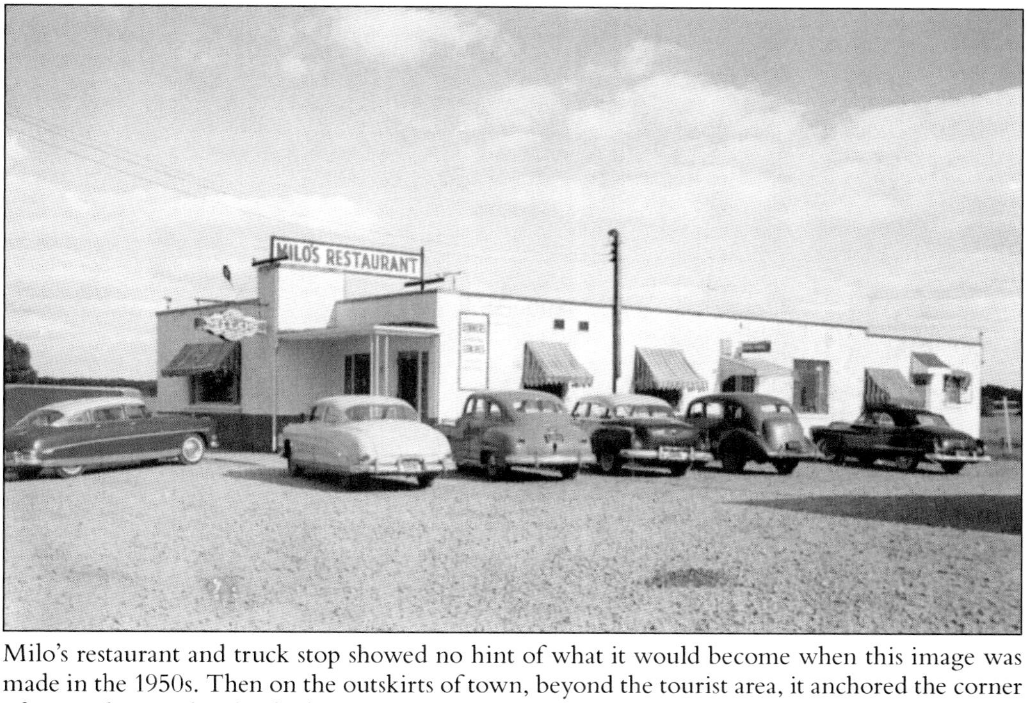

Milo's restaurant and truck stop showed no hint of what it would become when this image was made in the 1950s. Then on the outskirts of town, beyond the tourist area, it anchored the corner of East Lake Road and Lakeshore Drive. Today, it is a larger popular eatery known as Schooners, near the Finger Lakes Performing Arts Center. (Photograph by Margery M. Elling.)

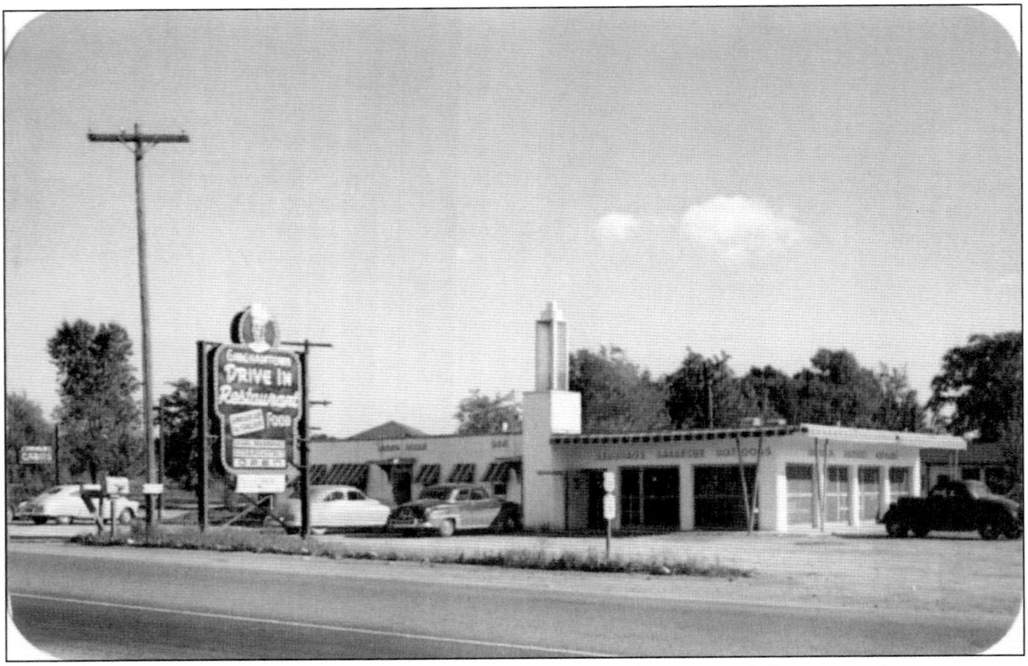

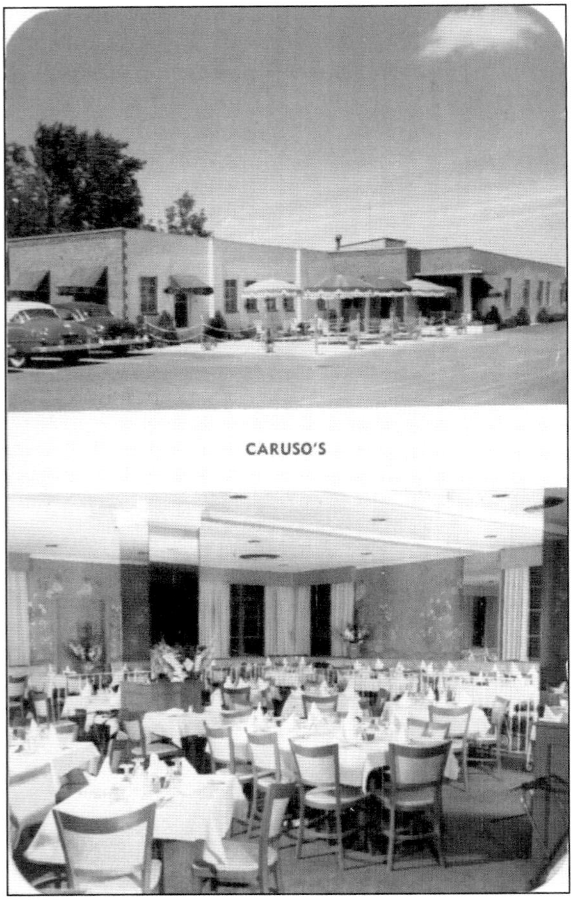

Before it was Schooners, the restaurant, first known as Milo's, was known as Ginghamtown. Next door was the Ginghamtown Motel. This is how it looked about 1960. The motel is now known as the Woodbridge Motel. (Courtesy of the Ontario County Historical Society.)

Caruso's restaurant, across from Kershaw Park, was a popular restaurant and party house. It was expanded several times after it was built in 1930. It was later called the Lakeshore House and Bella Lago, but its doors closed in 2008. Caruso's cuisine featured seafood and Italian-American dishes. On the back, the sender wrote, "Had dinner at this place tonight. Sure was good." (Photograph by Margery M. Elling.)

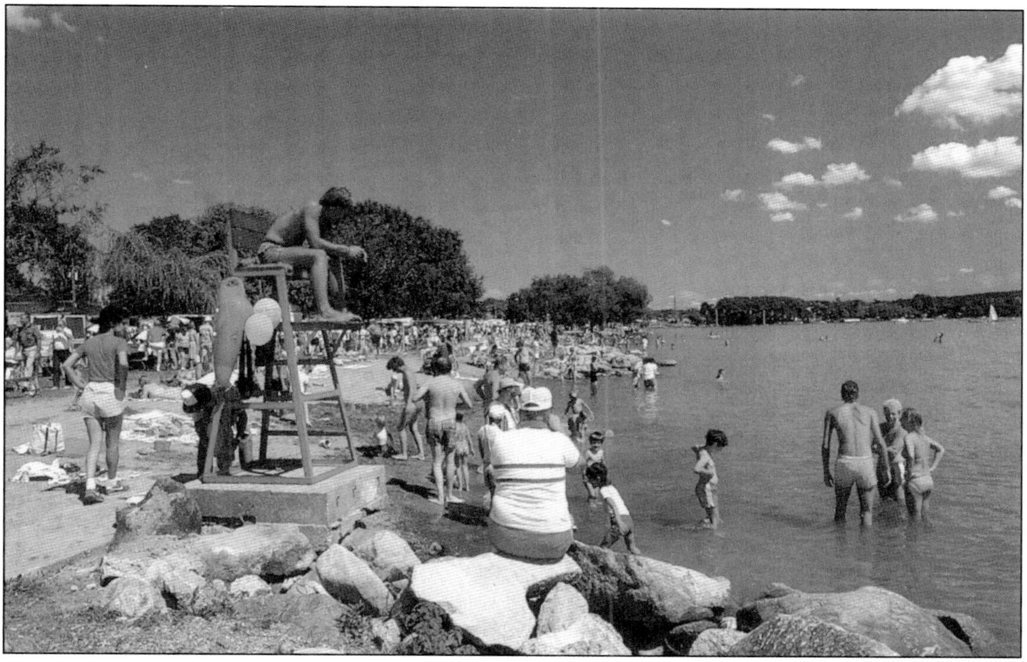

Kershaw Park opened in 1936. Named for Public Works commissioner John Kershaw, it sits on fill land. Dr. Charles Booth began promoting the park in 1925. During the 1930s, the park became a project of the Works Project Administration. Until the 1970s, the entire length of the park was open for swimming. (Photograph by Bill Banaszewski.)

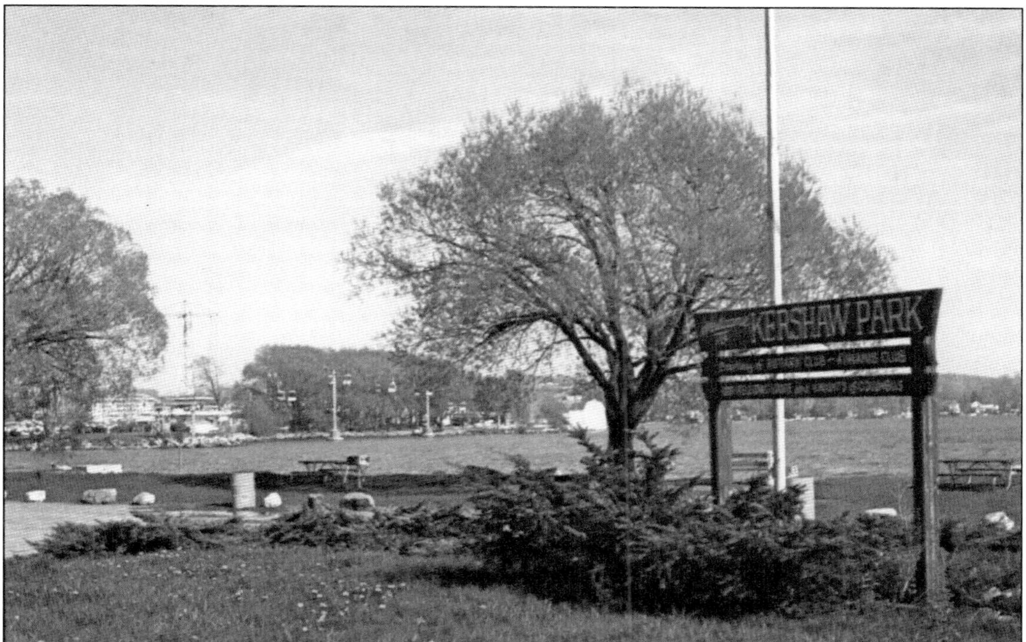

At the east entrance to Kershaw Park, a flagpole and welcome sign reminded visitors that the Canandaigua Rotary Club, the local Kiwanis Club, Odd Fellows Lodge, and Knights of Columbus all contributed to the creation and maintenance of the park. (Photograph by John Guyette.)

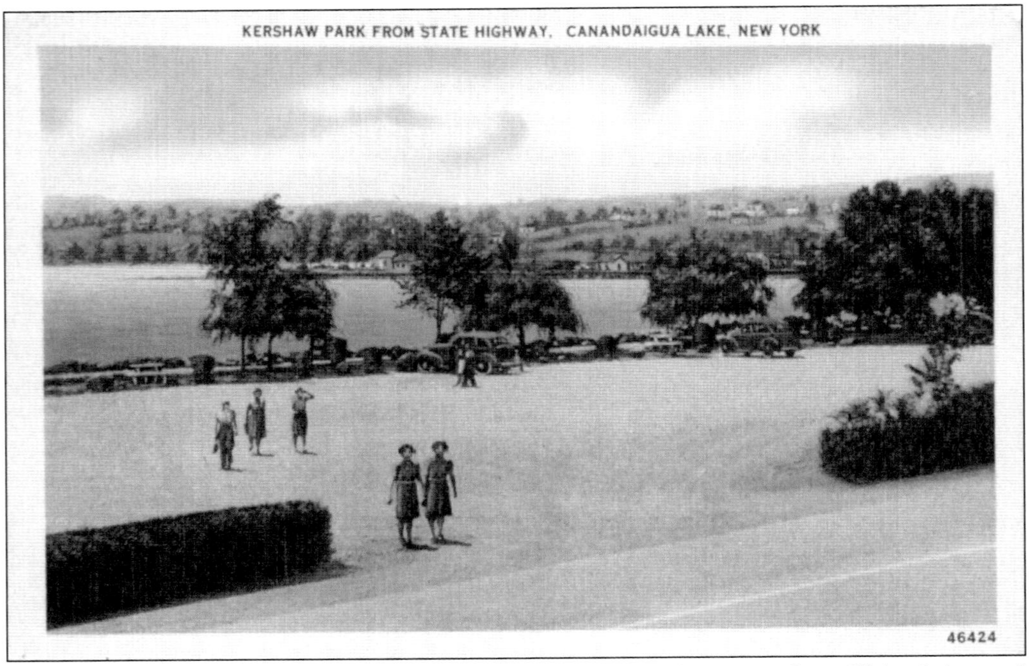

This postcard shows Kershaw Park as it looked when it was first created on fill land dumped into Canandaigua Lake. For many years, there were large gravel parking lots in the park close to the water.

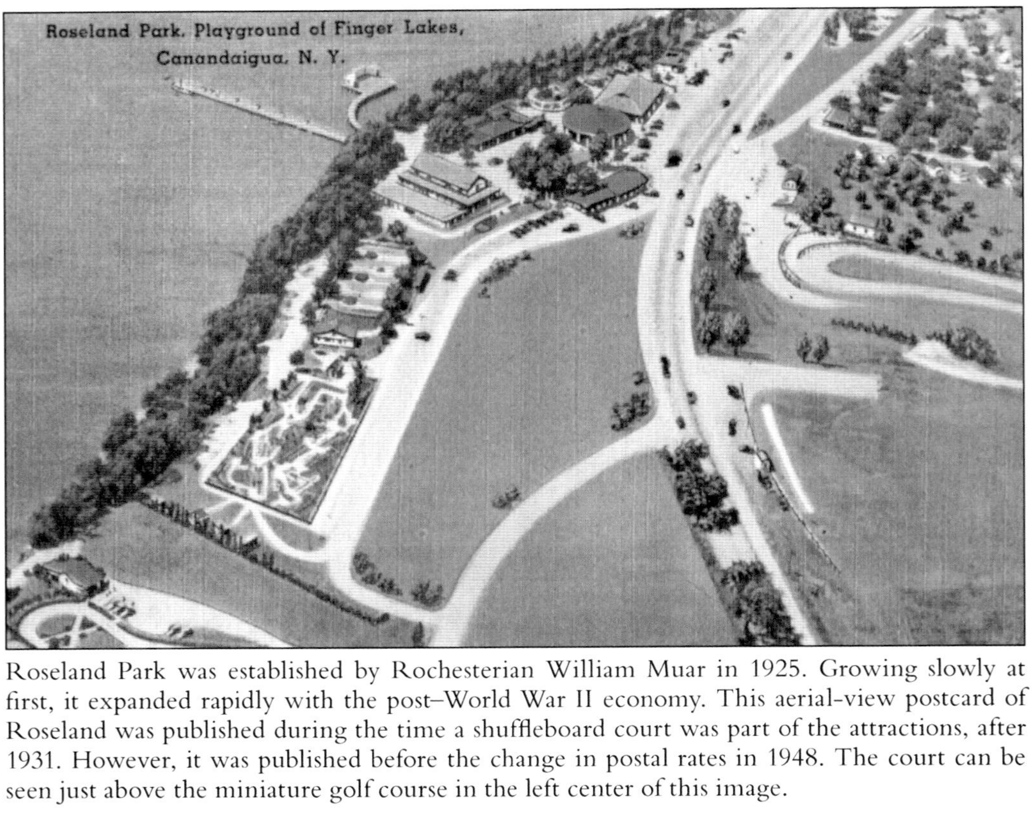

Roseland Park was established by Rochesterian William Muar in 1925. Growing slowly at first, it expanded rapidly with the post–World War II economy. This aerial-view postcard of Roseland was published during the time a shuffleboard court was part of the attractions, after 1931. However, it was published before the change in postal rates in 1948. The court can be seen just above the miniature golf course in the left center of this image.

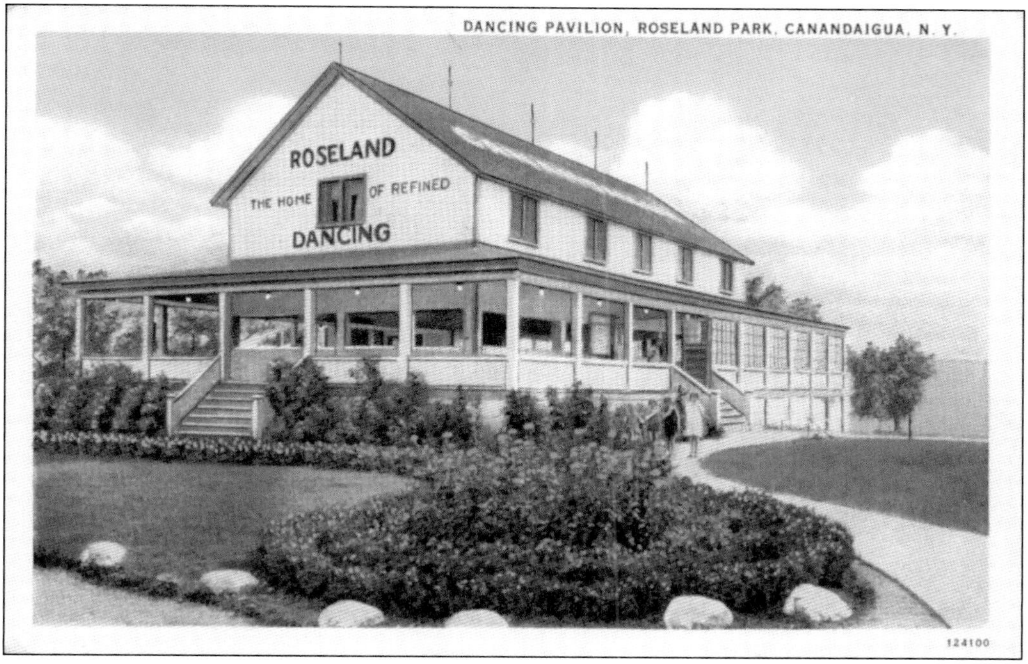

The old barn that became the dance pavilion at Roseland was part of the original Garrett farm. It had once been a livestock barn. William Muar first made it a dance hall, then a funhouse with 1950s-era pinball machines and mechanical entertainment devices. Dancing was popular at sites around the lake, and this hall was a major attraction. Its very name reminded young people of the glamorous Roseland Ballroom in New York City. This postcard dates from about 1950. (Courtesy of the Ontario County Historical Society.)

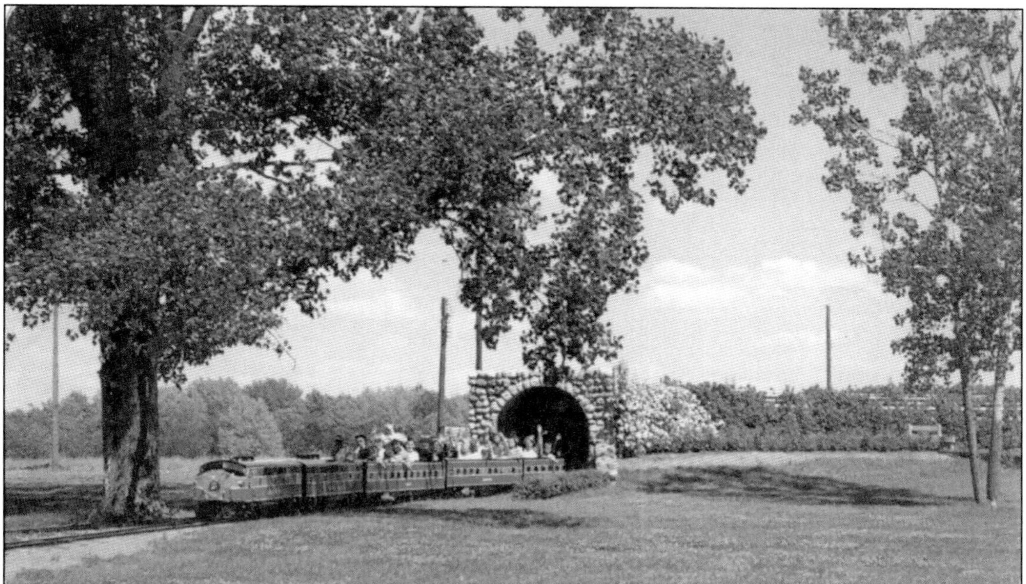

The "Playground of the Finger Lakes" added the Roseland Pacemaker to its rides in 1950. The miniature train left a circle of track, not far from the old outlet bridge, and followed a route over the outlet and through the picnic grove that Bill Muar created across Lakeshore Drive from his amusement park. This tunnel was located near the outlet dam. (Photograph by Margery Elling.)

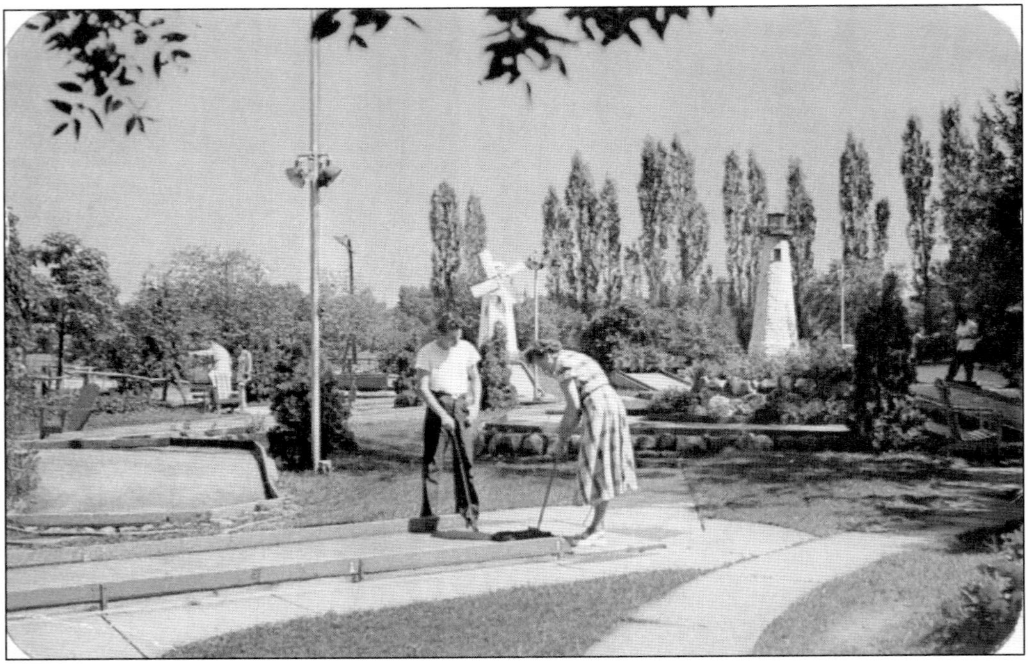

The miniature golf craze came to Roseland Park in 1930. An ornate landscaped-garden course, it was one of the most popular features of the park. At the east end of the park, the miniature golf course was next to the country club. The roller coaster was eventually located just to the left of this scene. This postcard was postmarked in 1958. (Photograph by Margery M. Elling.)

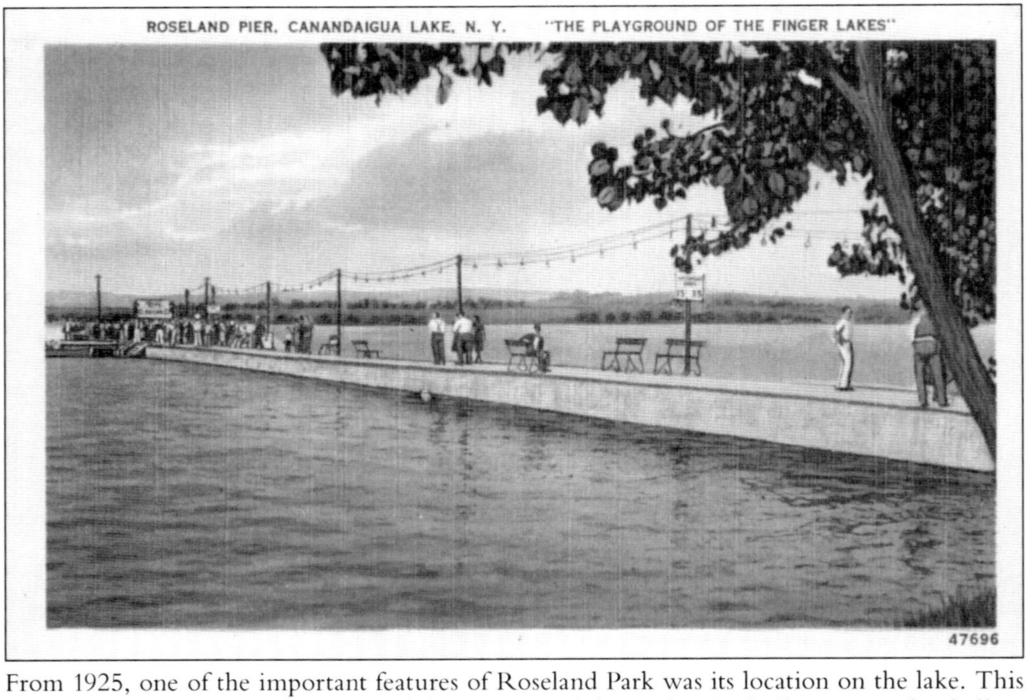

From 1925, one of the important features of Roseland Park was its location on the lake. This linen postcard was probably produced about 1945 and shows the pier built out over the shallow water to allow passengers to get on the tour boats.

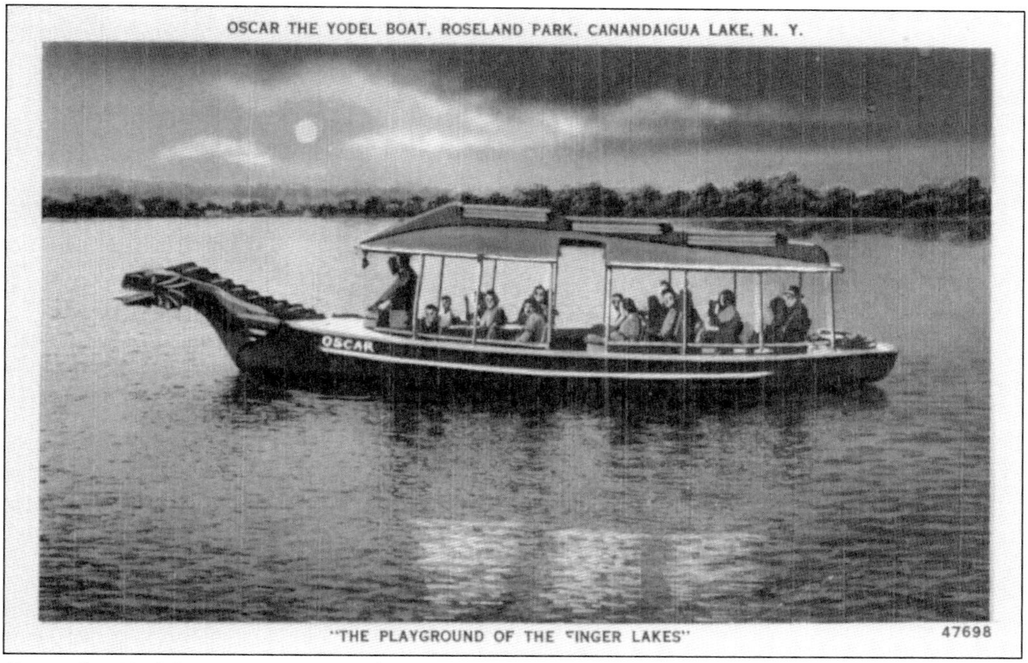

Oscar, the Yodel Boat, was one of the most unusual craft on the lake. For those too old for more exciting rides, it provided pleasant summer cruises on the actual lake. This postcard was produced about 1945.

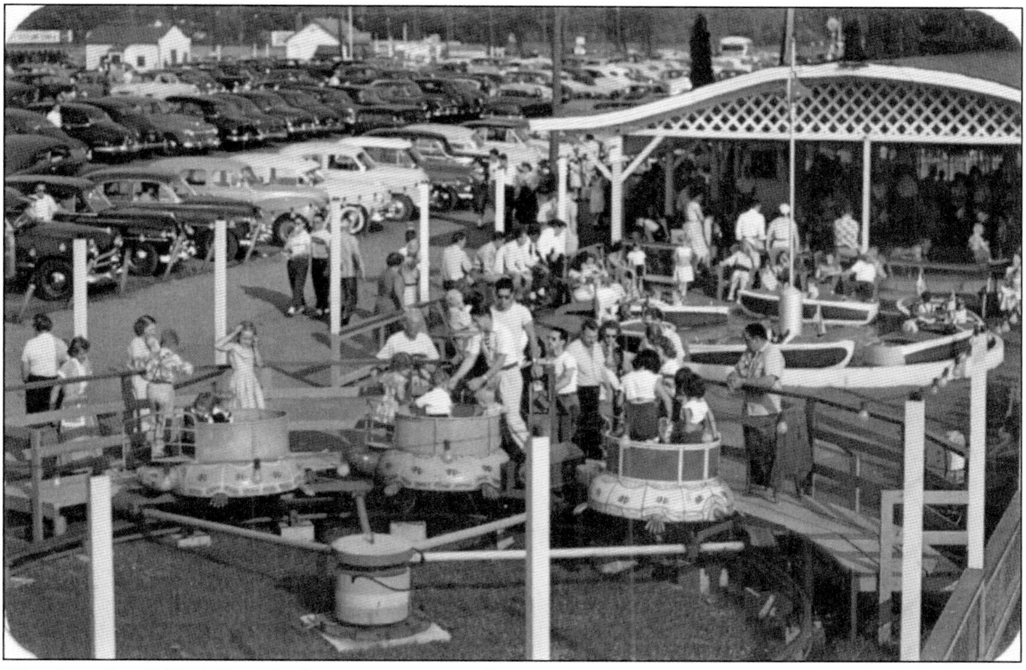

The Roseland "kiddie rides" were increasingly popular during the baby boom after World War II. In the foreground of this postcard, some youngsters get ready to enjoy the Flying Turtles ride. The parking lot attests to the end of the war years and rationing. This postcard was produced about 1955. (Photograph by Margery M. Elling.)

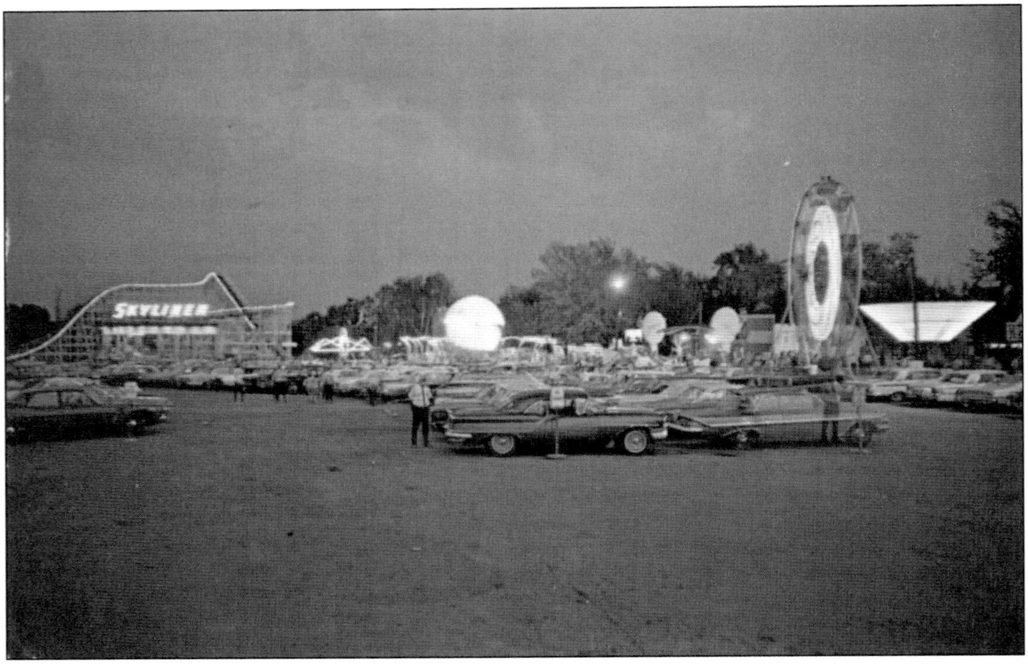

The Skyliner roller coaster was added to the Roseland attractions in 1960. In this evening scene, showing many automobiles from the early 1960s, crowds continue to enjoy Roseland Park under thousands of colored lights. (Photograph by G.W. Scott.)

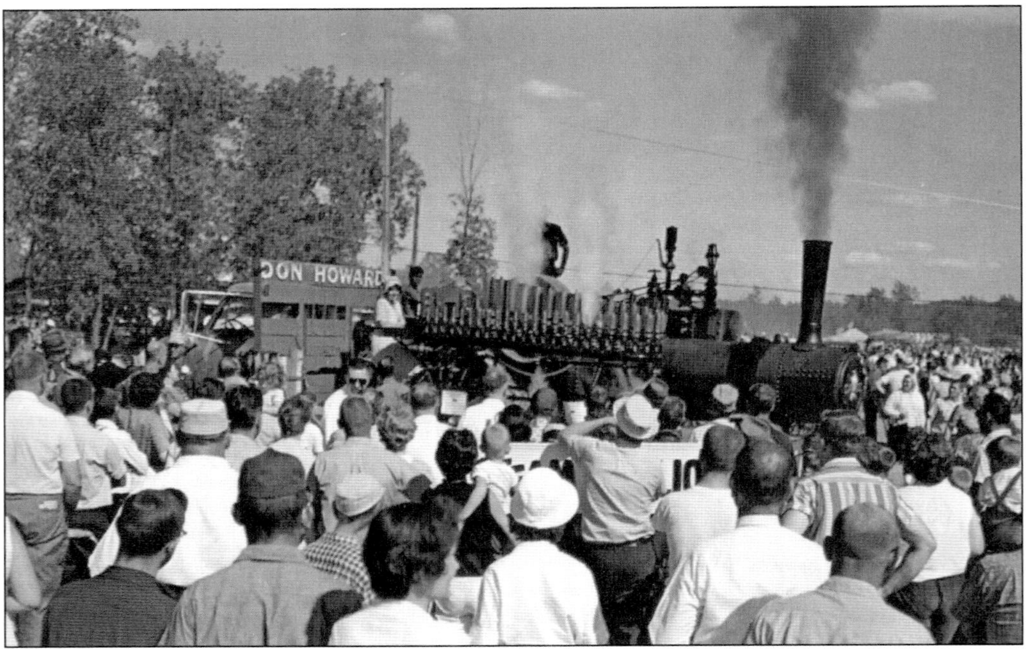

The New York State Steam Engine Association was formed in 1960. It promotes and encourages interest in antique vehicles powered by steam or other fuels. In 1964, the annual Pageant of Steam was held at Roseland Park. This postcard shows the popular steam calliope playing on the back of a truck loaned by Don Howard's farm equipment business. The original photograph was taken for the Scott Studio.

Six

Around the Lake

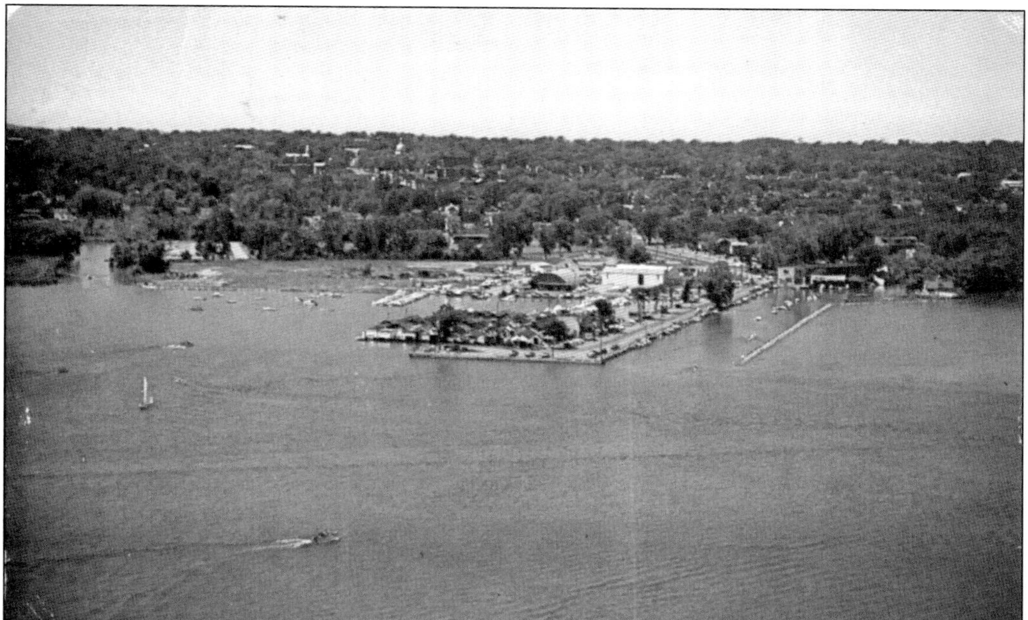

The Canandaigua City Pier has been serving boaters, fishermen, and sightseers since 1853. It has been reconstructed several times, and once had railroad tracks extending its full length. This early-1960s postcard shows the pier when there were no slips in the channel to the right of the pier. At the time this postcard was made, the Inn-on-the-Lake, now located to the left of the pier, had not been built.

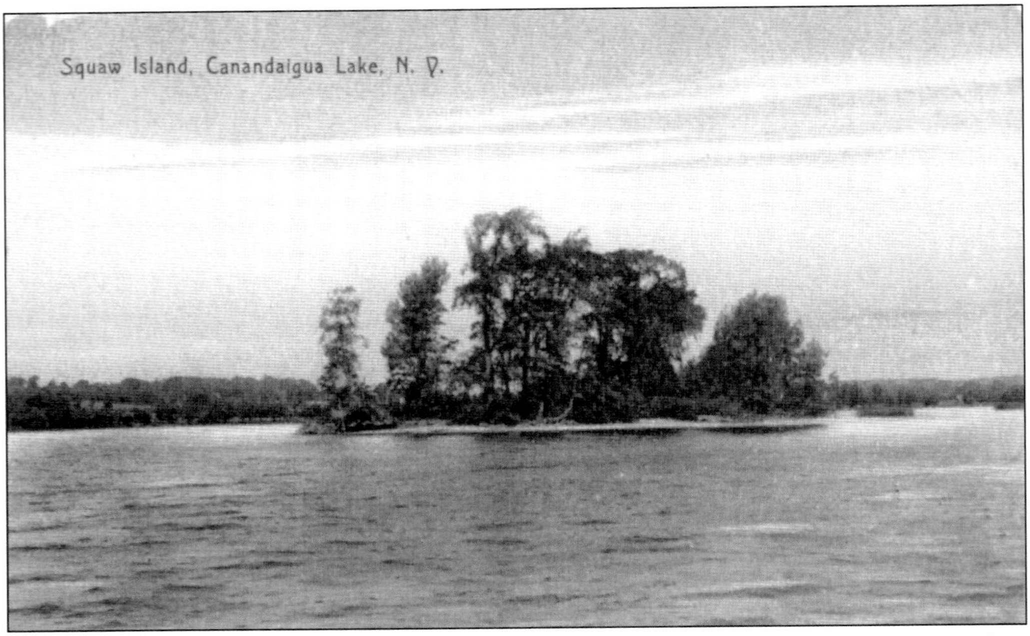

Squaw Island takes its name from a tale about Seneca women and children hiding there when Sullivan's army burned the Indian village of Canandaigua in 1779. In 1900, Dr. John M. Clark of the state museum conducted a study of a peculiar rock formation found around the island. Mary Clark Thompson had a boulder monument erected on the island in 1919. It describes the scientific significance of the island.

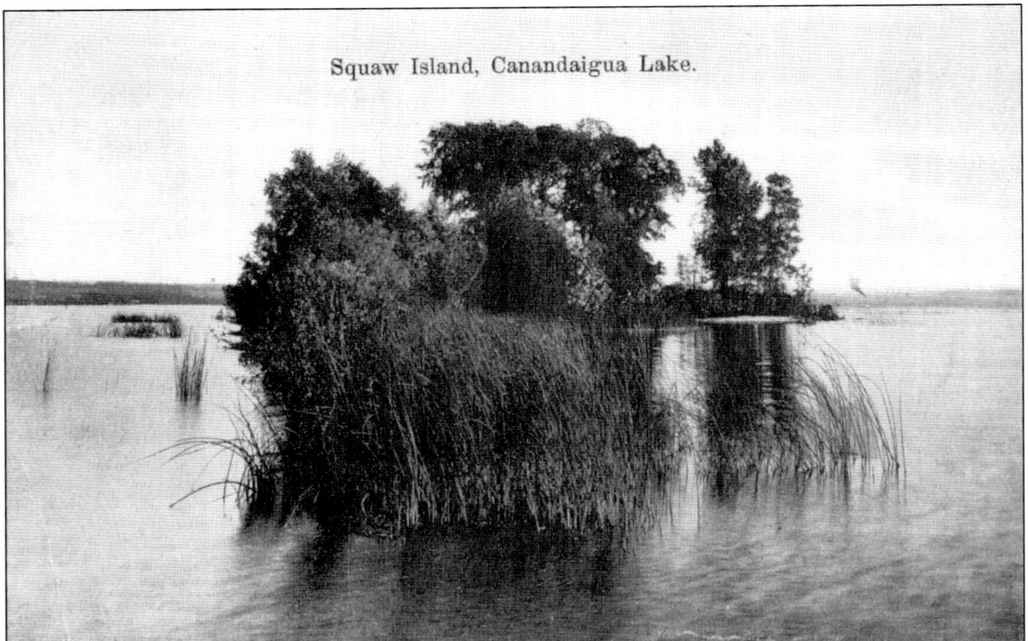

This picture of the island was taken from the shallow water covering the sand bar connecting the island to the mainland. Postmarked 1908, it shows the island slightly larger than it is today. Erosion from boat wakes, together with the higher water levels maintained by the dams on the lake outlet, have submerged much of the original island.

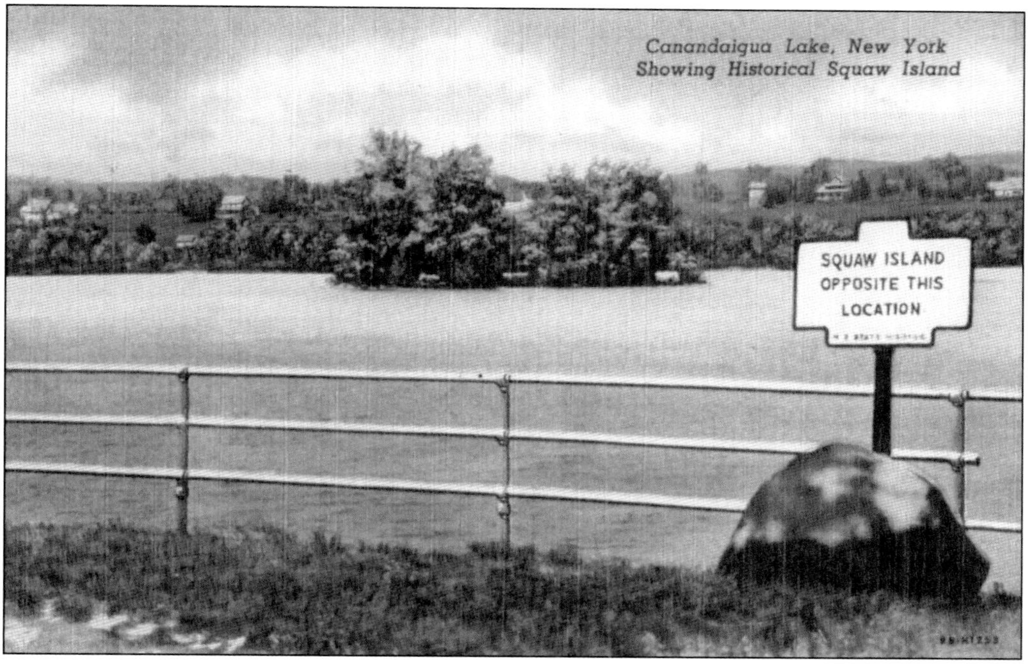

The State Highway Department erected this marker at the end of City Pier. Removed decades ago, it is now in the collection of the Ontario County Historical Society. Stories of native women and children taking refuge on the island during the Sullivan Expedition in 1779 have been known since at least the 1850s. The island is an important geological site because of the "water biscuits," limestone formations created around algae filaments, that form there.

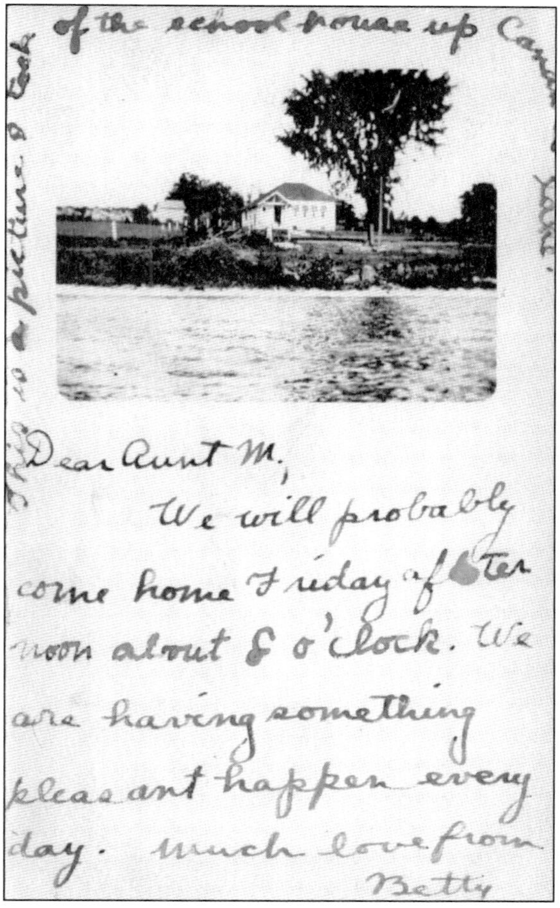

On Labor Day 1920, Dr. Charles Booth organized a work party of local residents to develop a public beach in front of the District No. 9 schoolhouse on the West Lake Road. This image shows the second building built in 1906. A popular town park today, this rare image shows just how rough the area around Butler Road was back then. (Courtesy of the Ontario County Historical Society.)

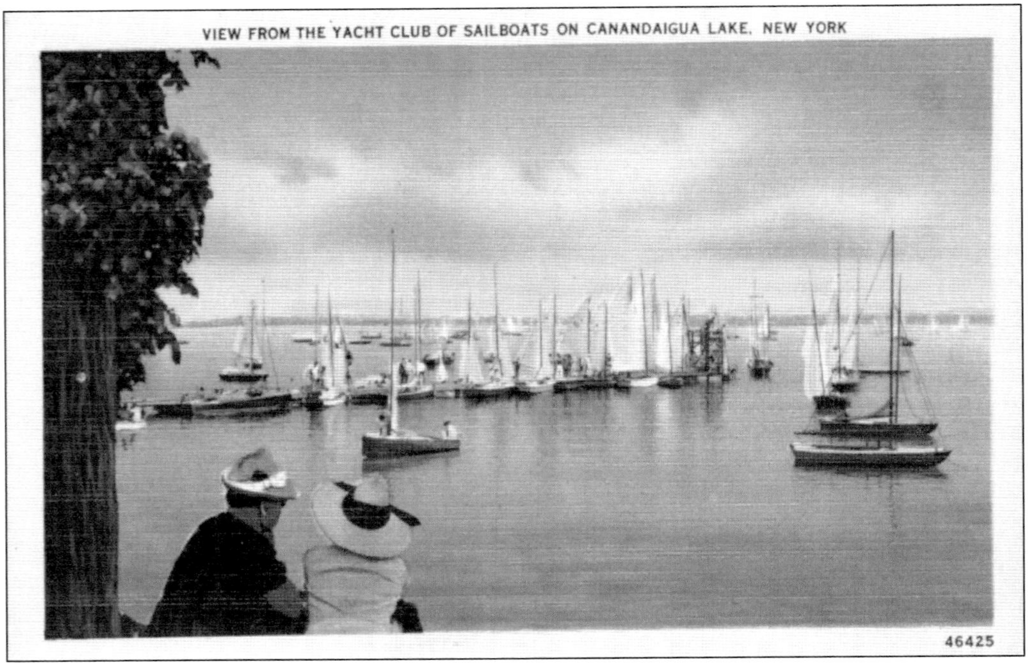

The Canandaigua Yacht Club was formed at the turn of the 20th century. After a few years it became inactive, and then it was revived in 1930. From 1930 to 1939, it was located in Booth Cottage, then Mentieth Point and Thendara. It moved to the former home of Maj. F.O. Chamberlain in 1939. This postcard shows the fleet at its current location as it looked in the mid-20th century.

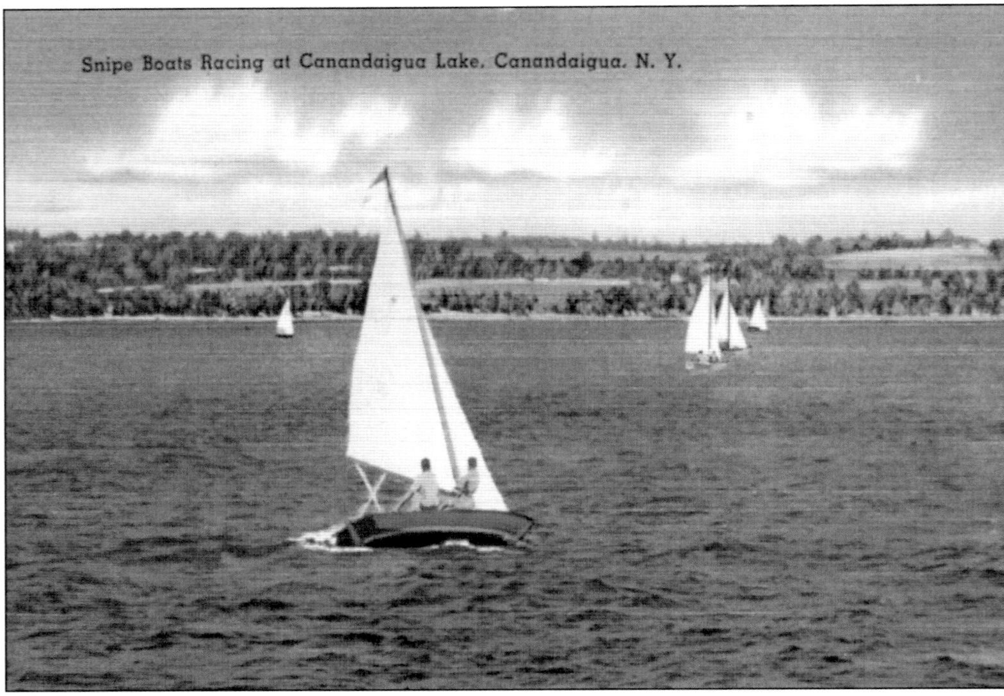

William Crosby designed the Snipe-class sailboat in 1931. A 15.5-foot, two person sailing dinghy, it is now recognized as an international-class sailboat. More than 30,000 Snipe boats have been produced. This linen postcard was probably produced in the 1950s.

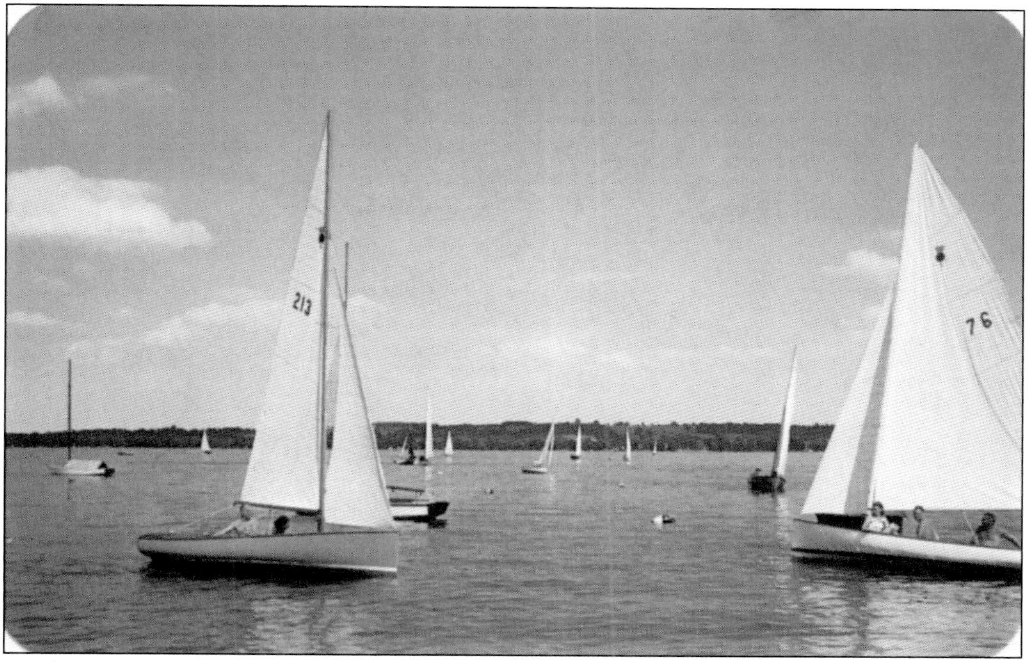

By the 1960s, the yacht club was growing, boats were getting larger, and the races were more competitive. This postcard from that time shows part of the fleet coming in from a race. (Photograph by Margery M. Elling; courtesy of the Ontario County Historical Society.)

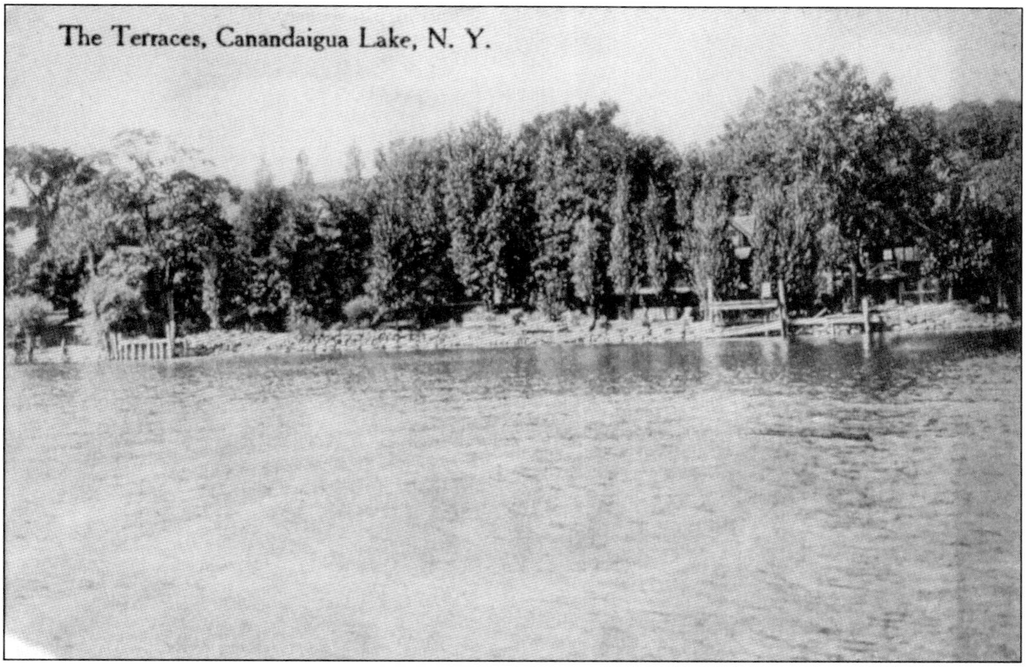

The Terraces was the name given to a stretch of lakeshore between Red Dock, just south of the present-day water works, and Tichenor Point. The long stone wall, or terrace, can be seen in this postcard, published about 1910. Most people named their cottages back then, and many of them became well-known landmarks.

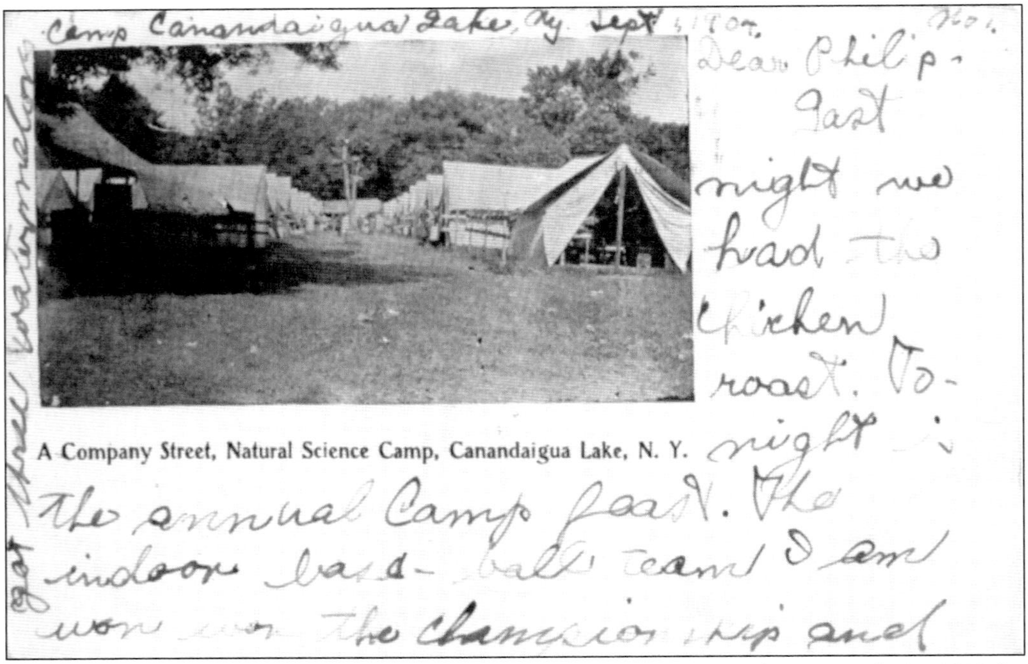

The Natural Science Camp was established on Tichenor Point on the west side in 1890 by Professor Airey, of Rochester Mechanic's Institute, now the Rochester Institute of Technology (RIT). A boys' camp at first, it later admitted young women. The camp was an example of progressive education where learning was promoted through hands-on experience. The camp moved to Keuka Lake in 1906. (Courtesy of Raymond and Barbara Henry.)

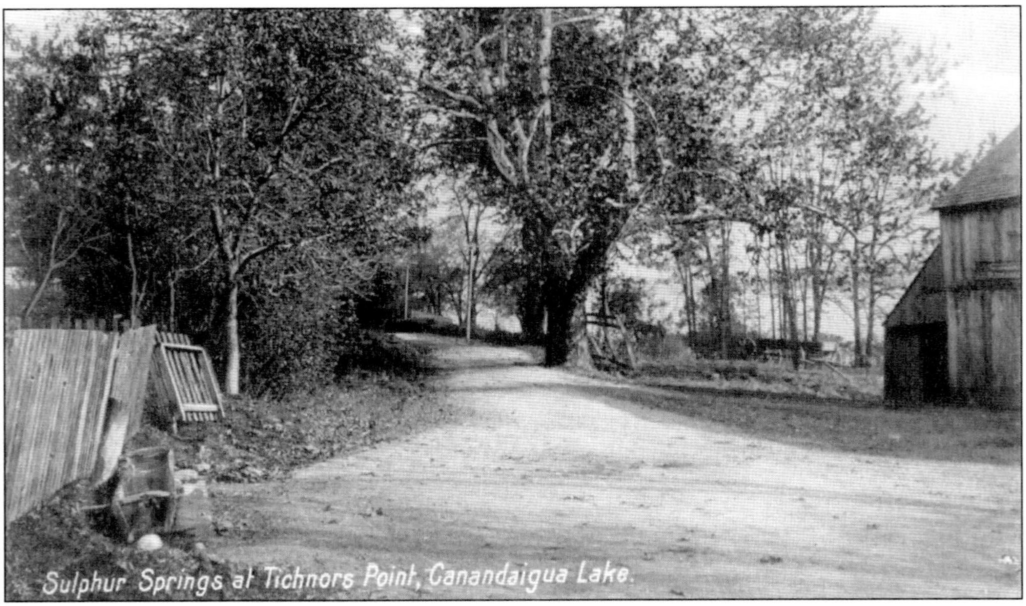

The sulphur spring was one of the features of the Natural Science Camp and Tichenor Point. Stories from the camp tell of campers being thrown into the sulphur water as punishment for rule infractions. Like many other points on the lakeshore, Tichenor's Point was subdivided into cottage lots in the 1920s. This postcard was postmarked in 1909, shortly after the Natural Science Camp closed.

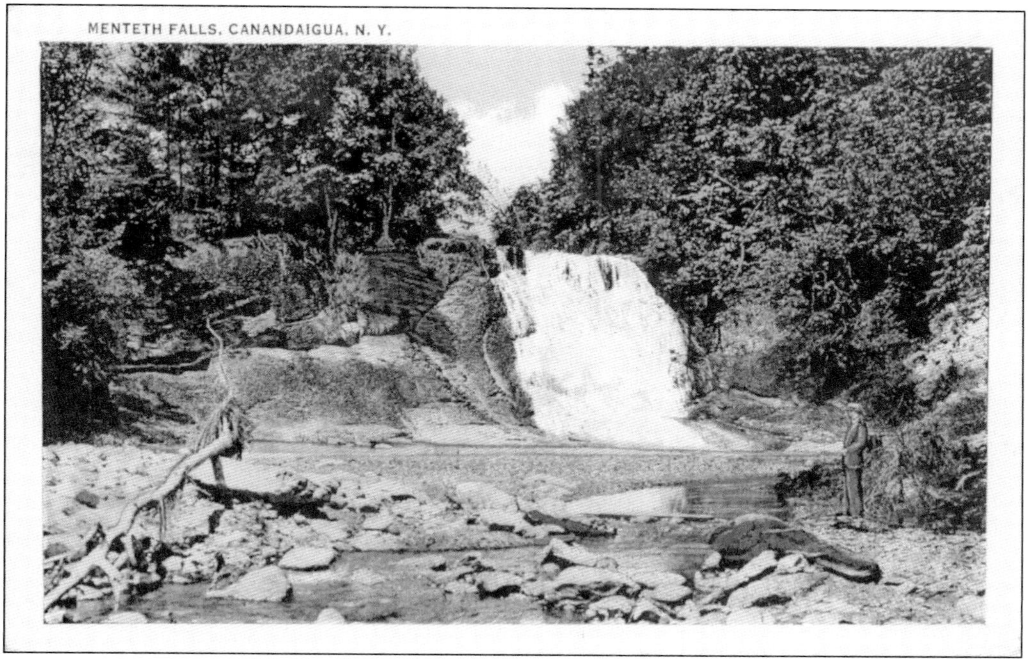

Mentieth Point is named for a pioneer family of Scots. Visitors often came by steamboat to hike the glen and see the falls. From 1919 to 1950, Catholic girls from nearby Camps Graynook and Madonna explored the glen. Today, the point is filled with cottages. The glen and its falls are seldom seen.

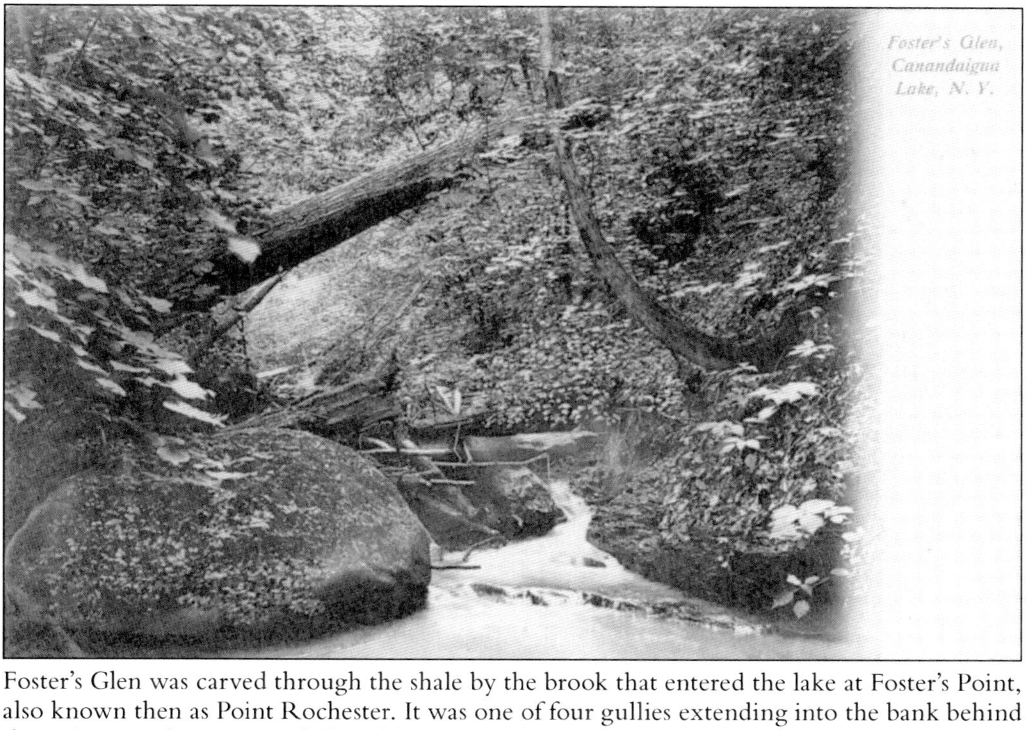

Foster's Glen was carved through the shale by the brook that entered the lake at Foster's Point, also known then as Point Rochester. It was one of four gullies extending into the bank behind the point. Much more tangled, and less visited than other glens, it was still a well-known and picturesque location.

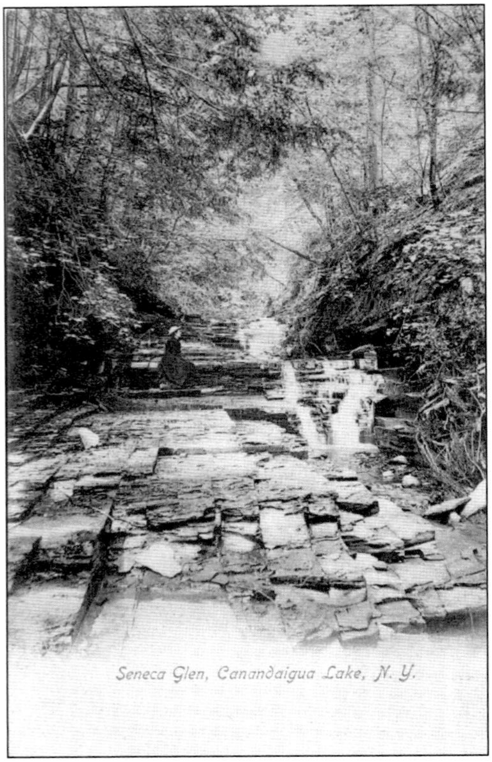

Seneca Glen extended back from Seneca Point into the hillside. The many visitors to the old Seneca Point Hotel could easily hike much of the scenic shale glen.

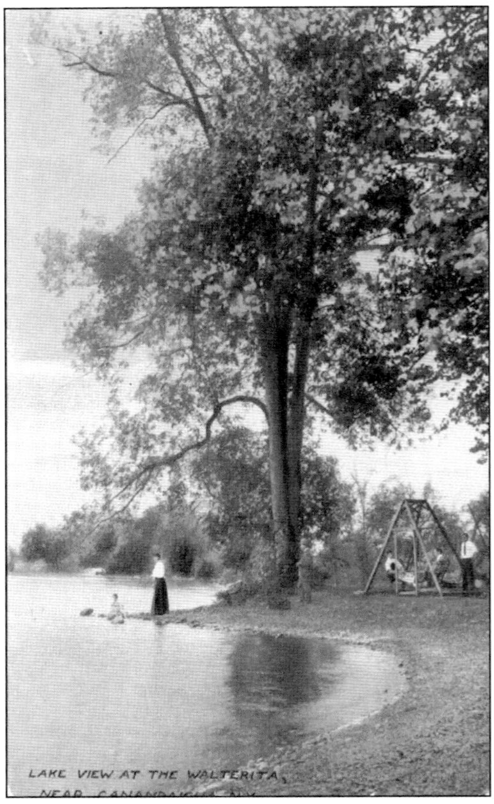

Lakeshore hotels, like the Walterita, provided a relaxing atmosphere for middle-class families at the turn of the 20th century. The pleasures of a few days or weeks along the lake were basic; wading in the water, sitting in the swing, fishing, or using a rowboat. The shore was quiet and natural a century ago.

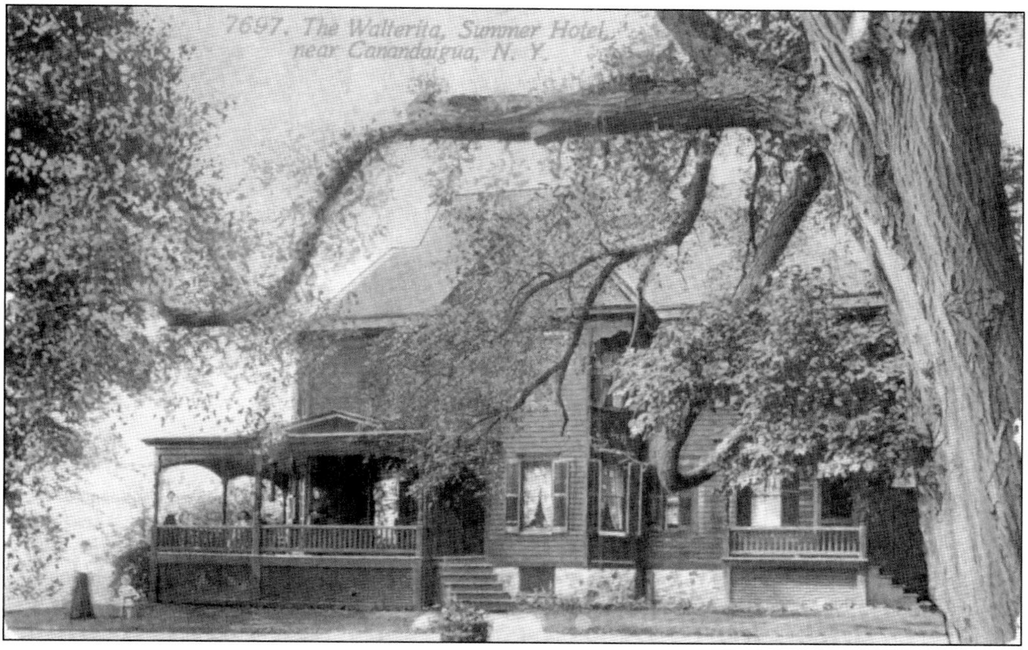

The Walterita Hotel was one of several small resort hotels located around the lake. After the hotel closed, it was cut into three sections, each of which became a separate cottage. (Courtesy of Ray and Barbara Henry.)

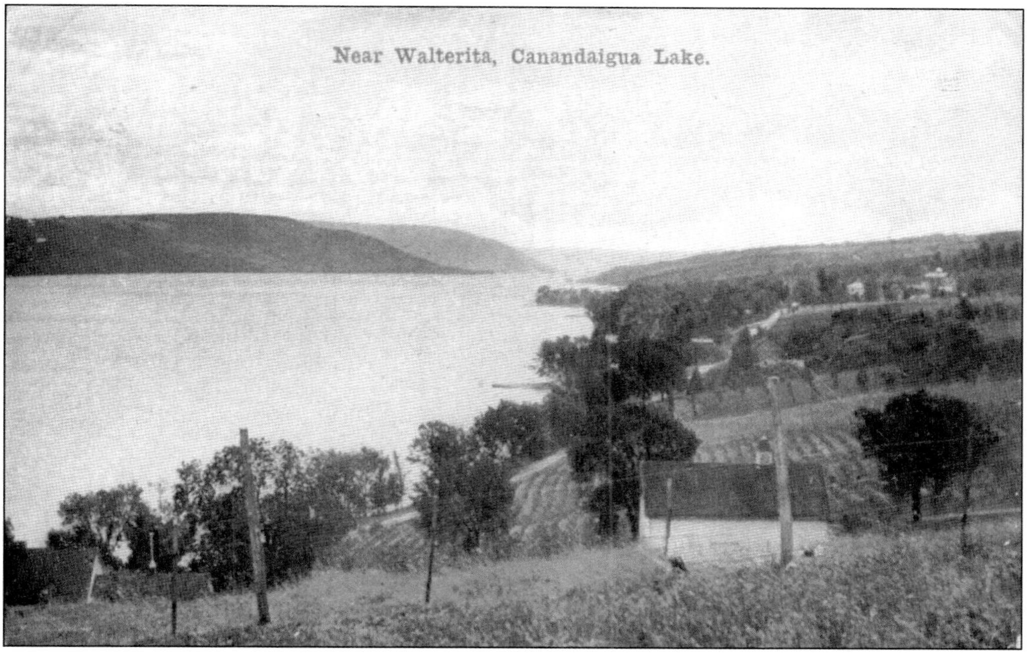

Built in 1905 near the intersection of Wells-Curtice and West Lake Roads, the Walterita was a well-known summer hotel. When this picture was taken, the west shore of Canandaigua Lake was mostly agricultural land. Today, this area is filled with cottages and homes.

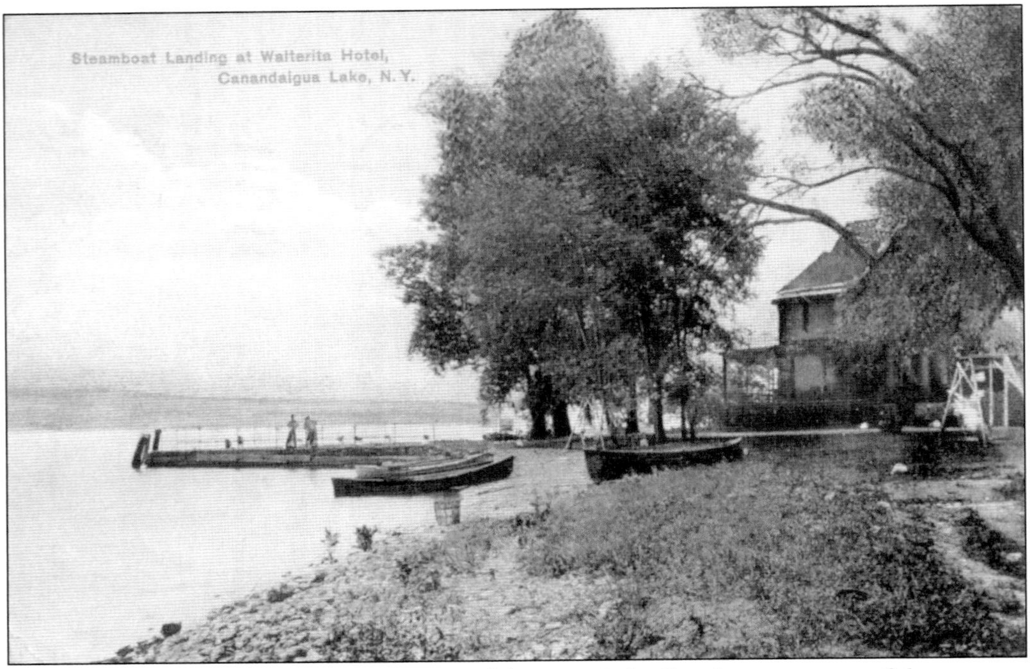

In the days before the grading and paving of the West Lake Road, most guests of the summer hotels arrived by steamboat. This postcard shows the steamboat dock at the Walterita Hotel. It does not extend very far into the lake because the steamboats were shallow-draft vessels and could come close in to shore.

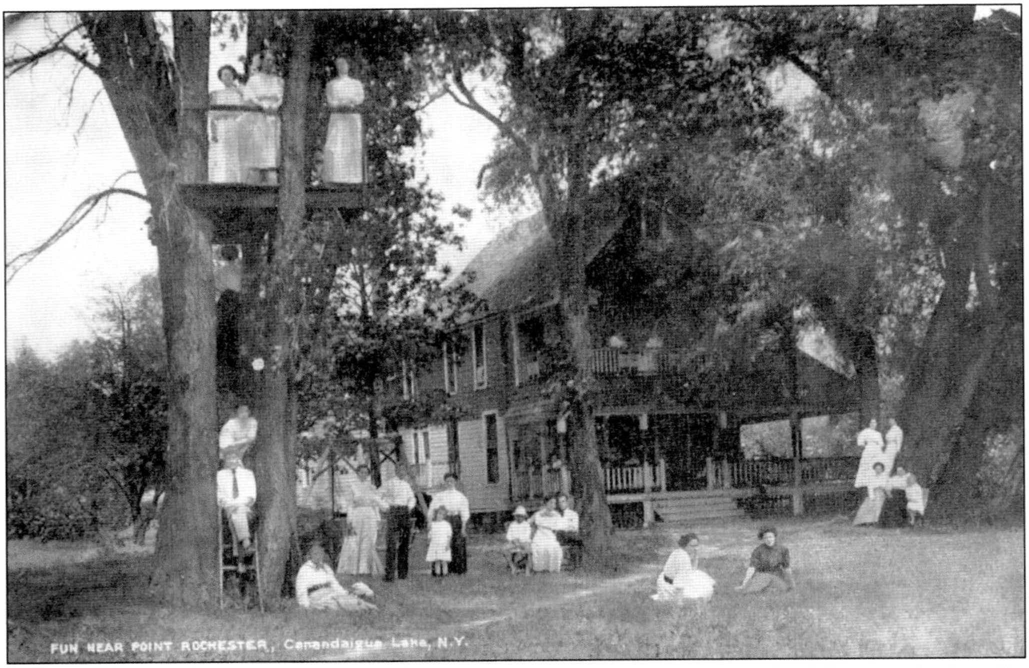

This family gathering at Point Rochester shows how relaxed life up the lake was during the summer a century ago. However, looking closely, one can see that everyone is wearing his or her Sunday best. It must have been quite a feat for the ladies in long dresses to get up in the tree house.

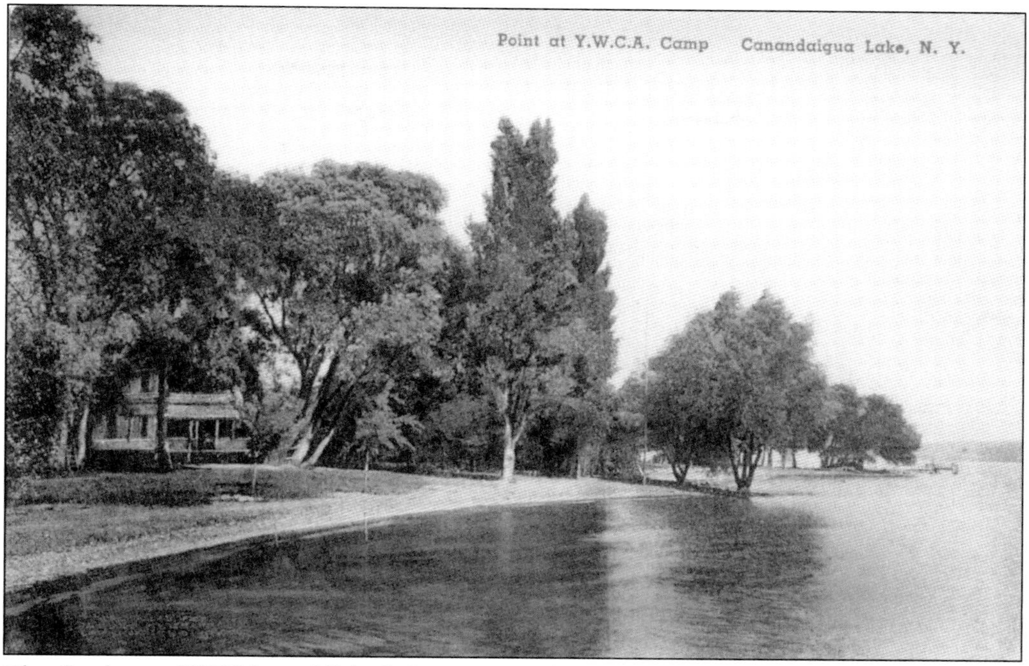

The Rochester YWCA established Camp Onanda on Point Rochester in 1919. The camp closed, was purchased by the Town of Canandaigua, and became Onanda Park in 1988–1989. From 1982 to 1988, this point was the location of Camp Good Days and Special Times for children suffering from cancer. The point is still called Point Rochester by local residents, although it had several other names in the past.

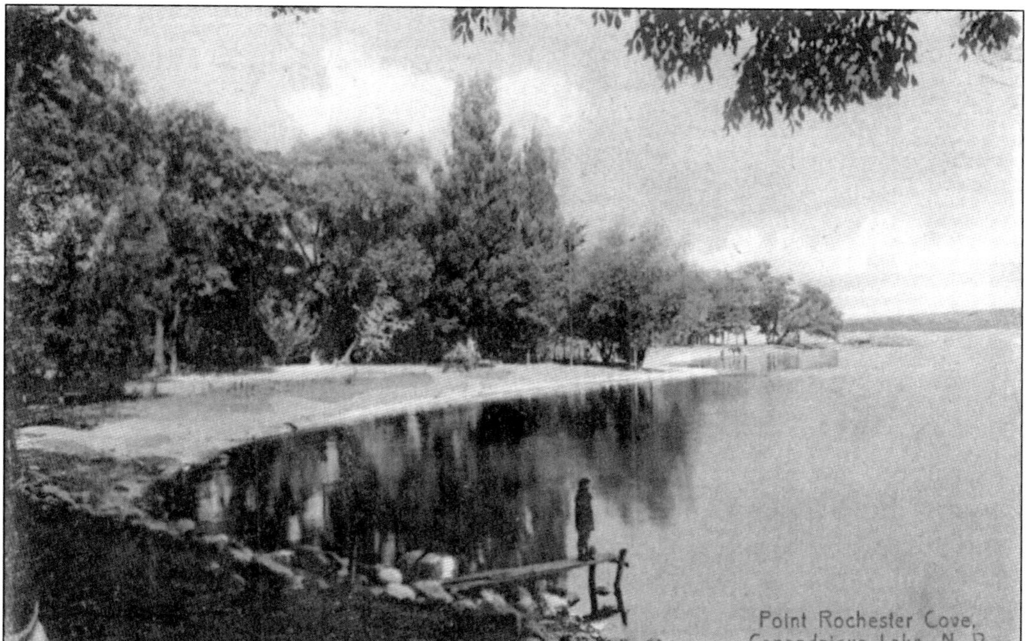

Point Rochester cove is the location of Onanda Park and the former camps. This postcard was postmarked in 1909. The writer noted that she had "been out rowing every day, going in a launch up to the Head of the Lake this morning. Having a great time."

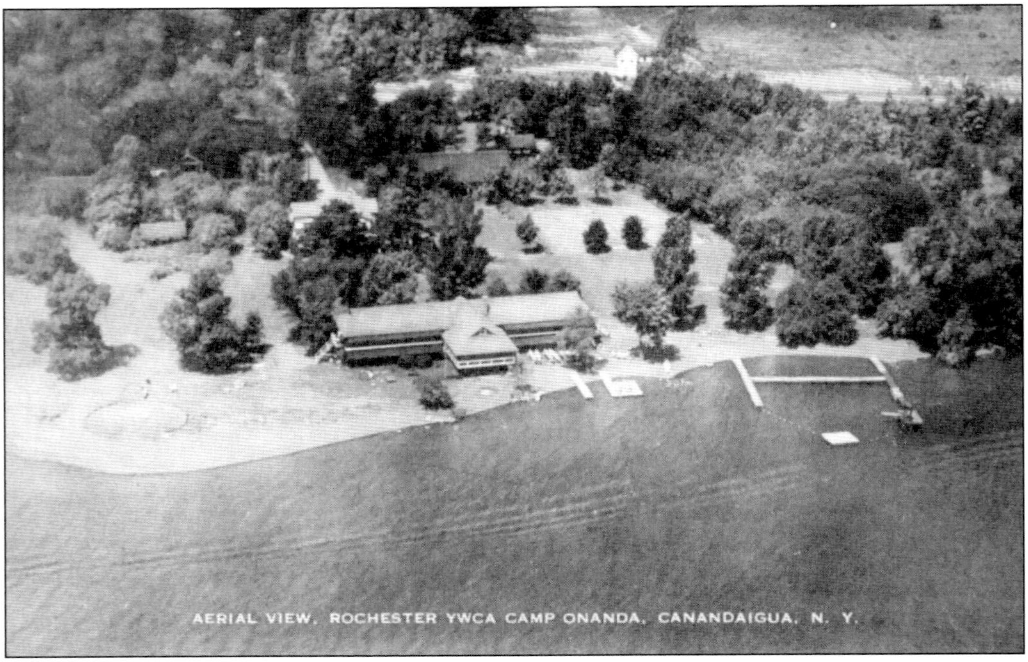

This aerial view of Camp Onanda was probably made in the 1930s. The large building near the shore was cut apart, and the sections became several other buildings that continue to be used by visitors to the town park.

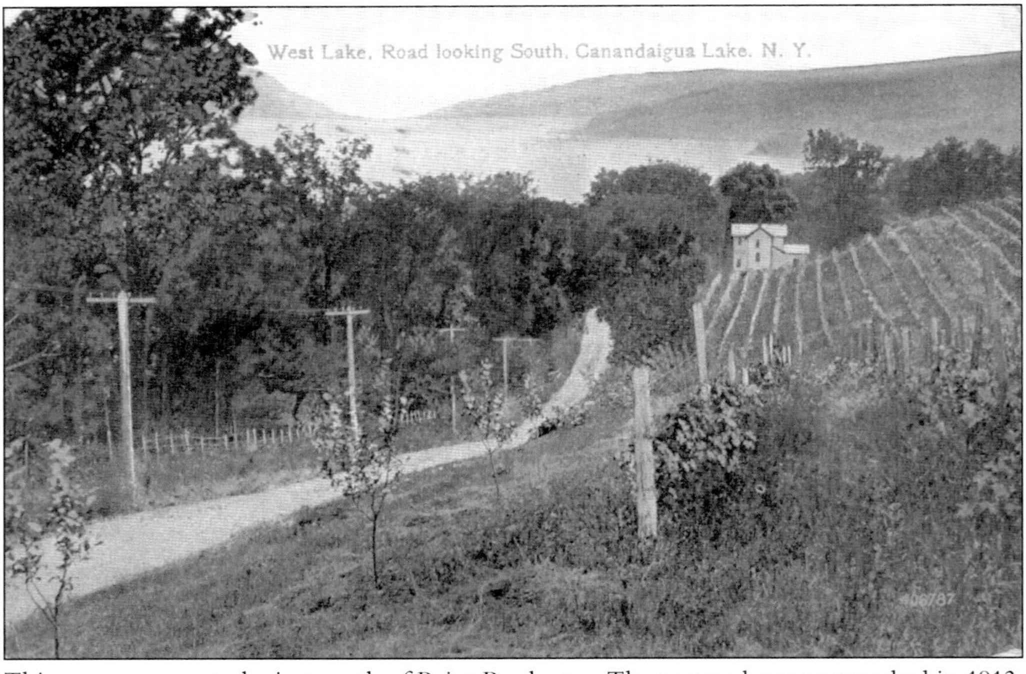

This scene appears to be just north of Point Rochester. The postcard was postmarked in 1913. Telephone service extended down the West Lake Road by the time this postcard was published. However, the road was still gravel and dirt, and the area was mostly used for agricultural purposes. The lakeshore was a quiet, relaxed place in those days. The sender of the postcard wrote, "I am having a lovely time here. Am going to stay all summer."

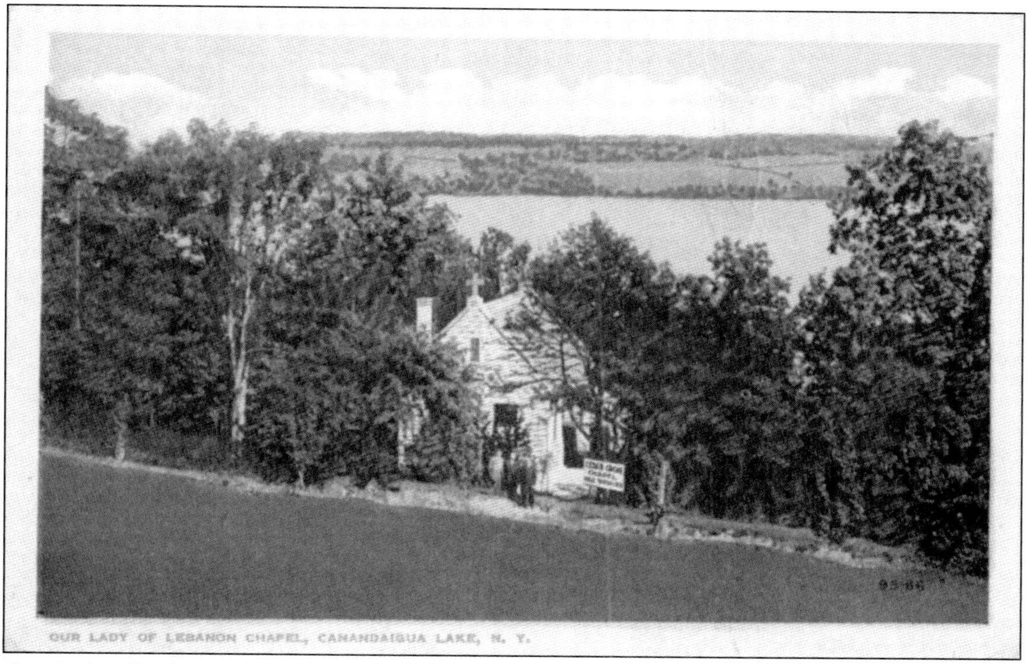

Our Lady of Lebanon Chapel was established by the Rochester Catholic Diocese for the benefit of cottagers and the young women at nearby Camp Graynook. Located at the intersection of Wells-Curtice Road and the West Lake Road, it was closed in by the mid-1930s. By then, Camp Graynook had closed. For the past half century, the old chapel has been a summer home.

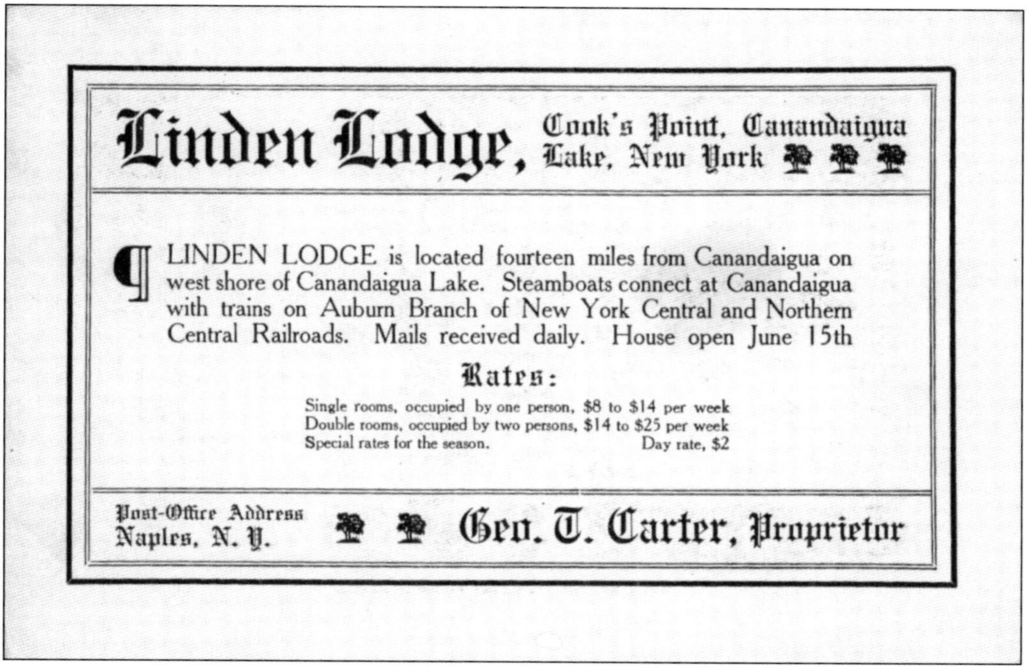

Linden Lodge was the final name of the hotel on Cook's Point. Its quiet seclusion attracted visitors from around the northeast. As this advertising postcard indicates, the cozy hotel was well connected to the outside world.

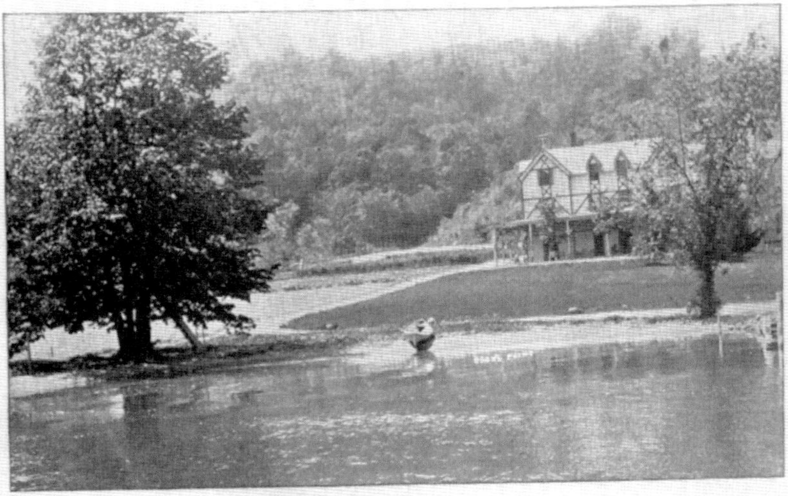

BEACH IN FRONT OF LINDEN LODGE

The Cook family first came to this point in 1863. Here, they built "Elm Lodge." Robert D. Cook later built a year-round house and opened vineyards planted by a German immigrant, Jake Wolters. In later years, Cook's wife ran a popular resort at the house when her husband had financial problems. "Linden Lodge," the final name of the Cook's Point resort, was closed and demolished in 1914.

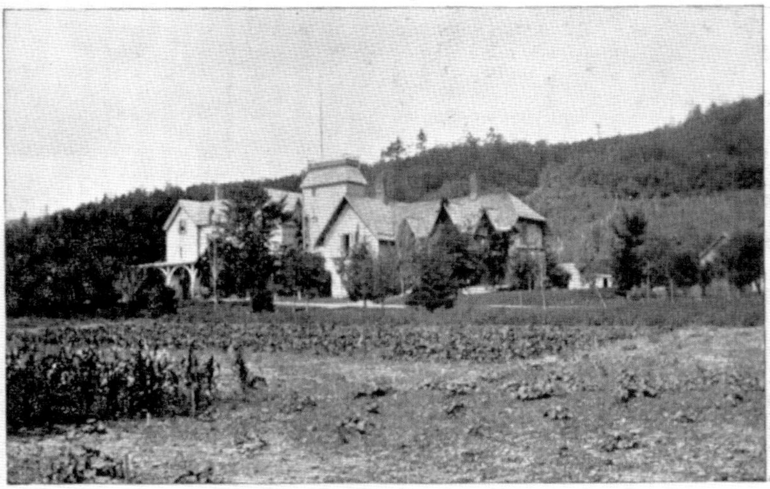

LINDEN LODGE, CANANDAIGUA LAKE, N. Y.

The hotel on Cook's Point was much like other small hotels along the lake a century ago. Accommodating only a few guests at a time, it provided simple, comfortable, and personal service, much like modern bed-and-breakfast lodging. There were no baseball games or horse races on Cook's Point.

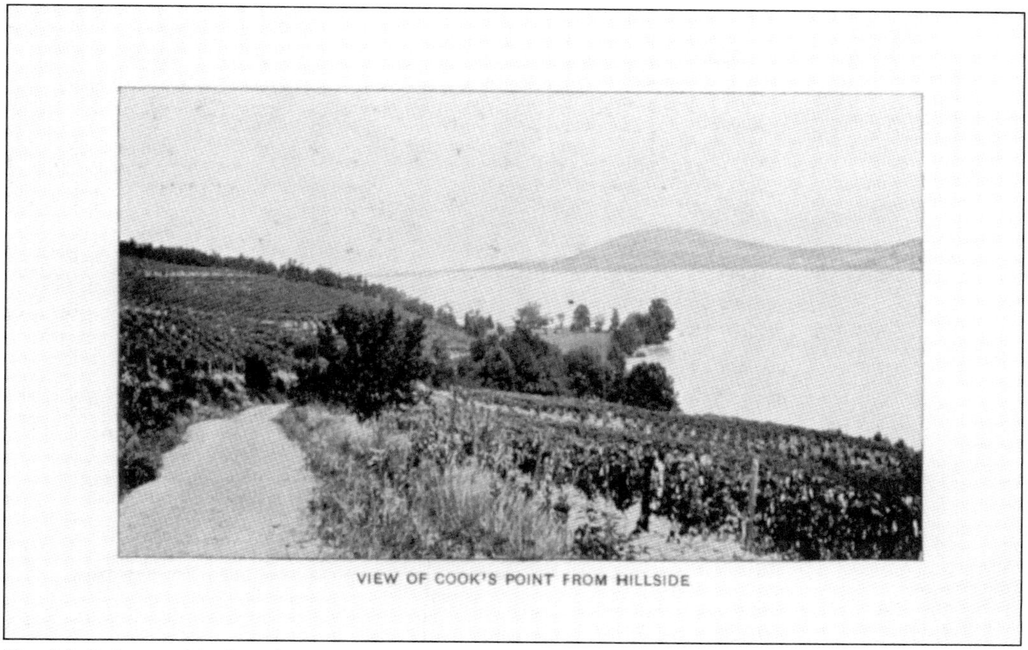

Cook's Point and its hotel were just south of the much larger Seneca Point. A major steamboat stop, Seneca Point welcomed many guests on a typical summer day. Unlike the Seneca Point Hotel, Cook's Point and "Linden Lodge" catered to small family gatherings seeking quiet, seclusion, bathing, fishing, and boating.

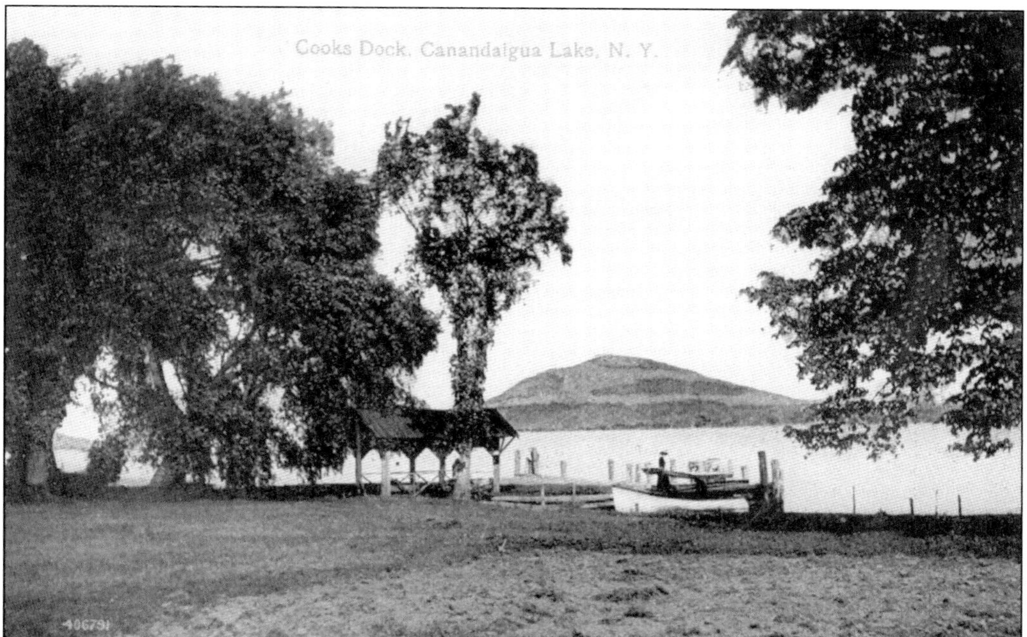

Serene isolation was one of the main attractions of the hotel on Cook's Point. Known far and wide, the hotel received Adm. Arent Schuyler Crowninshield, of the US Navy, as a guest in 1904. The admiral's wife, Mary, was a well-known Geneva author.

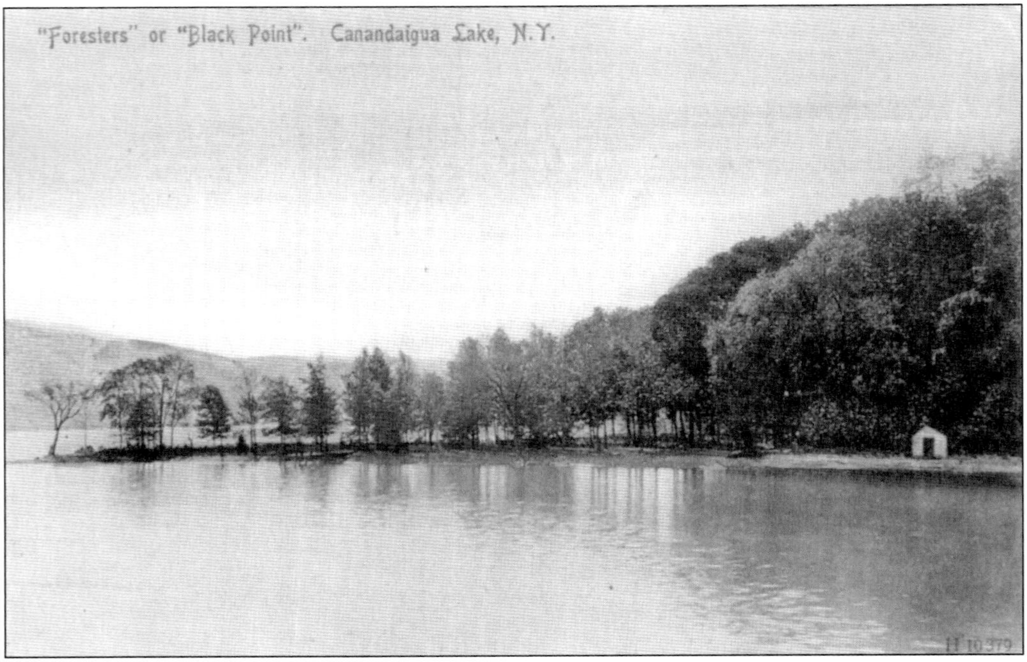

Black Point was the site of two early social clubs, the Foresters and the Black Point Association. The use of the two large cabins, erected on the north and south shoulders of the point, was shared by the members of the clubs, extended families, and businessmen from Canandaigua. Black Point was an established steamboat stop. Most of the point was subdivided into private cottage lots in 1948.

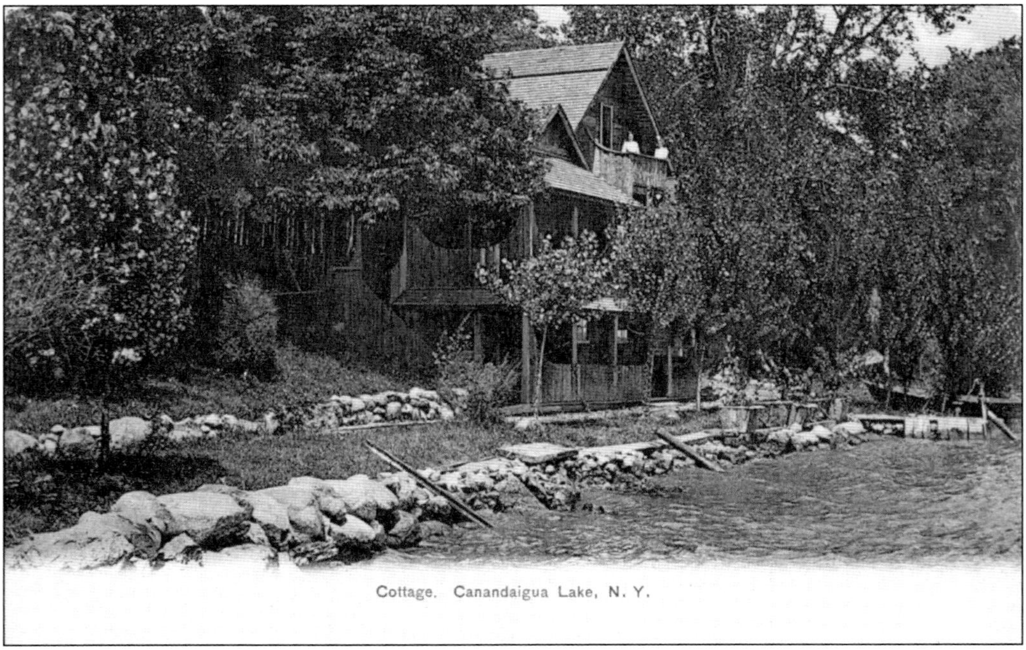

This unidentified cottage was probably located on the west side along the southwest shore. It was unusual because of its close proximity to the water. The rustic architecture used weathered boards for siding and railings. This postcard was published prior to 1907.

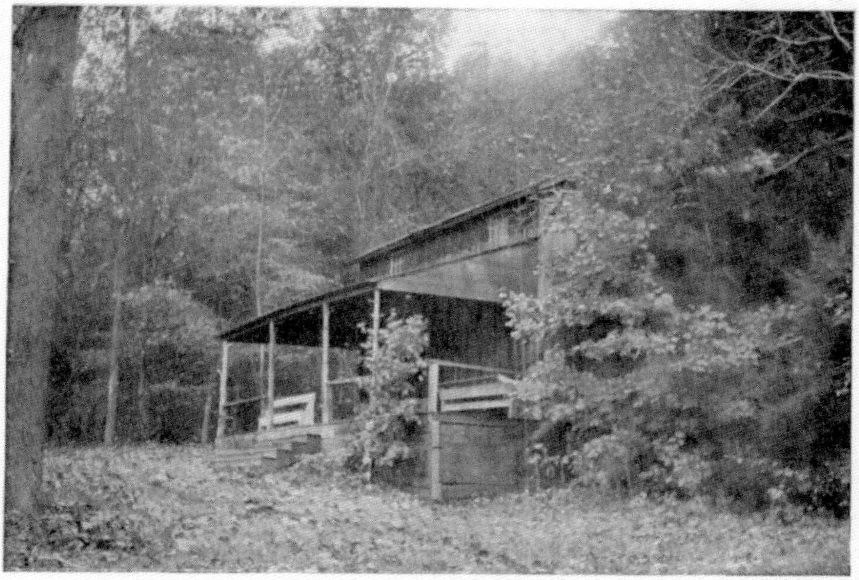

WALTON CABIN, CANANDAIGUA LAKE.

Much changed, the Walton Cabin still stands along the lake on Walton Point, just south of Stemple's Landing. One of the oldest structures on the lakeshore, it originally served the Canandaigua Walton Club, comprised entirely of lawyers. Walter S. Hubbell, the last survivor of the club, sold the cabin in 1911. The cabin was built about 1864.

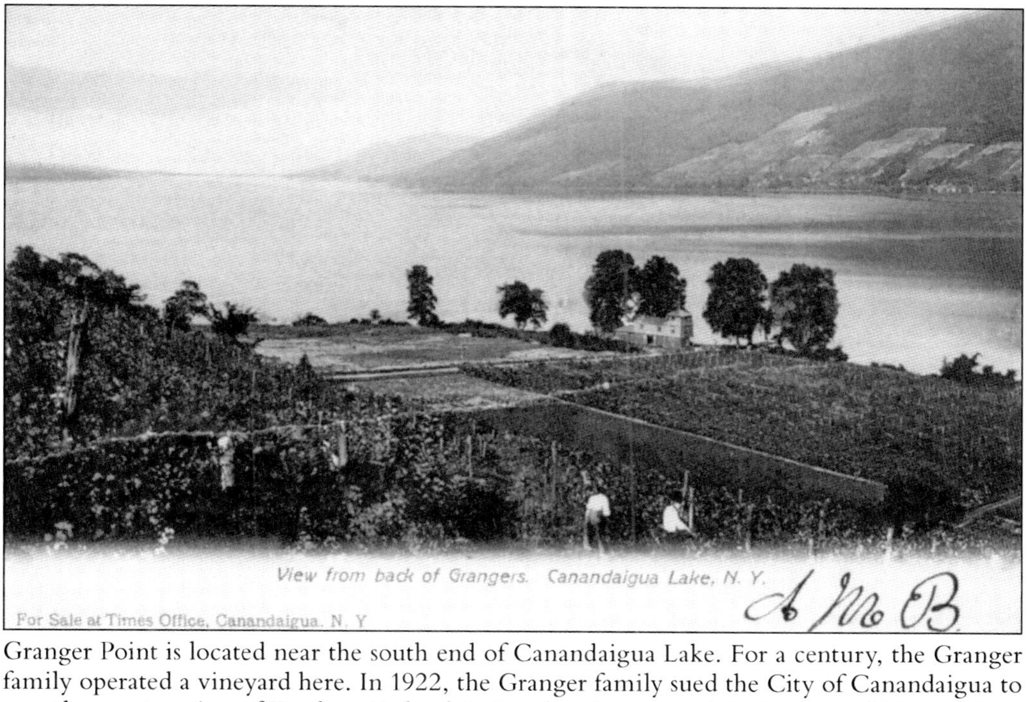

Granger Point is located near the south end of Canandaigua Lake. For a century, the Granger family operated a vineyard here. In 1922, the Granger family sued the City of Canandaigua to stop the construction of Kershaw Park, claiming that they owned the bottom of Canandaigua Lake. They did have a deed to the bottoms of several lakes and rivers, but New York's Court of Appeals ruled that land under navigable waterways was state property.

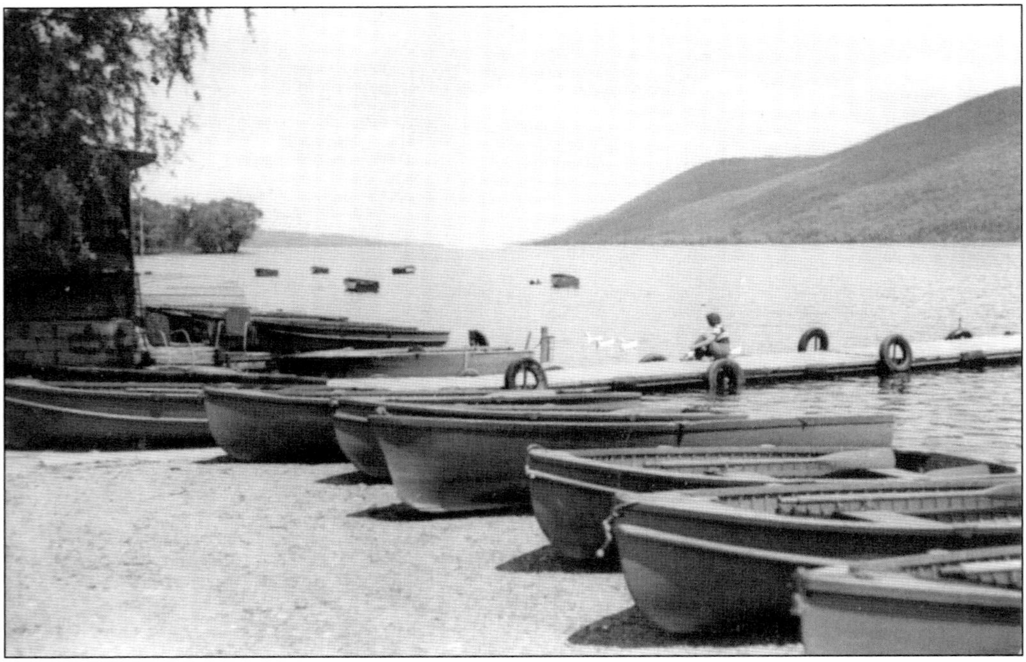

These rowboats, and small craft visible in the background, are reminders of how pleasure boating has changed on Canandaigua Lake. Dating from the early 1960s, this postcard shows the shore, moorings, and quiet water at the south end of the lake at Woodville. A South Bristol town park is now located in this area. Woodville craftsmen were once known for the production of wooden boats. (Photograph by Margery M. Elling.)

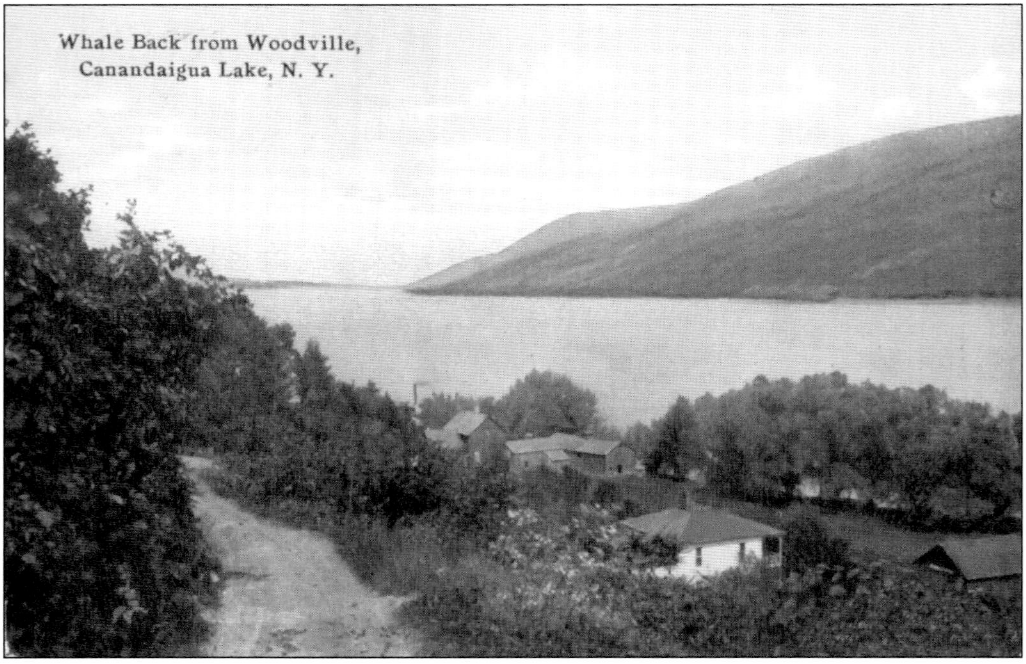

"Whale Back," the hill visible across the lake in this view, is also known as South Hill. That hill, across Vine Valley from Bare Hill, contains archaeological evidence of the origins of the Seneca people, called "the people of the hill."

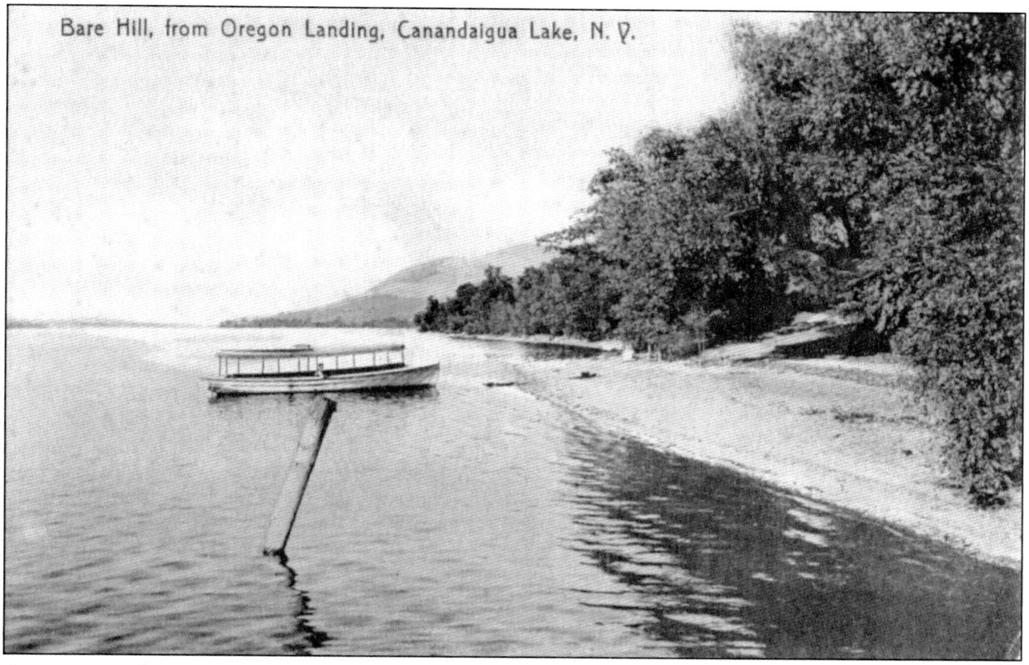

Oregon Landing is located in Yates County, on the southeast shore of Canandaigua Lake, about a mile below Vine Valley. It is the site of one of the few log cabins left on the lake. Shown in this picture is one of the naphtha steam launches that began appearing on the lake in the late 19th century. Naptha is a petroleum fuel similar to gasoline.

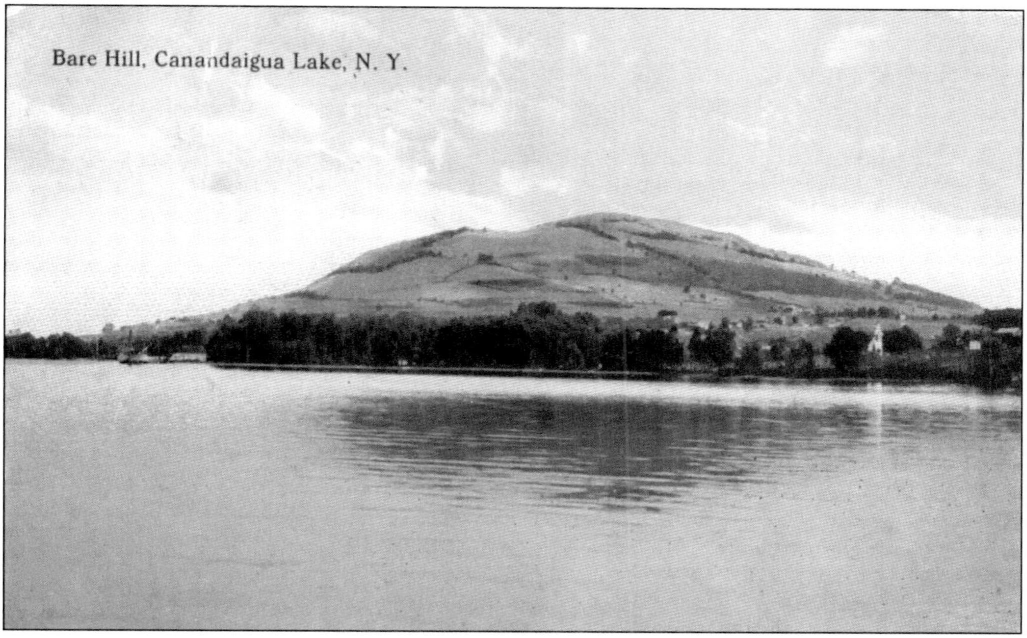

Bare Hill is the legendary origin of the Seneca people. Legend says that the hill was bare because a huge snake rolled down the hill, killing all the vegetation. As it rolled, the snake disgorged the heads of its victims. Rocks resembling heads can be found around the lakeshore. The lack of vegetation probably resulted from clear cutting for pioneer farms and vineyards. The summit of Bare Hill is now protected by the state.

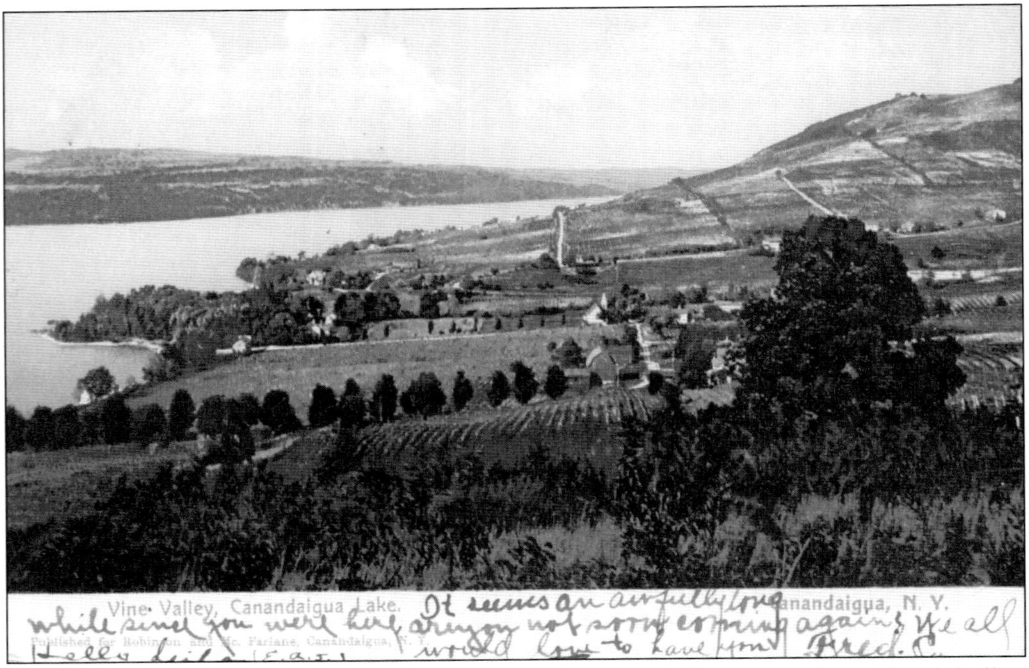

Vine Valley, shown in this postcard image, is formed by Bare Hill to its north and South Hill to its south. A quiet farming community and lake port serving the nearby villages of Gorham and Rushville, it was often called Middlesex Landing. The state museum excavated a Hopewellian village site here in 1922. Late in the 19th century, a private park called "Willow Grove" was created here, complete with a dance hall and picnic grounds.

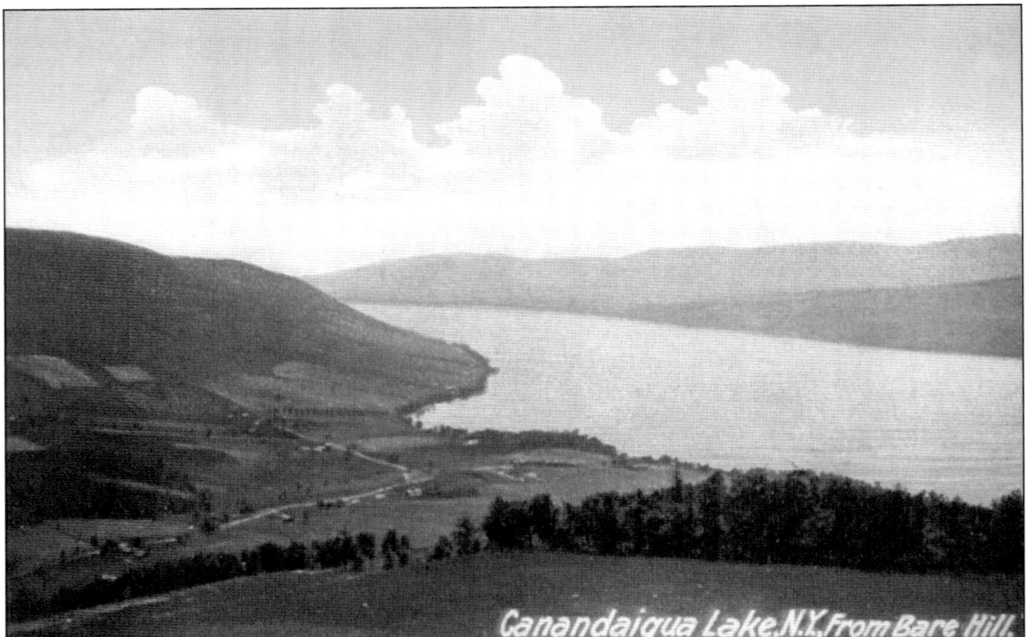

This view of Vine Valley shows the wooded point that served as a steamboat landing. The extensive vineyards and cultivated fields on the slope of Bare Hill are also clearly visible in this undivided postcard, which was published prior to 1907.

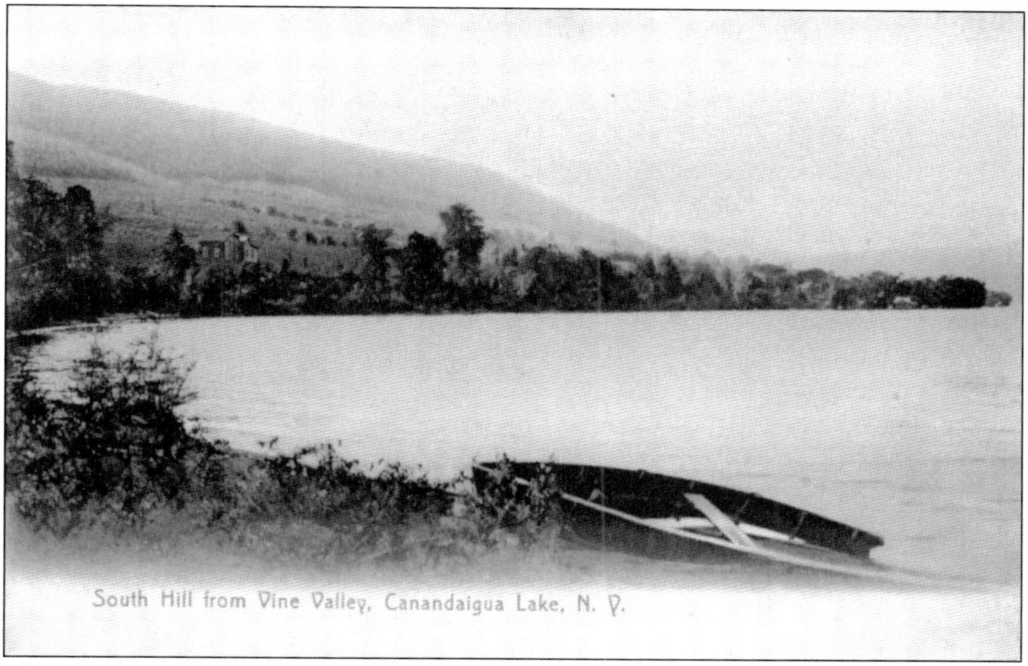

This scene from the beach at Vine Valley shows what a quiet rural setting the area was. It was known as Middlesex Landing for many years. Just out of view was a substantial steamboat pier. This postcard has a divided back, and the blurred postmark appears to be 1910.

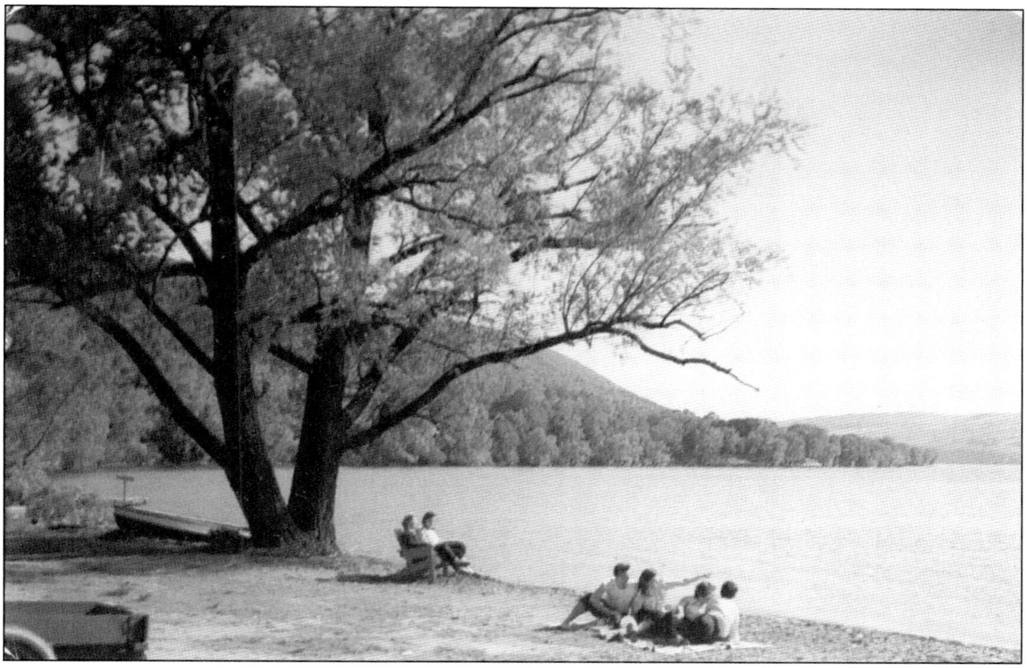

The relaxed scene shown here is the public beach at Vine Valley on the east side of Canandaigua Lake. Much of the beachfront at Vine Valley is known as Willow Grove. However, outside that private park is this beach area that is now a town park belonging to Middlesex. This postcard dates from the early 1960s. (Photograph by Margery M. Elling.)

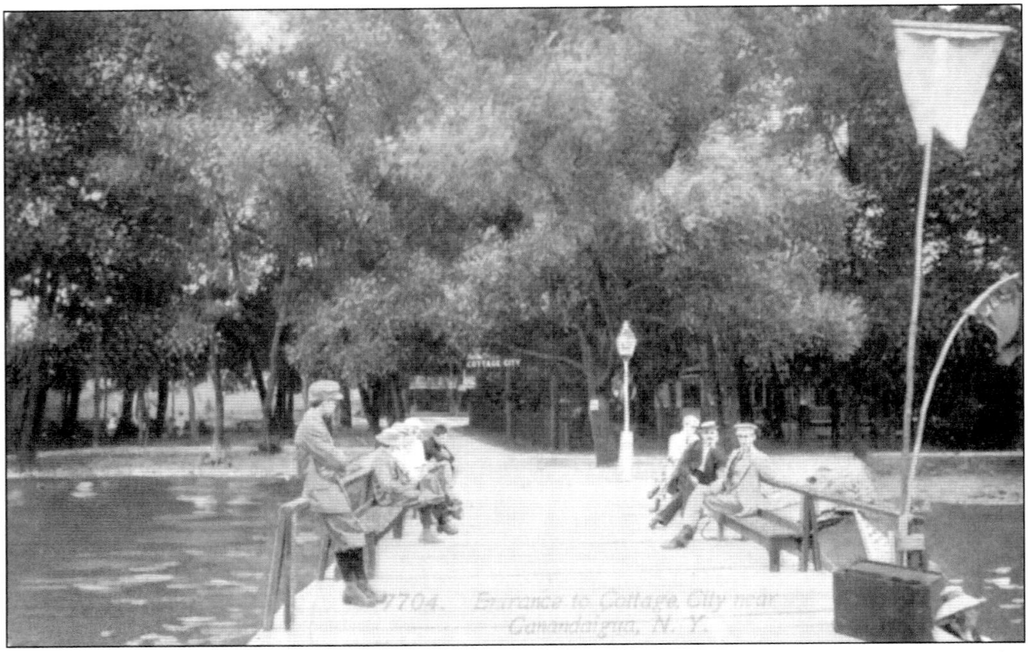

Cottage City began as a steamboat stop, hotel, and dance hall, operated by Richard Gage. The first cottage was built in 1878. Gage's Landing began to be called Cottage City in 1895. In this view, one can see the large pier made necessary by the number of passengers coming and going from Cottage City. The flag used for hailing steamboats is visible at the right side.

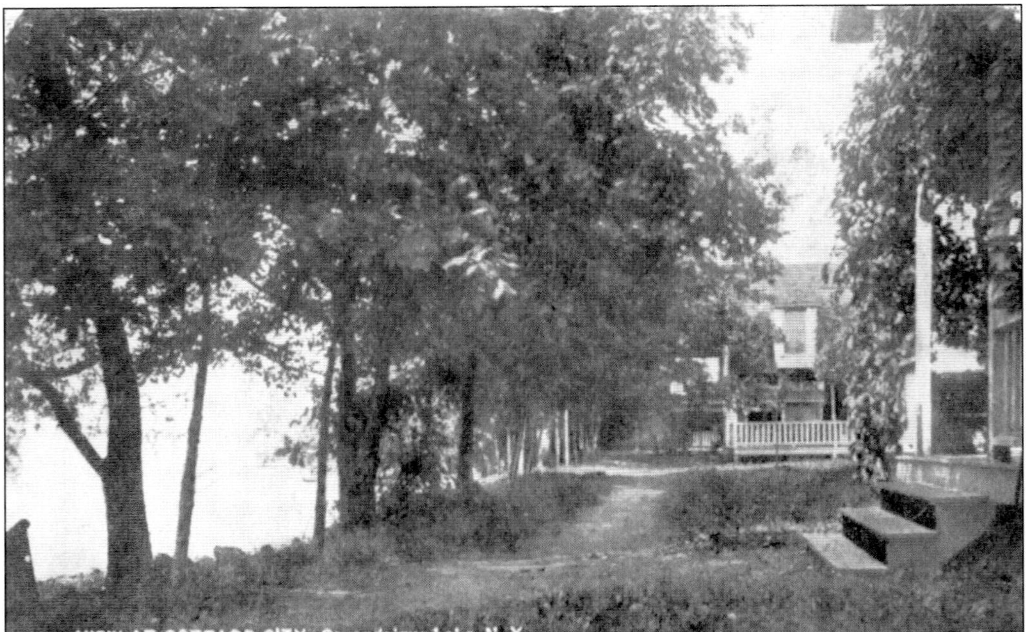

In this postcard, cancelled in 1911, the walk along the lakeshore and the close cottages can be seen. Cottage City retains much of its charm today, except that the shore is dotted with pleasure boats and the streets are paved. (Courtesy of the Ontario County Historical Society.)

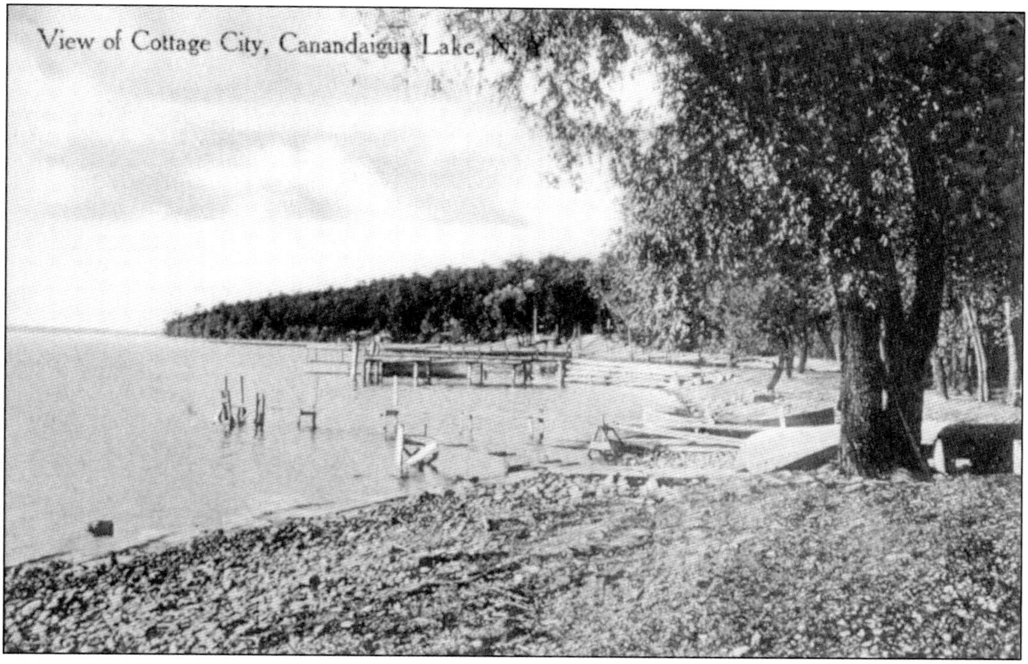

This view of Cottage City shoreline clearly shows the large dock built to accommodate steamboat traffic. A launch is just visible extending out from behind the dock. When this postcard was postmarked in 1920, the large steamboats were gone from the lake. (Courtesy of the Ontario County Historical Society.)

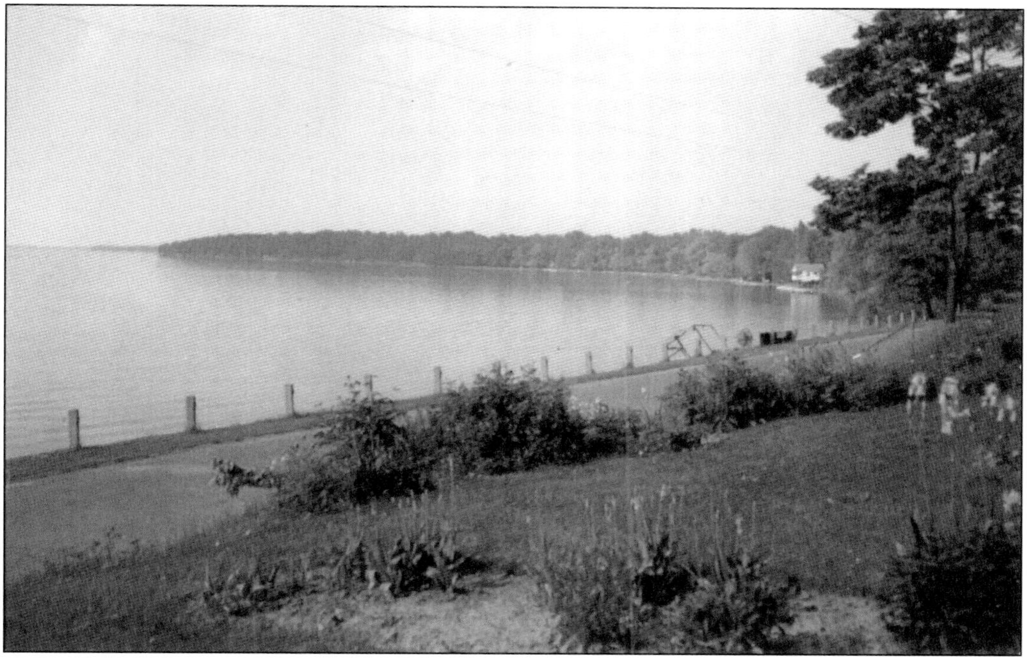

This stretch of the East Lake Road leads north from Gooding's Landing. It is about a mile south of the intersection of the East Lake Road and New York Route 364. Around the cove in the center background is Cottage City. (Photograph by Charles E. Cooksey.)

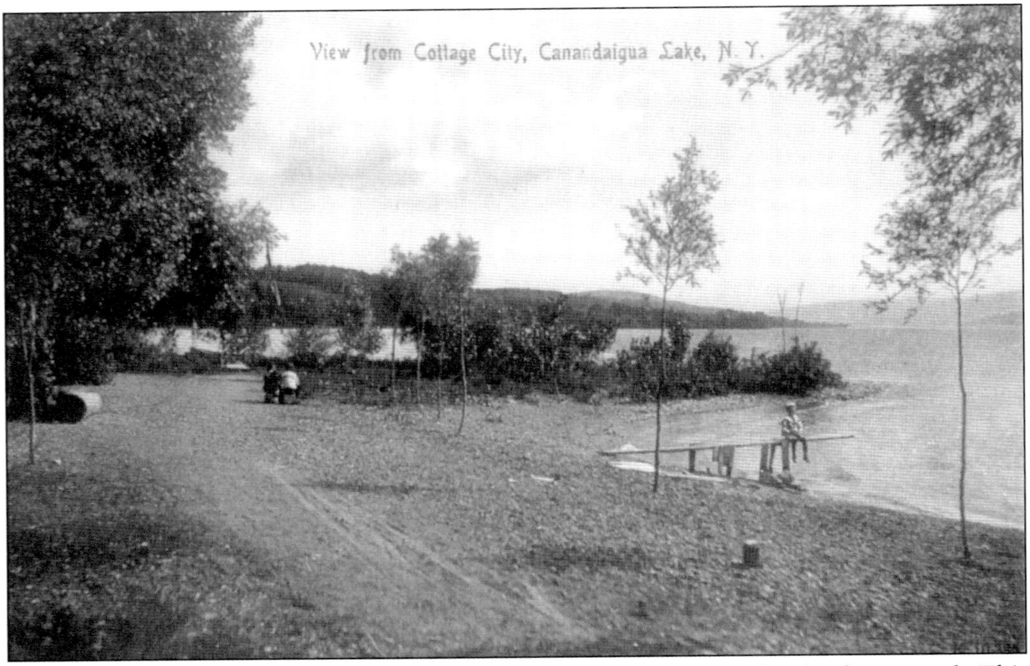

Looking south toward Gooding's Point, Cottage City can be seen in the foreground. This postcard shows the quiet summer atmosphere and slower pace of the early 20th century. Imagine, only one young man on the beach! (Courtesy of the Ontario County Historical Society.)

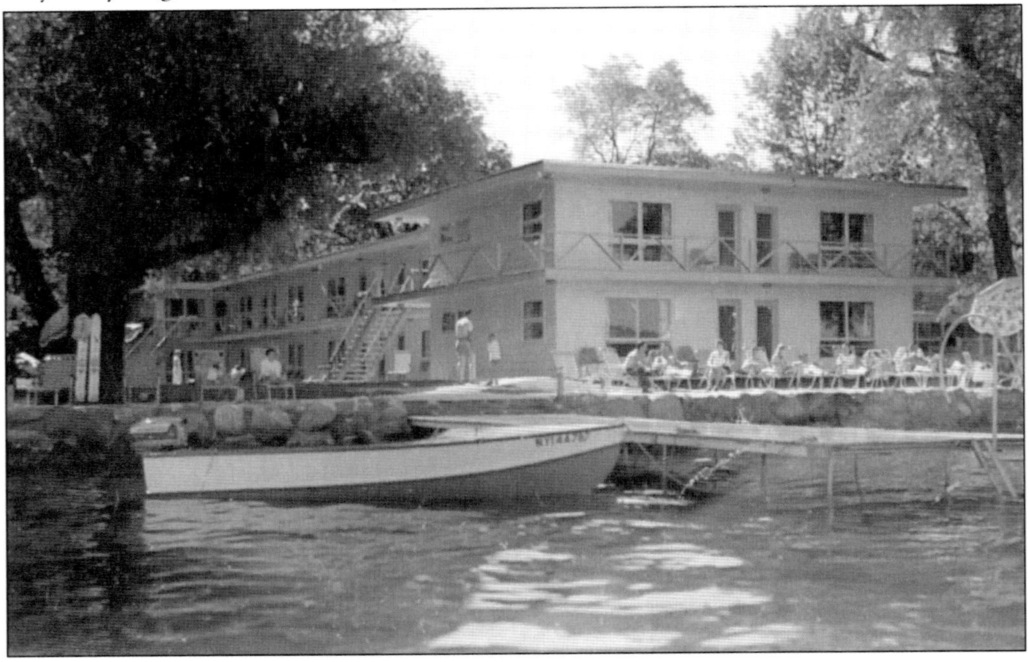

The Sunaqua Resort was opened at Gooding's Landing on East Lake Road in the early 1960s, when this postcard was published. Billed as a "Florida-type" resort apartment complex, it offered its residents boating, bathing, and waterskiing. Mr. and Mrs. Charles Zurick were the original owners. Sunaqua continues to offer lakefront apartments today. (Photograph by Charles E. Cooksey.)

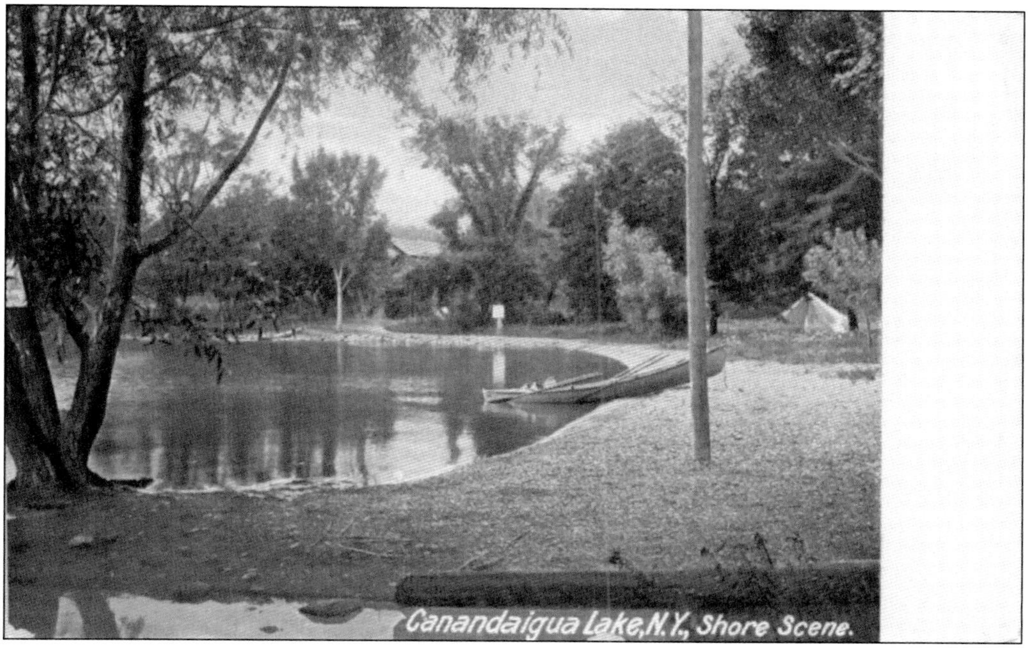

The location of this shore scene is unknown, although it was probably on the east side of the lake. Rowboats and tents were common ways to enjoy the lake in the early 20th century. People could row to a deserted section of the shore and set up camp.

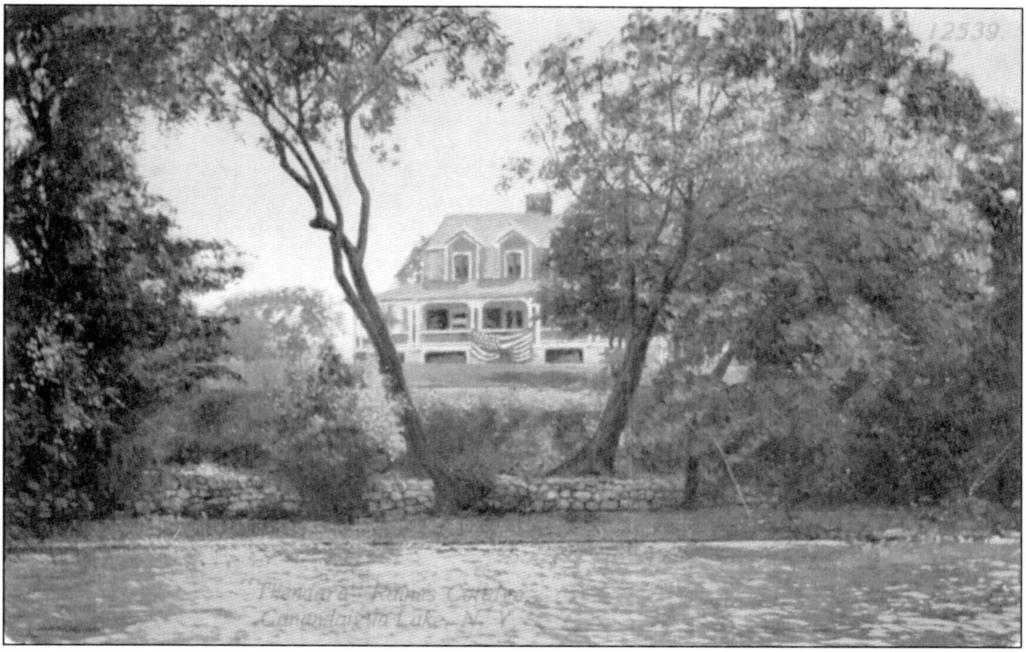

Thendara, the summer home of Sen. John Raines, was completed in 1909, a few months after Raines's death. Over the years, it has been a private residence, a summer resort, a popular restaurant, and steamboat landing. For a short time from 1935 to 1939, it was the home of the Canandaigua Yacht Club. This postcard is postmarked 1913.

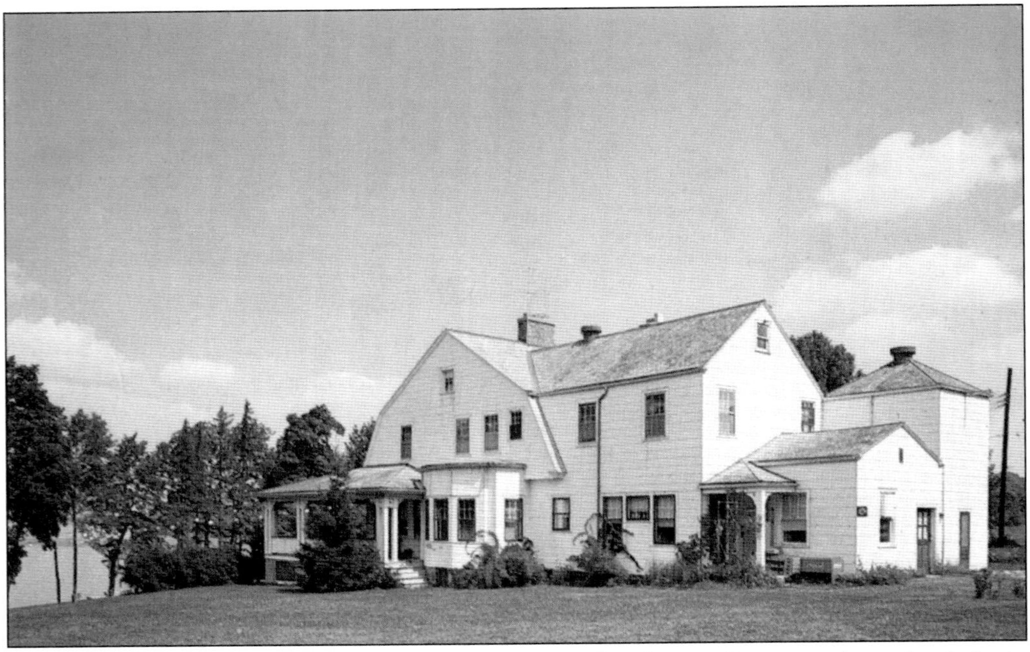

In this photograph, taken by Bill Bard, one can see Thendara as Greenwood-on-the-Lake in the early 1960s. The reverse of the postcard mentions spacious guest rooms, a television lounge, and comfortable porches. Housekeeping cottages and mobile home accommodations were also available on the grounds.

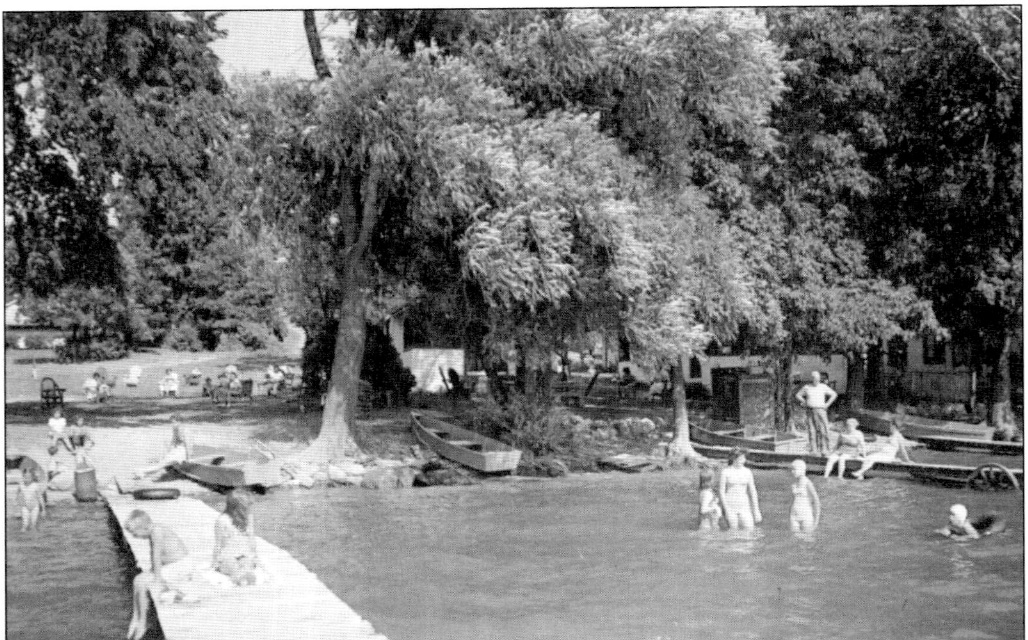

McCormick's Orchard Rest was located at the former 207 East Lake Road, just north of Deep Run. This picture was taken about 1960. In addition to cottage rentals, the resort offered boat rentals, bait, pizza, chicken, ice cream, and fish boxes in the lake directory that year. Note the small rowboats that were popular in the days before jet skis.

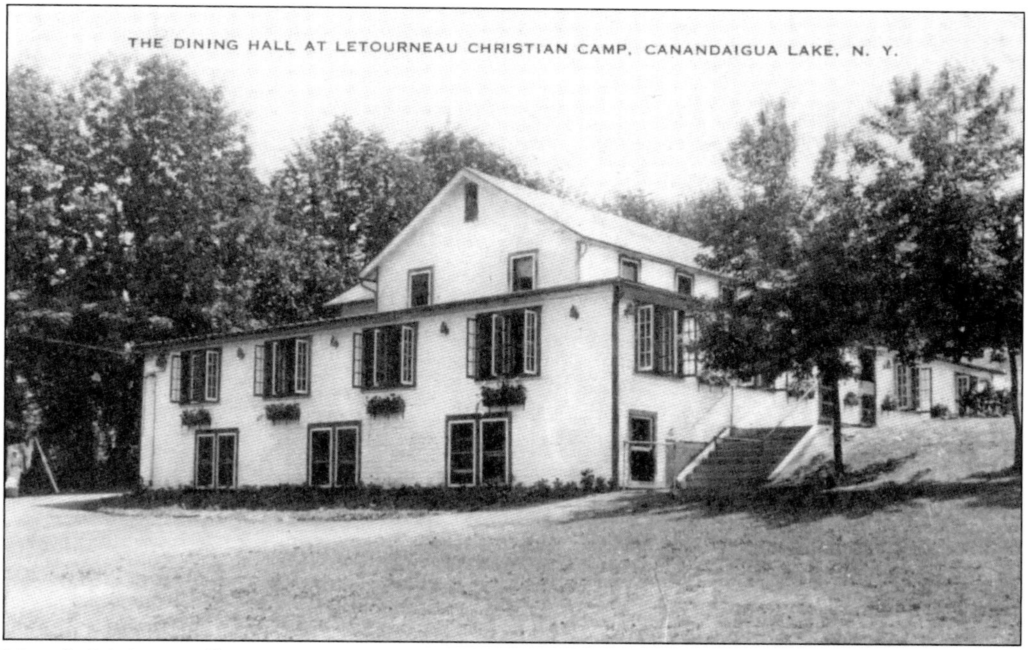

Here is Dining Hall at Camp LeTourneau. Postmarked July 23, 1952, the writer said, "I am just getting ready for swimming. It has been raining up here. That is all for now."

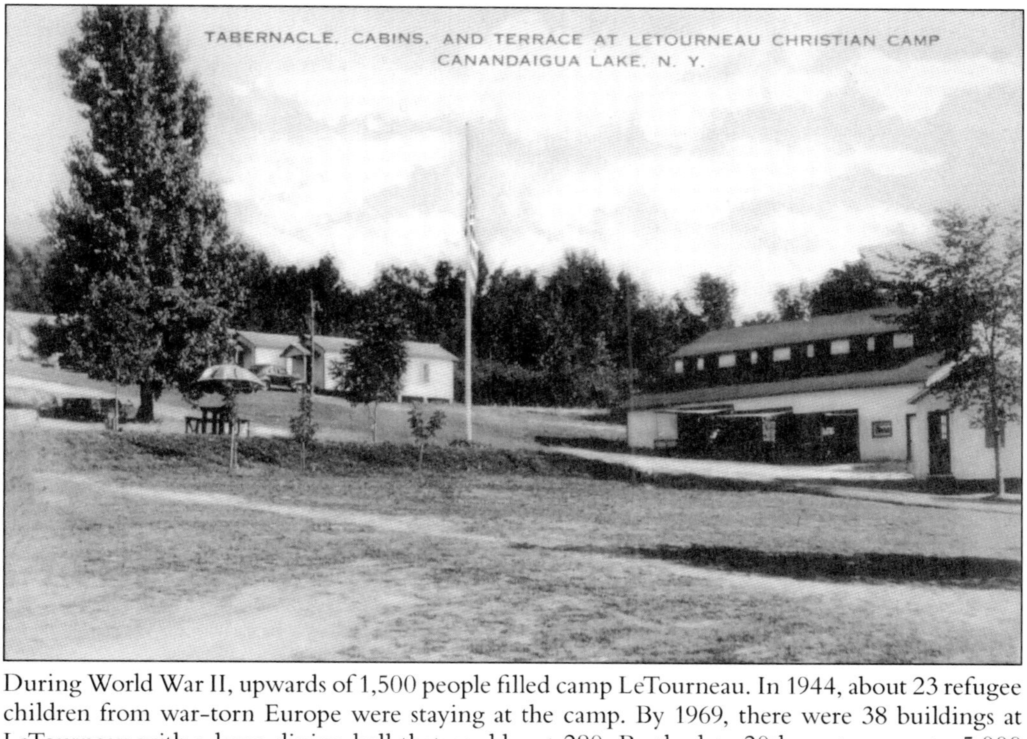

During World War II, upwards of 1,500 people filled camp LeTourneau. In 1944, about 23 refugee children from war-torn Europe were staying at the camp. By 1969, there were 38 buildings at LeTourneau with a large dining hall that could seat 280. By the late 20th century, up to 5,000 campers (adult and youth) came annually.

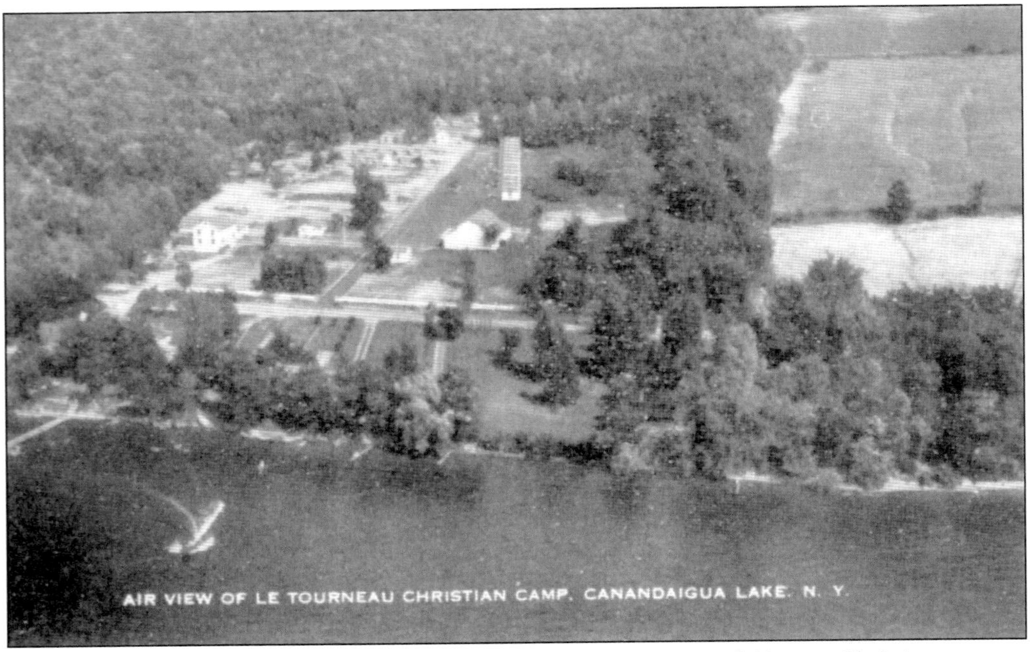

INTERIOR VIEW OF THE TABERNACLE

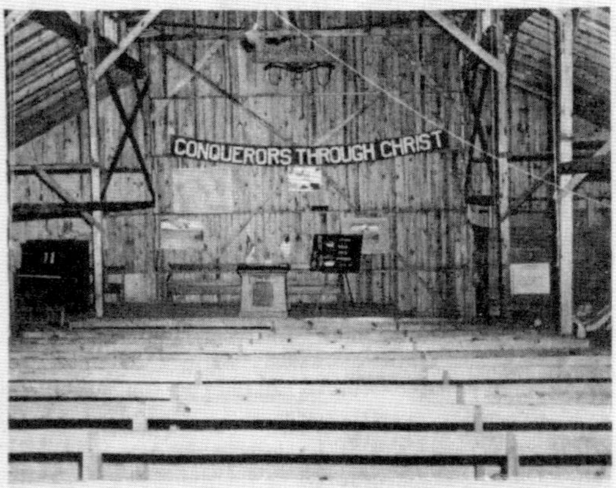

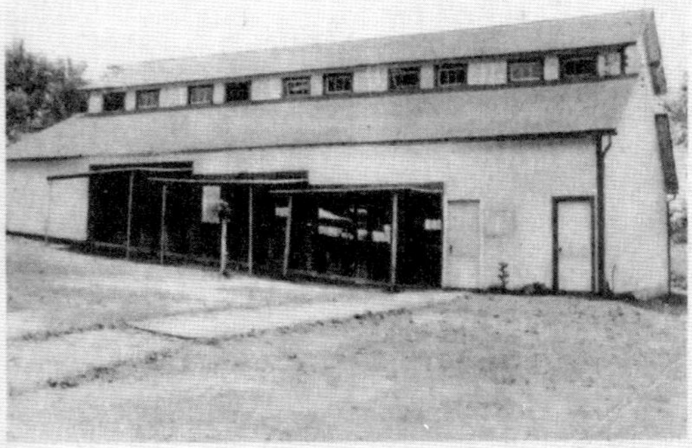

THE TABERNACLE—LETOURNEAU CHRISTIAN CAMP. CANANDAIGUA LAKE, N. Y.

The original 22-acre Christian camp and conference center was dedicated on July 4, 1934. Rev. George Alden Cole, of Buffalo, preached a sermon in the morning. County judge Horace Fitch welcomed visitors in the afternoon. Hon. Clinton N. Howard, the "famed orator of Rochester," delivered the main address of the day. A musical festival took place in the evening. The original plan, reported in local papers, included 200 cottages and a year-round home for unemployed ministers or those needing some rest.

The Conference Center was an abandoned Depression-era farm, owned by the Perrin family, when Dr. Harold Strathearn and Don and Howard Joss purchased the property in 1934. It was originally called Tabernacle-on-the-Lake. In 1939, industrialist R.G. LeTourneau made a major contribution to the development of the camp. The camp and conference center is owned and operated by Interstate Evangelistic Association, founded by Dr. Strathearn in 1929.

Seven

Roads and Automobiles

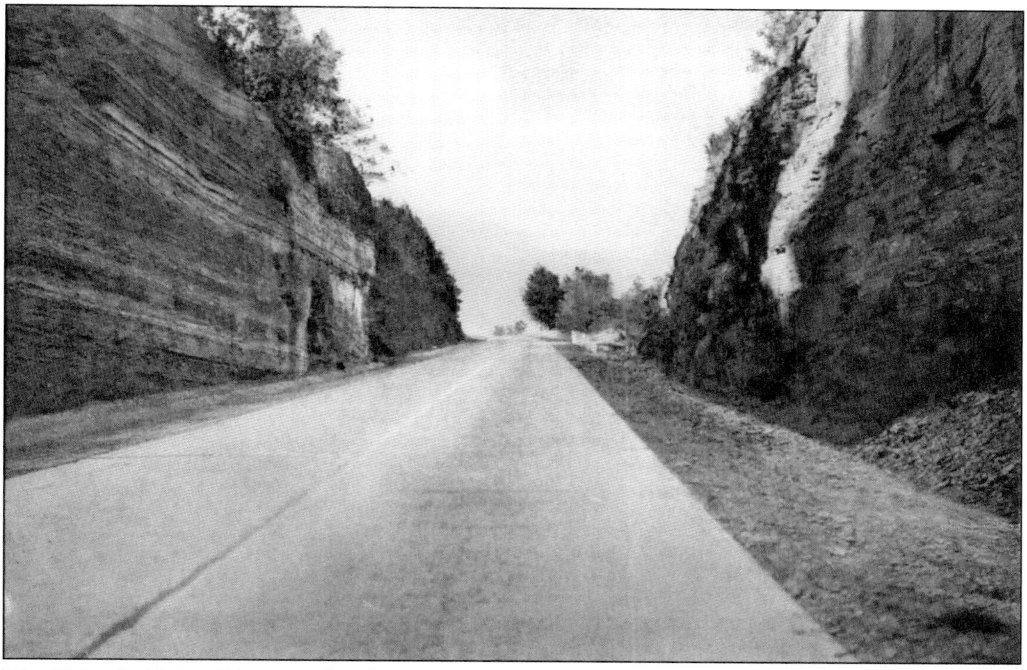

The "Maxfield Cut," just north of Woodville, was completed to Bristol Springs in 1925. At the time, it was considered the second most difficult road construction project in New York state, next to the Storm King Highway along the Hudson River. The cut was named for a prominent Naples family whose Maxfield Bank promoted business, banking, and transportation. The Maxfield Cut put Woodville on a main road to Naples.

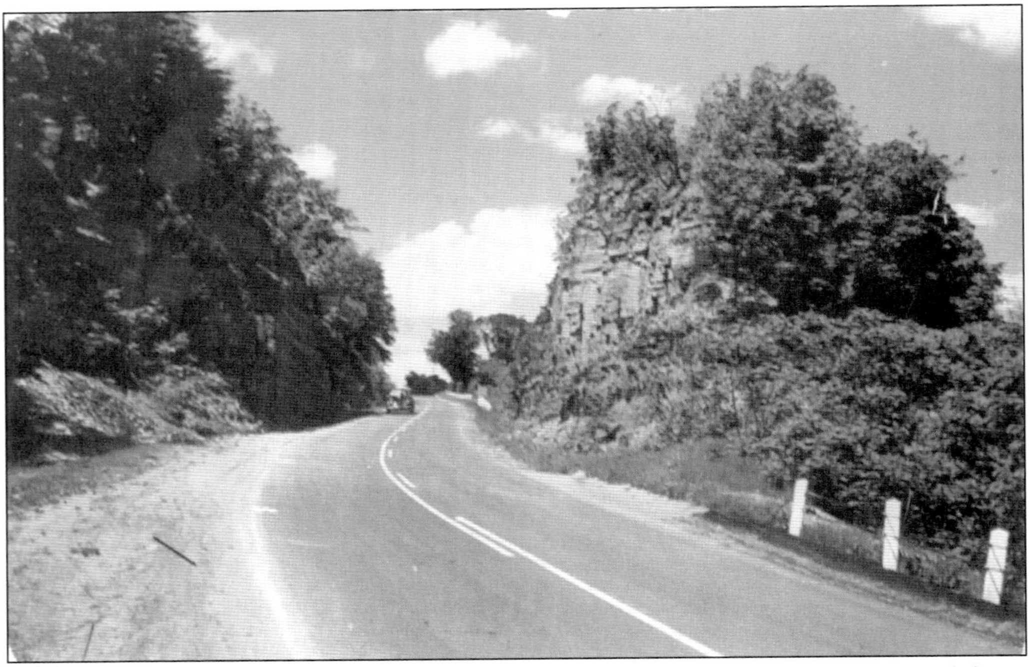

This image of the Maxfield Cut was made about 25 years after the road was completed down to Woodville. It looks much like this today. The photographer for this postcard was Ralph O. Stratton, who worked with Margery M. Elling.

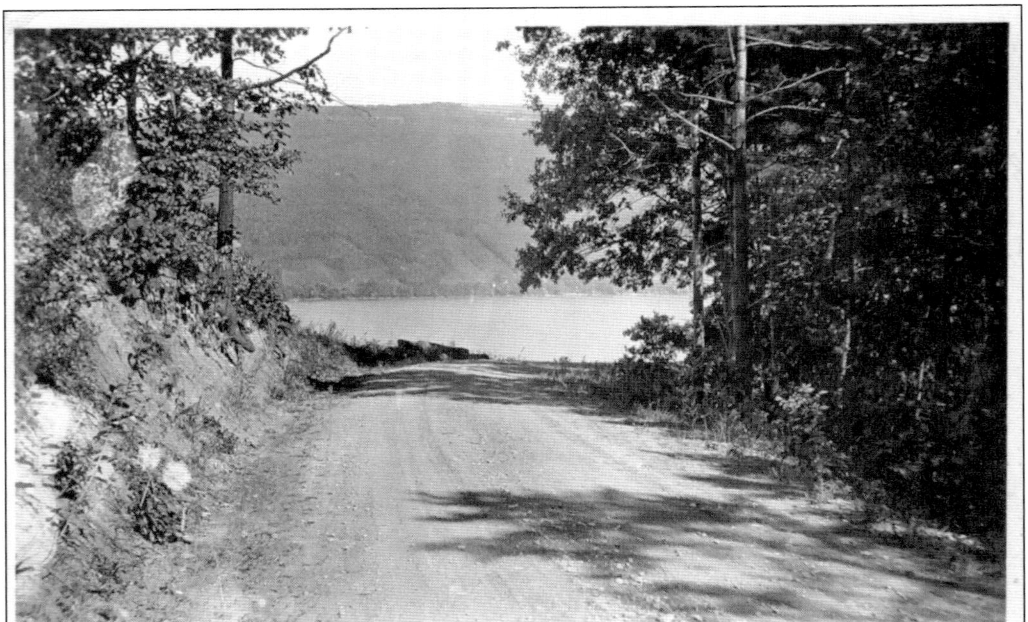

This postcard is labeled only as "road to Naples." It provides a good idea of the steep and winding route early motorists and wagons had to take between Naples and Bristol Springs before the Maxfield Cut was completed.

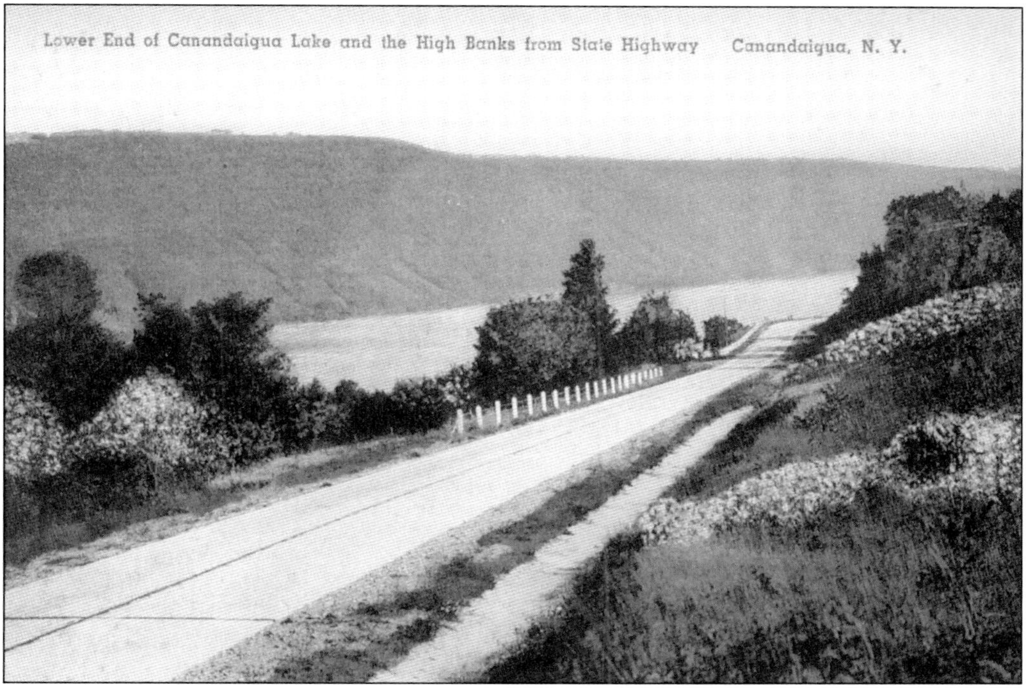

This postcard shows the newly paved state highway that is now New York Route 21 in the town of South Bristol. Just around the bend to the right is the spectacular Maxfield Cut.

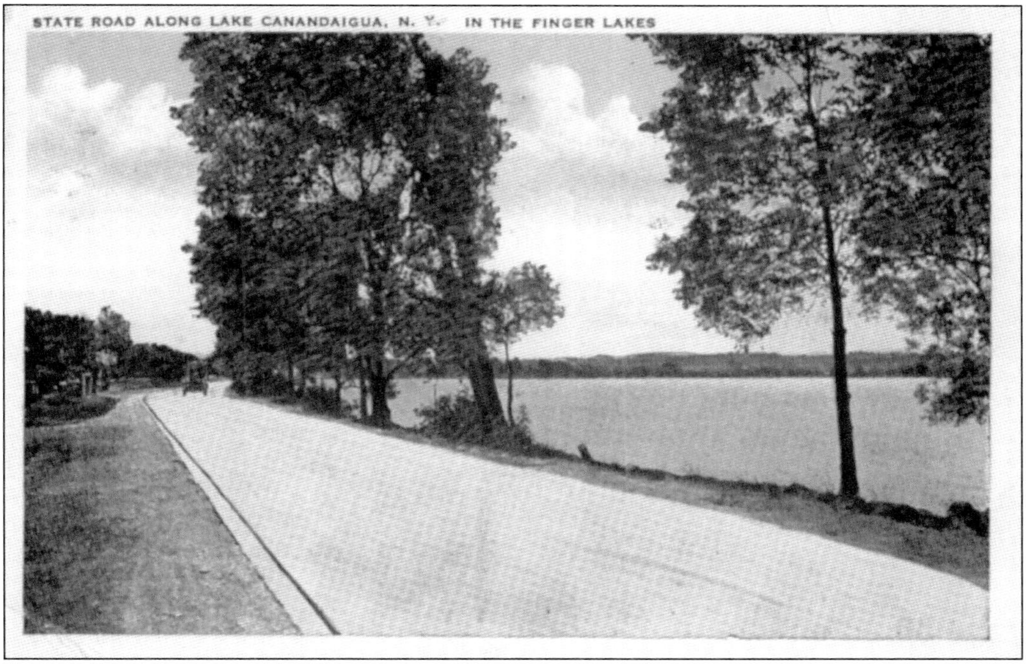

While this road is identified only as a "state road," it is probably Lakeshore Drive, Canandaigua. Routes 5 and 20 ran very close to the lake until Kershaw Park was completed. This postcard provides a real sense of how much the northern lakeshore has changed since 1925. A local newspaper once lamented that paving lakeshore drive was a waste of money since few people would want to travel there.

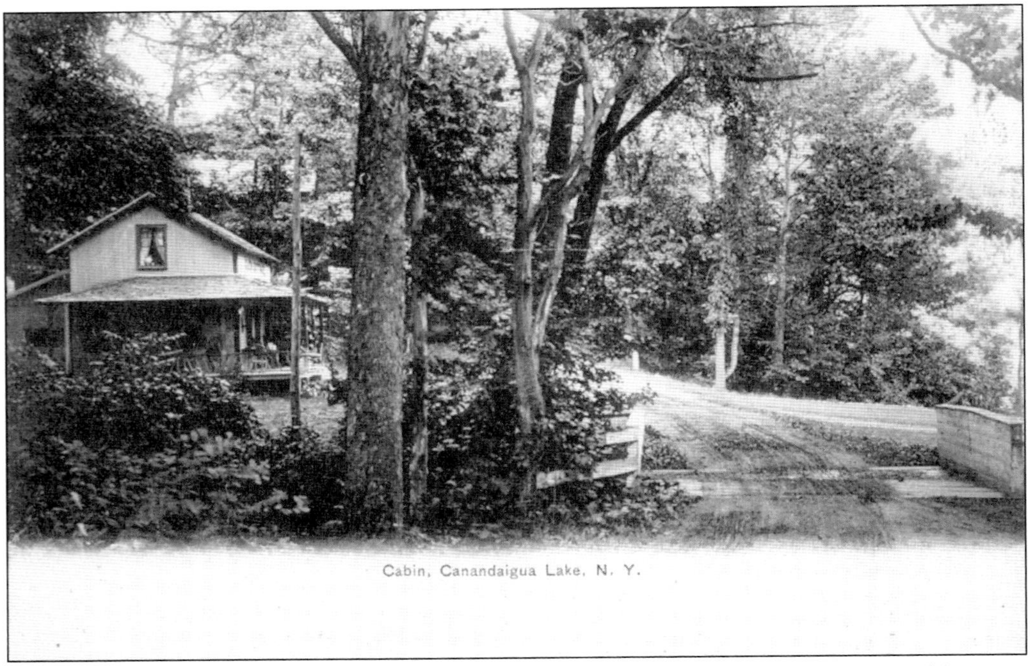

This scene is probably along the West Lake Road, now County Road 16, near Mentieth's Point. Spending the summer "up the lake" was much more rustic and quiet a century ago. There were fewer people and little to no traffic, except for farm wagons.

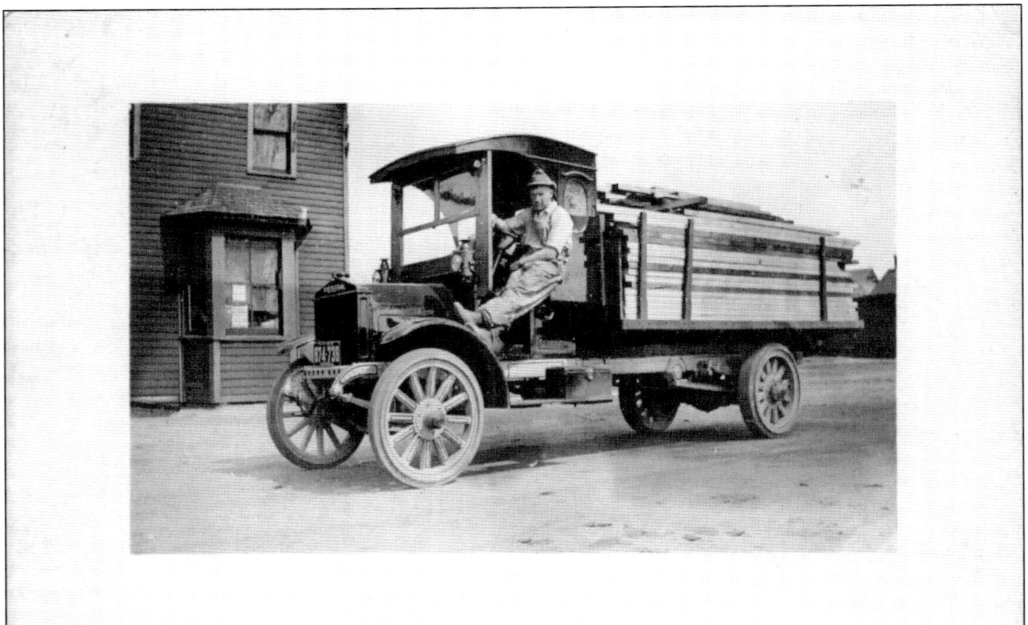

This Federal truck is loaded with lumber and probably about to make a delivery for one of the Canandaigua lumber yards, possibly Davidson's, just under the bridge on West Avenue. The New York state commercial license plate can be seen. Since the Federal Motor Company did not manufacture trucks prior to 1910, this postcard dates from 1910 to 1920.

Eight

Steamboats, Trains, and Trolleys

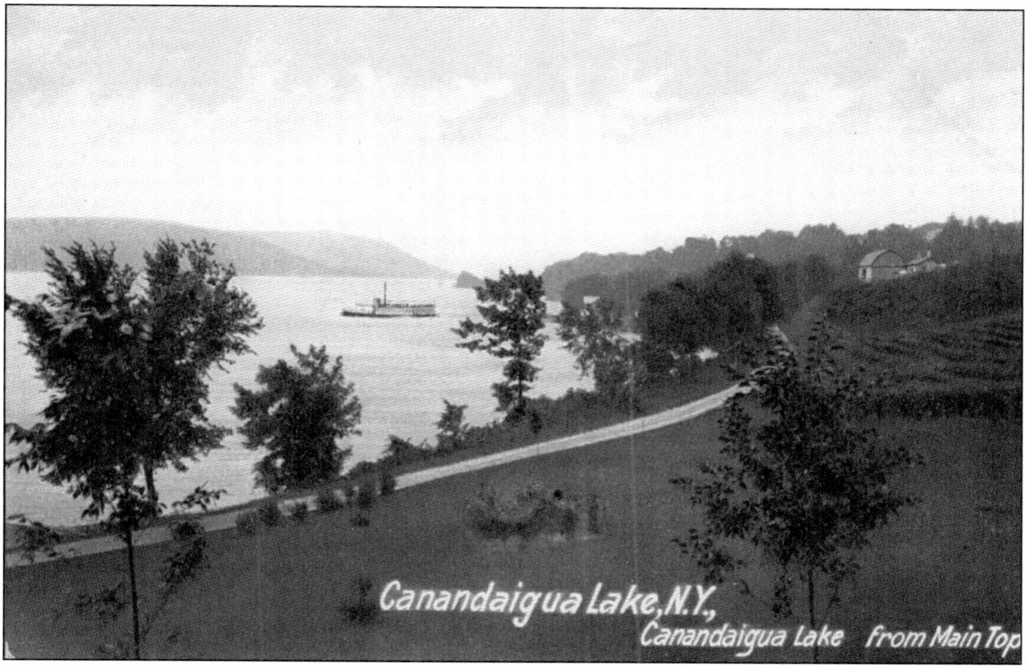

Regular steamboat service operated on Canandaigua Lake from 1845 to 1924. This view of the West Lake Road shows a boat leaving a dock just south of Main Top. Built in 1887 by Dr. Henry Stewart, a former Navy surgeon, it was named for the hills behind Stewart's house. After Stewart died, his house became a small summer hotel called Main Top.

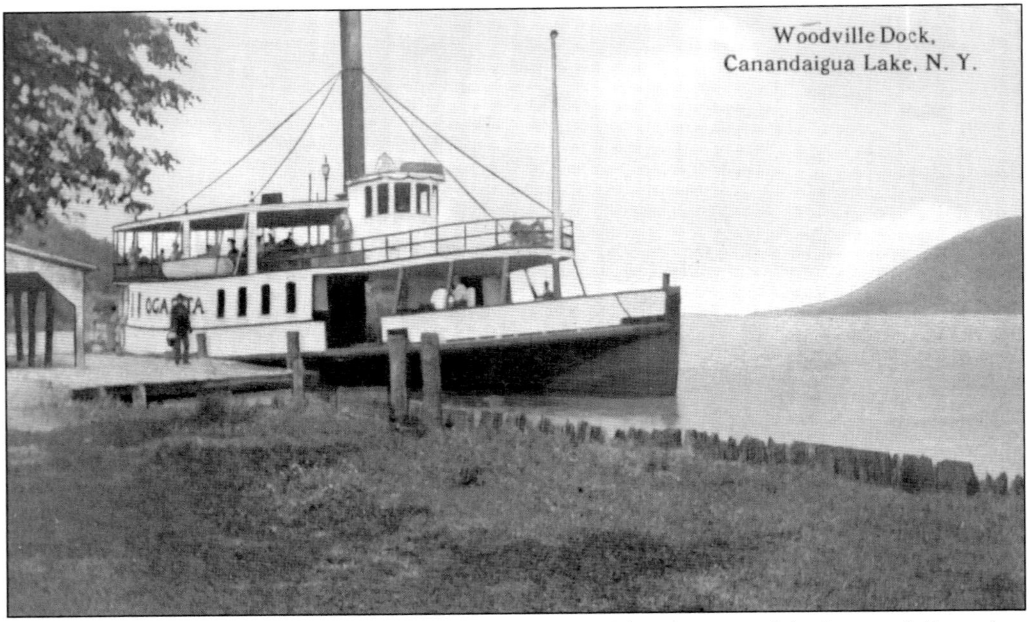

The dock at Woodville was a place where passengers and freight were picked up or delivered to the Naples area. The *Ogarita*, launched in 1889, burned at this dock on July 20, 1914. In 1894, the steamboat *Gennundewah* also burned at the Woodville dock. The *Ogarita* was named for the daughter of Frank B. Merrill, manager of the Canandaigua Water Works and namesake of Merrill Hose Co.

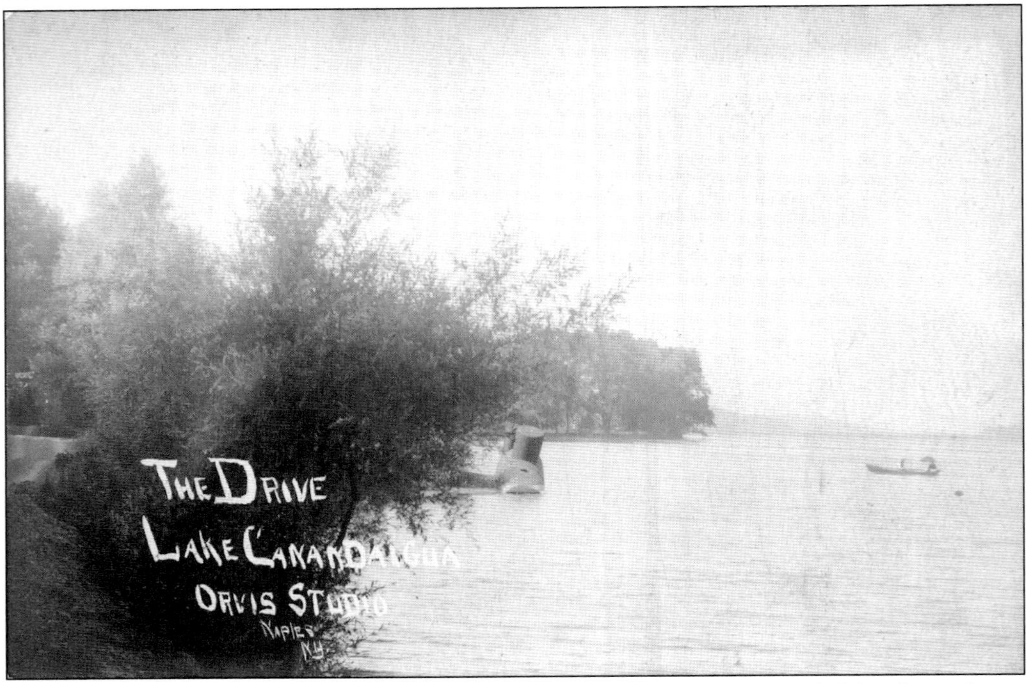

This postcard was postmarked in 1909. In the center of the picture is a tank-like object that is probably the boiler of the steamboat *Gennundewah*. That boat burned at Woodville in 1894. By 1914, the wreckage had drifted north to Hazel Del, just south of Granger Point. It silted in, and a point was formed around the wreckage.

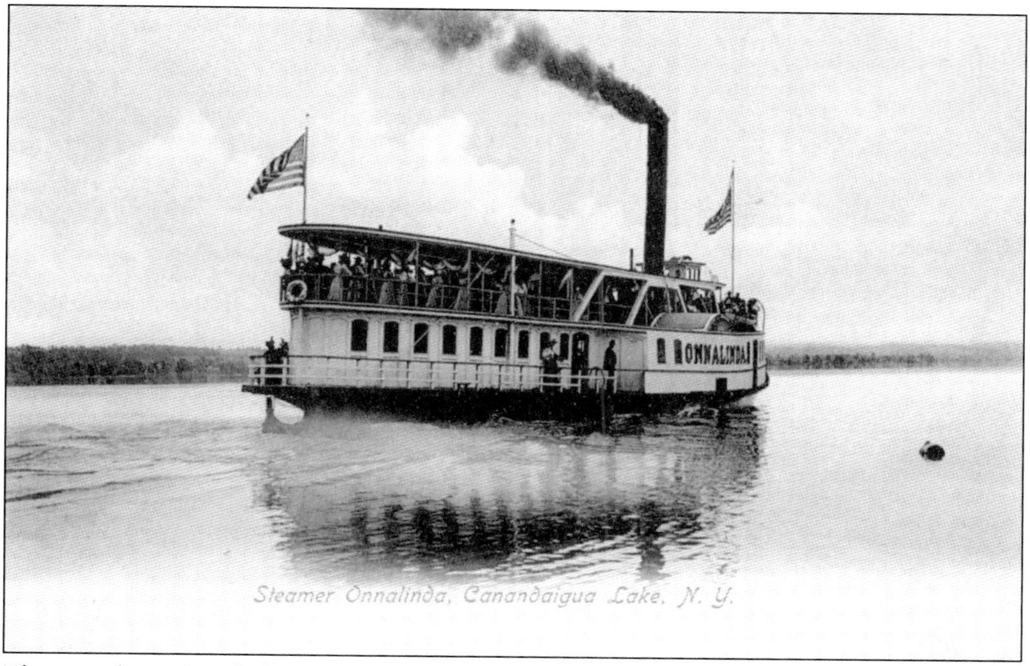

The steamboat *Onnalinda* was named for a book-length poem published in 1888. At 142 feet long and 42 feet wide, this steamboat was the largest boat to ply the waters of Canandaigua Lake. The hull of the *Onnalinda* was deliberately scuttled in the lake after it was partially dismantled in 1913. Its remains lie in the shallow water just to the north of Otetiana Point.

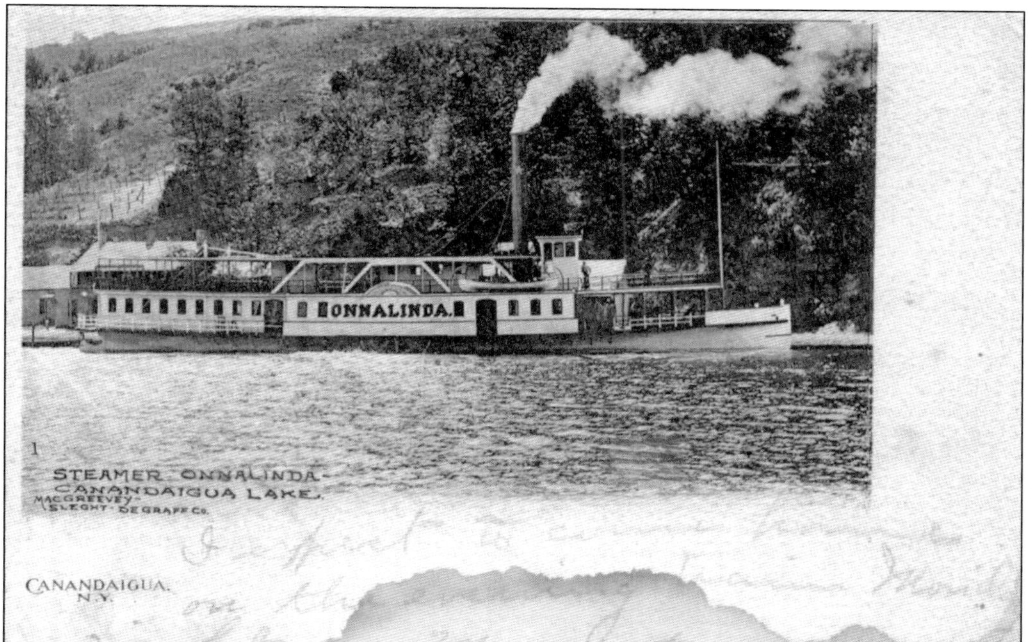

Postmarked in 1907, this postcard shows the *Onnalinda* at a dock, probably Woodville. It provides a good perspective on the length of this boat. The plume of smoke coming from the stacks of the steamboats served to alert people along the lakeshore that a boat would soon be coming.

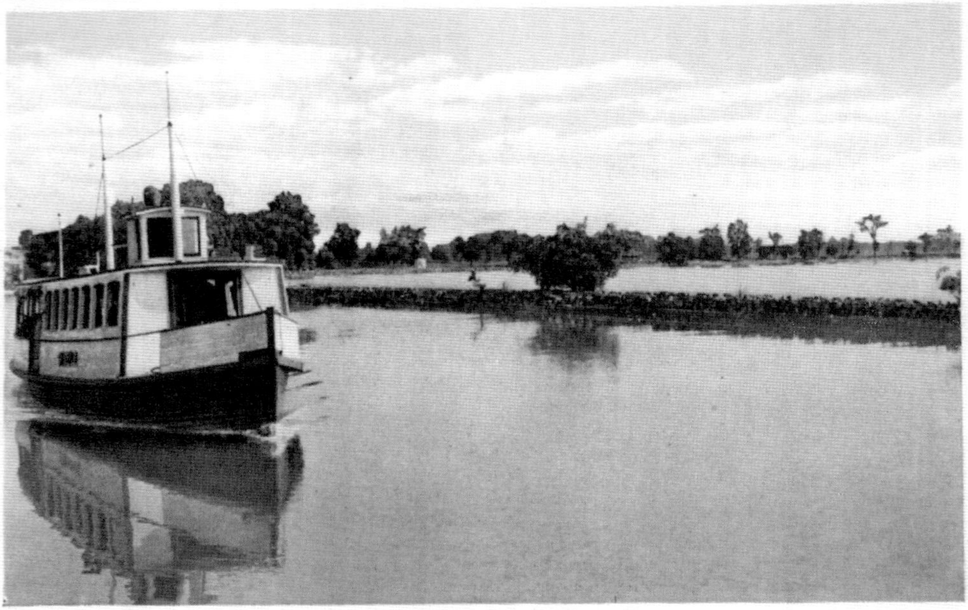

BOAT LEAVING WHARF, CANANDAIGUA LAKE, CANANDAIGUA, N. Y.

The boat leaving the pier in this image is the *Oriana*. At the center of the picture is the stone breakwater that calmed the waves in the steamboat basin. The old Swimming School is out of the picture to the left. The *Oriana* began service on the lake as the *Seneca Chief* (1887). It was still in service as a gasoline launch in 1919. This postcard was postmarked 1922.

SWIMMING SCHOOL, CANANDAIGUA LAKE, "WESTERN GATEWAY TO THE FINGER LAKES," CANANDAIGUA, N. Y.

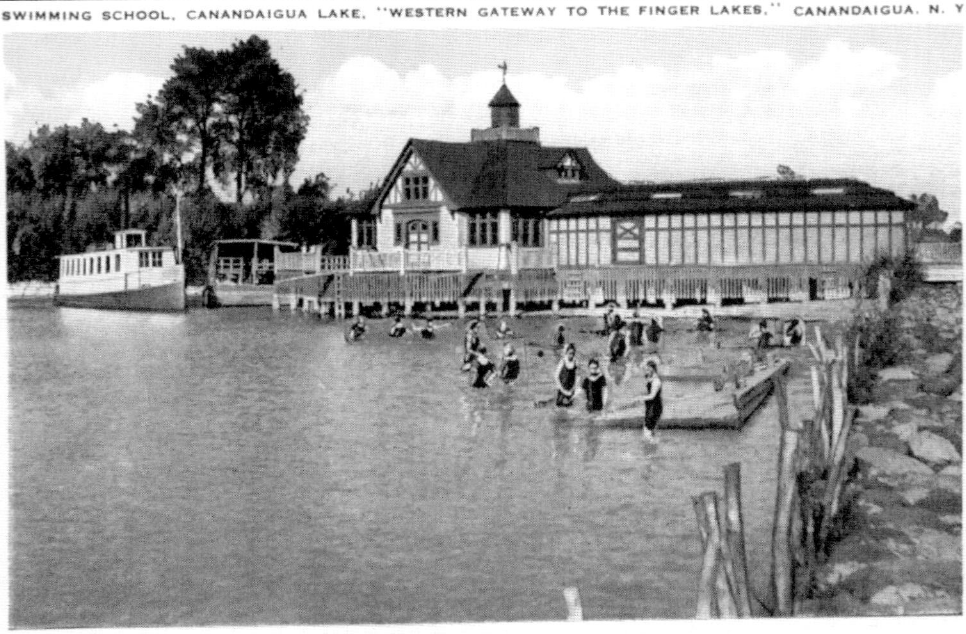

Perhaps no image shows the shallow draft of small boats like the *Oriana* better than this view. The boat is tied up to the shore at what was then a small park at the entrance to the Swimming School. At the time this postcard was made, swimmers could stand in very shallow water in the basin. Part of the breakwater can be seen along the right edge of the picture.

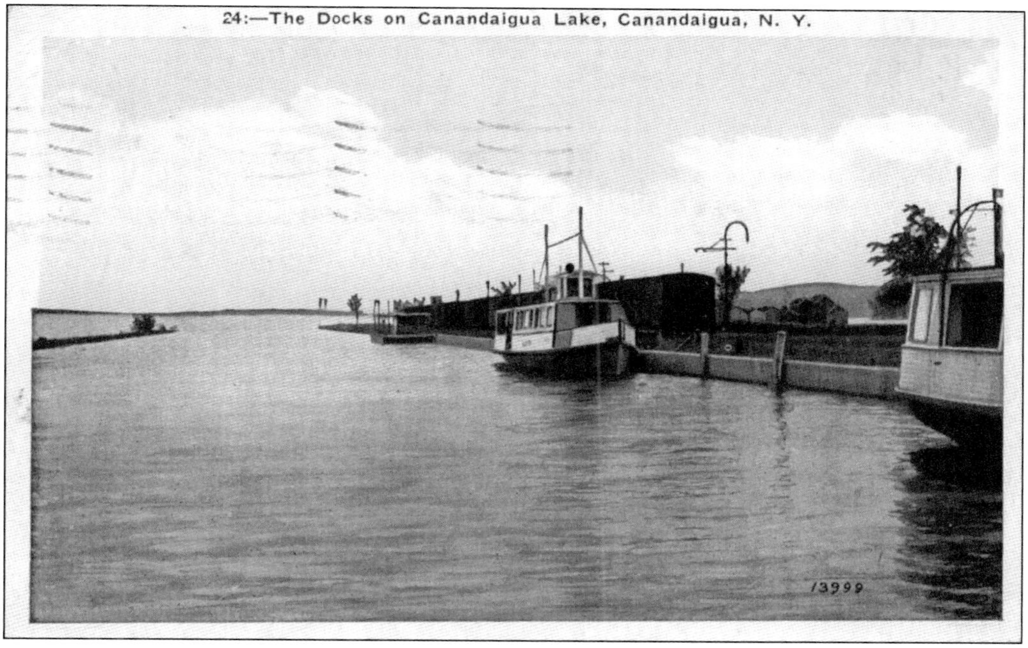

This unique postcard shows the *Oriana* tied up at the pier next to a string of railroad freight cars. Steamboats delivered freight directly to the Northern Central Railroad at its spur on the pier, built in 1882. Postmarked in 1932, this postcard shows the pier in the waning days of steamboat service.

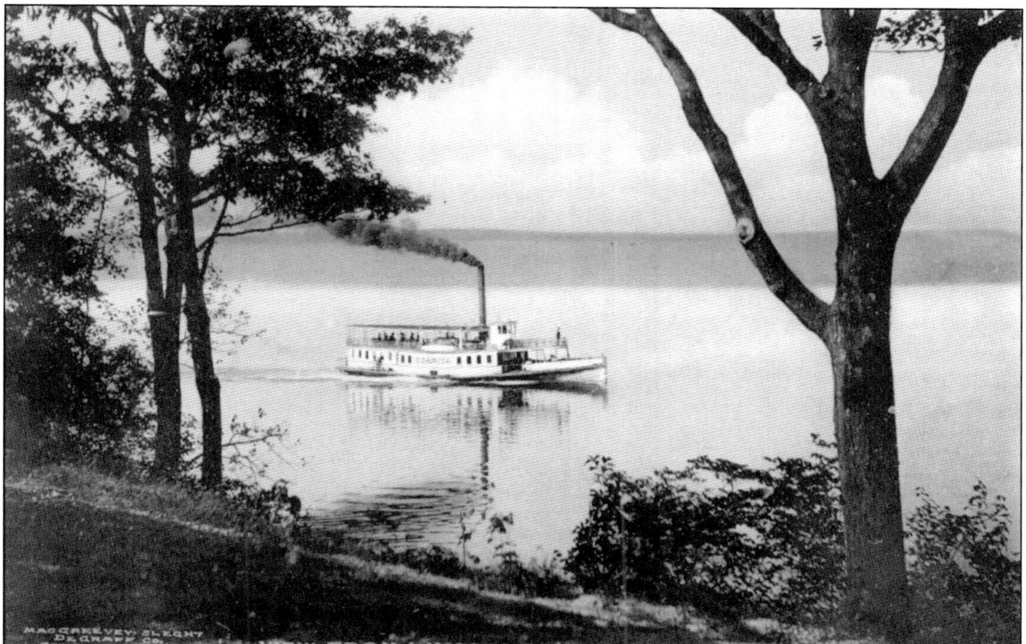

The *Ogarita* is steaming past the Lincoln Wood landing in this view. One of the older landings on the lake, it was named for the pioneer Lincoln family. The landing still exists, and a trace of the old access road can be seen just south of Thendara. This picture was probably taken from the back lawn of Senator Raines's cottage.

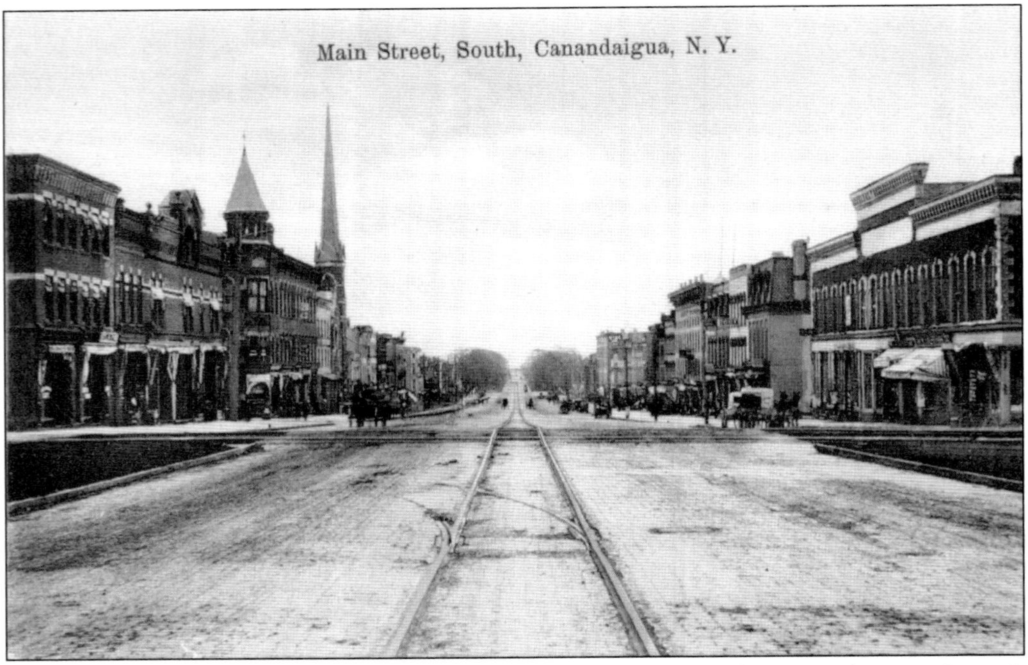

The Rochester and Eastern Rapid Railway began operating from Rochester, through Canandaigua, to Geneva in 1903. Paved roads and the advent of the automobile put an end to the trolley line in 1930. In Canandaigua, the tracks ran down the middle of Main Street.

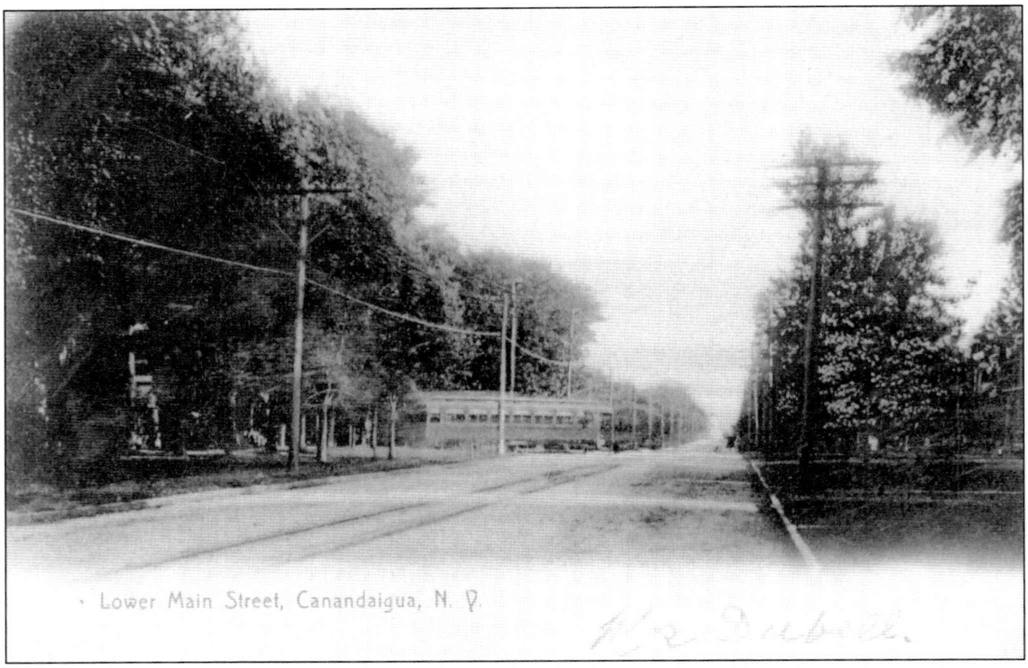

While the trolley line ran out onto the pier, and the power house was at the intersection of the pier and Lake Street, the main line to Geneva turned at Phelps Street and ran east along County Road 46, then called County House Road. This postcard shows one of the Rochester and Eastern cars leaving Main Street and heading east.

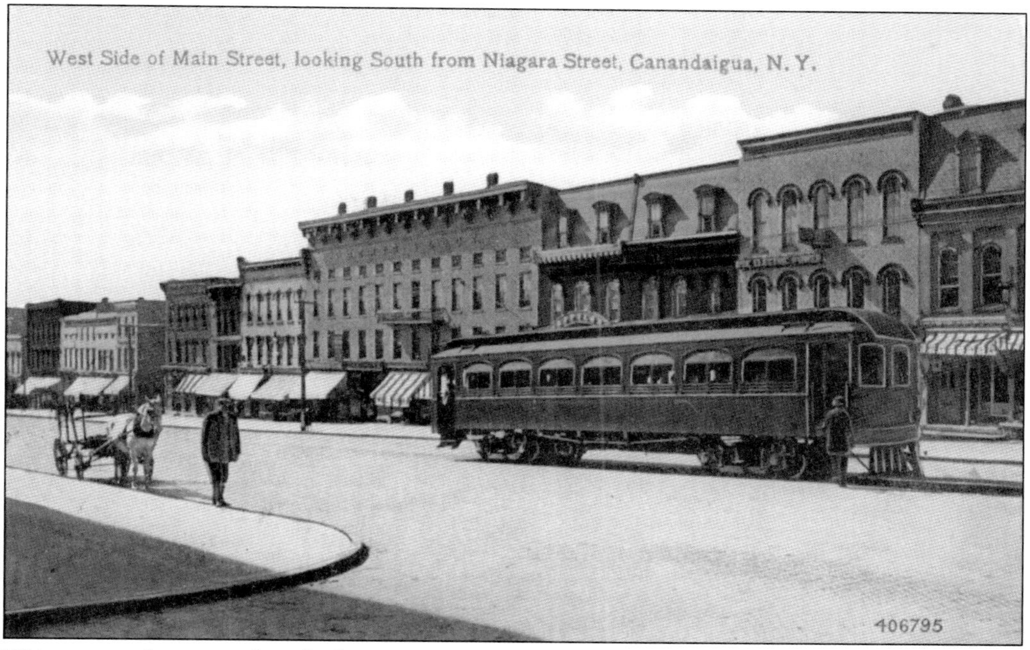

This postcard was produced after 1903 since a Rochester and Eastern car is featured picking up a passenger at the intersection of Niagara and Main Streets. No automobiles are visible, although the first motor vehicle arrived in Canandaigua in 1900. The "Route of the Orange Limited," as the Rochester and Eastern was known, provided quick service to stops all the way to Rochester.

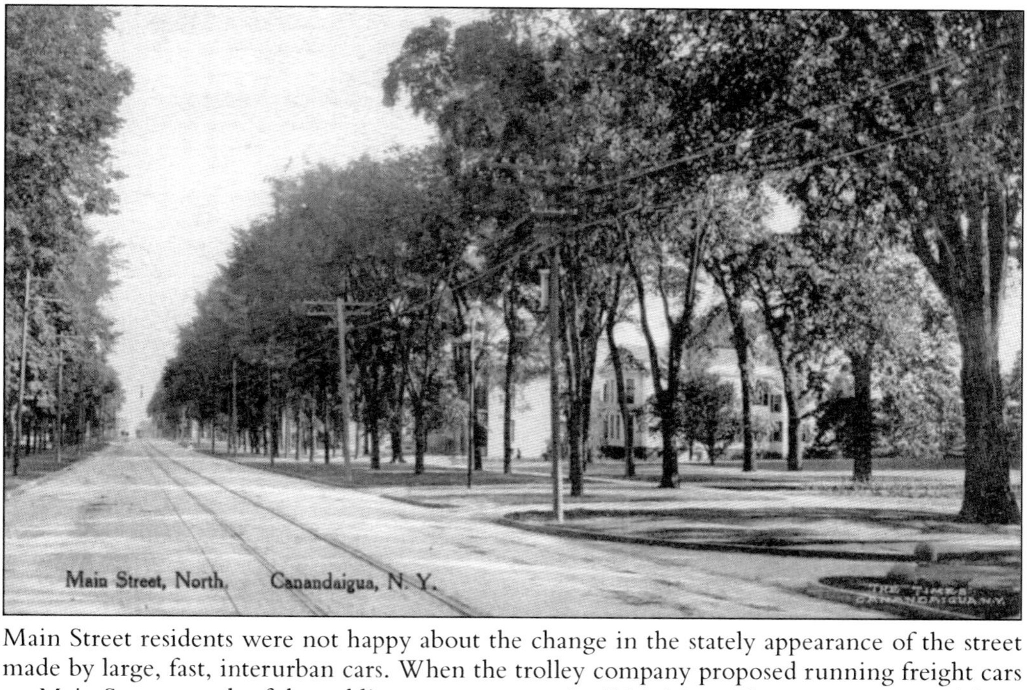

Main Street residents were not happy about the change in the stately appearance of the street made by large, fast, interurban cars. When the trolley company proposed running freight cars on Main Street, much of the public was very upset. In 1904, Mary Thompson sent word from London that she was willing to spend up to $10,000 to keep the trolley company from running freight cars on Main Street.

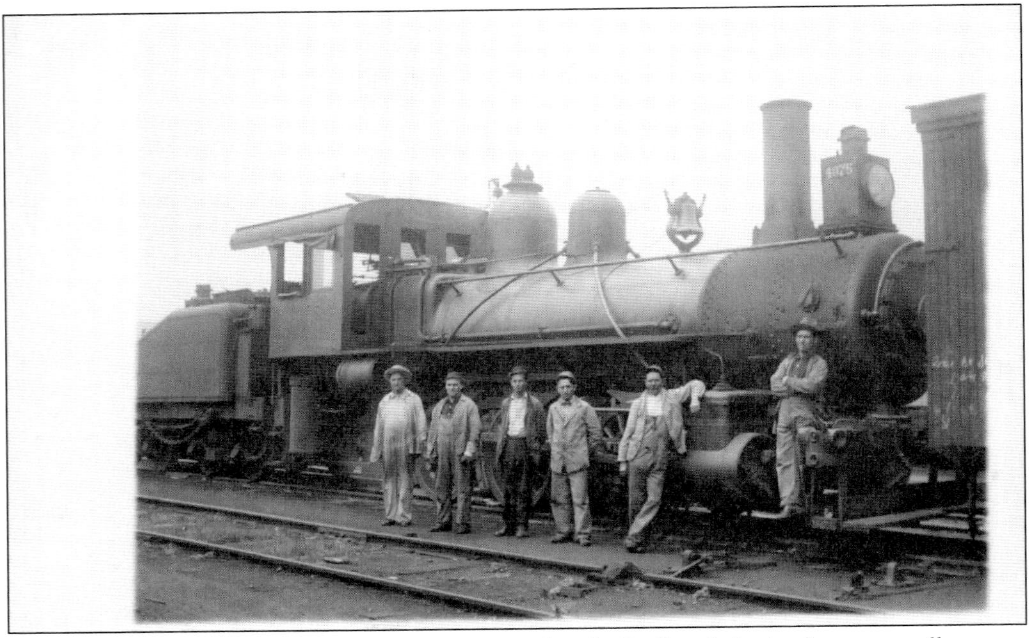

The Northern Central, later part of the Pennsylvania Railroad, had a large roundhouse, a separate freight station, and substantial freight and passenger business in Canandaigua. The line operated overnight Pullman service to Washington, DC, and a Railway Post Office that ran to Williamsport, Pennsylvania. The 0-6-0 Class B6 "shifter," shown here, was a well-known feature of the Canandaigua railroad yard.

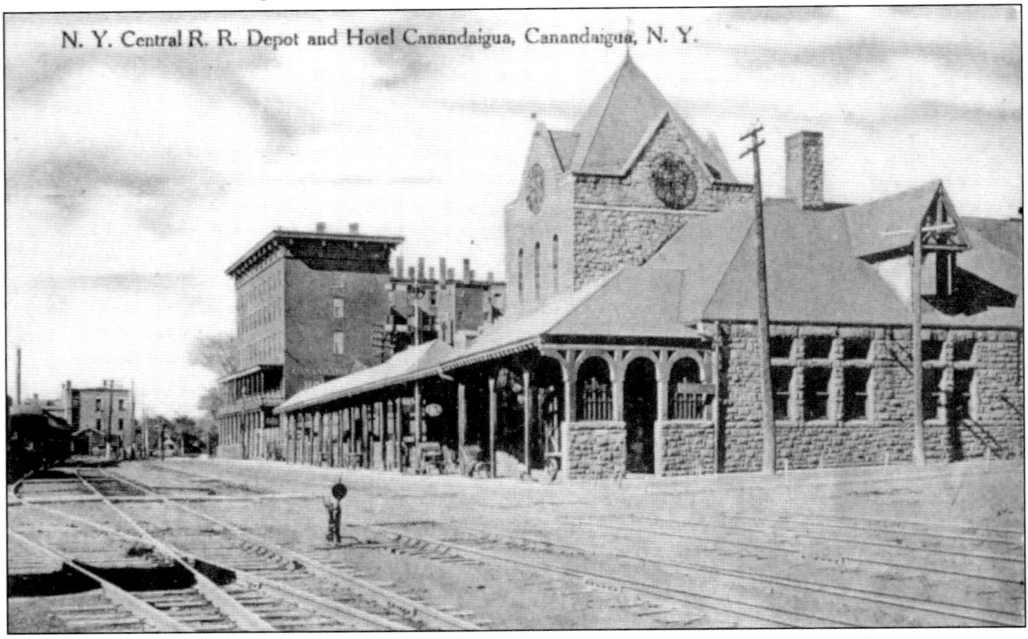

Frederick Ferris Thompson convinced the New York Central Railroad to build an impressive stone station in Canandaigua in 1890. Its passenger platform stretched all the way to the Canandaigua Hotel, the previous ticket office. A dozen trains left Canandaigua daily on the two New York Central lines that converged here. The station burned in 1968 and was eventually remodeled into commercial and professional offices.

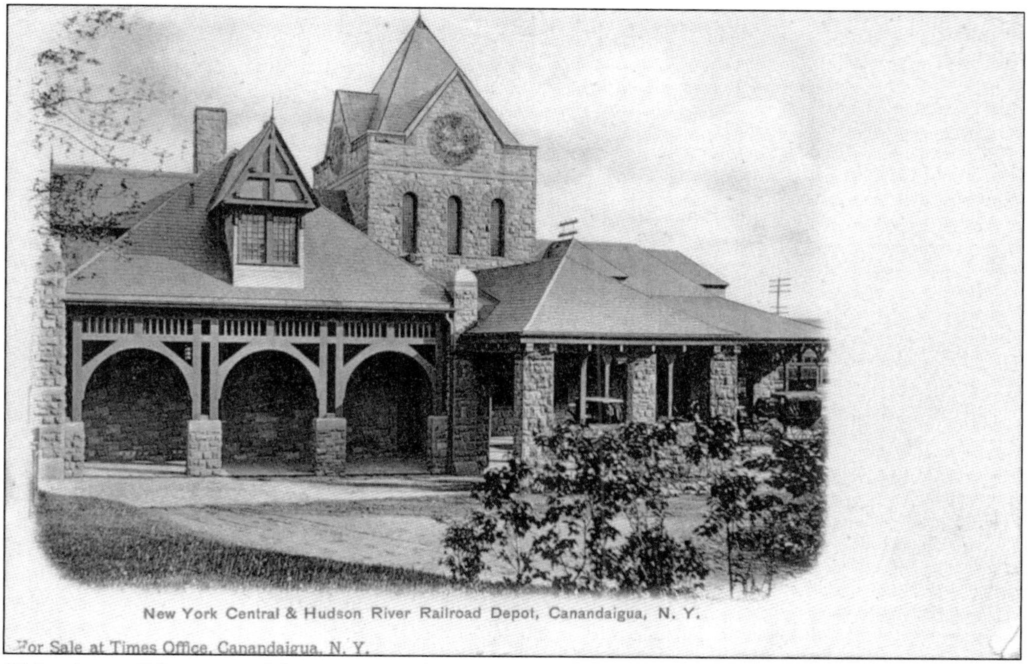

This view of the rear of the New York Central Railroad station was produced prior to 1907 since it is printed on an undivided postcard. This is the entrance passengers would have used to enter the building, buy tickets, and wait for a train.

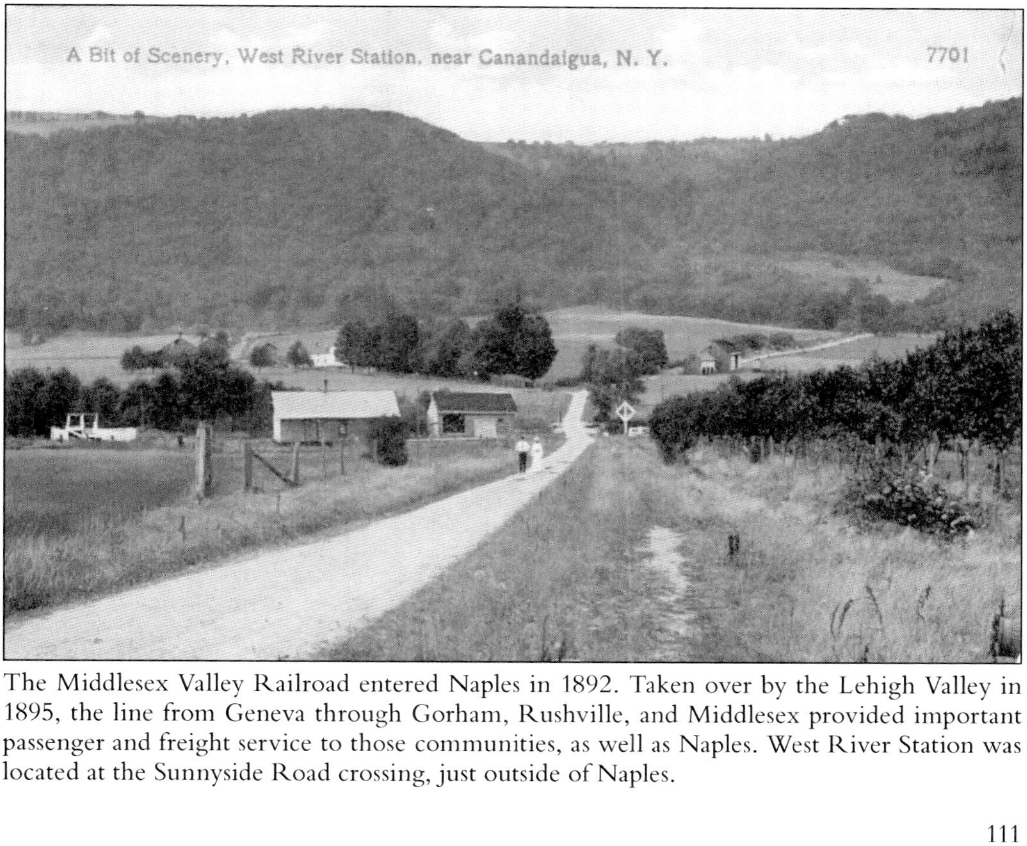

The Middlesex Valley Railroad entered Naples in 1892. Taken over by the Lehigh Valley in 1895, the line from Geneva through Gorham, Rushville, and Middlesex provided important passenger and freight service to those communities, as well as Naples. West River Station was located at the Sunnyside Road crossing, just outside of Naples.

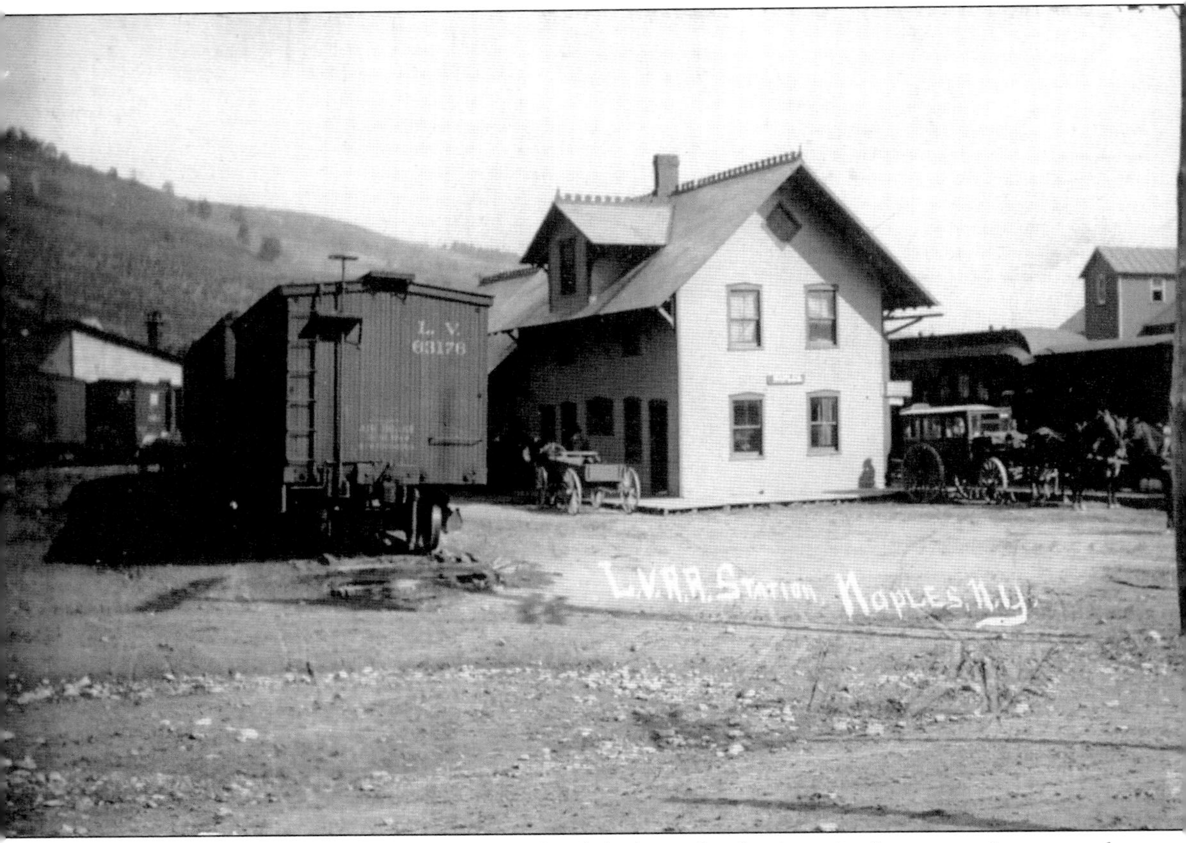

The freight and passenger stations in Naples did a booming business in the years prior to good roads. The Naples branch connected Naples to Geneva and the Lehigh Valley main line to the north. The line opened vast new markets to the wine and grape industry in particular.

Nine

Naples and Middlesex at the Head of the Lake

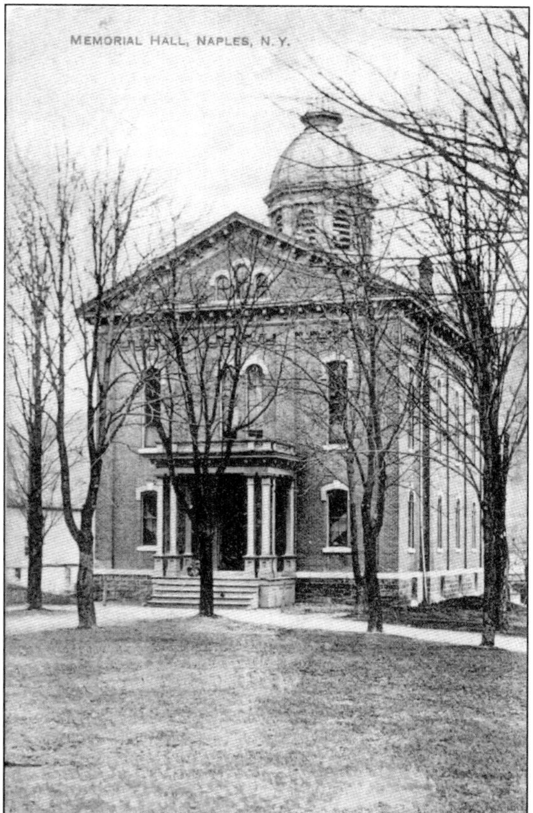

A total of 225 Naples men served in the Civil War, the highest rate of participation in the county. Naples built Memorial Town Hall to honor its soldiers in 1872. Memorial Town Hall was the scene of social, cultural, and athletic events for many years. It was renovated in 1976 after a quarter-century of use as a factory.

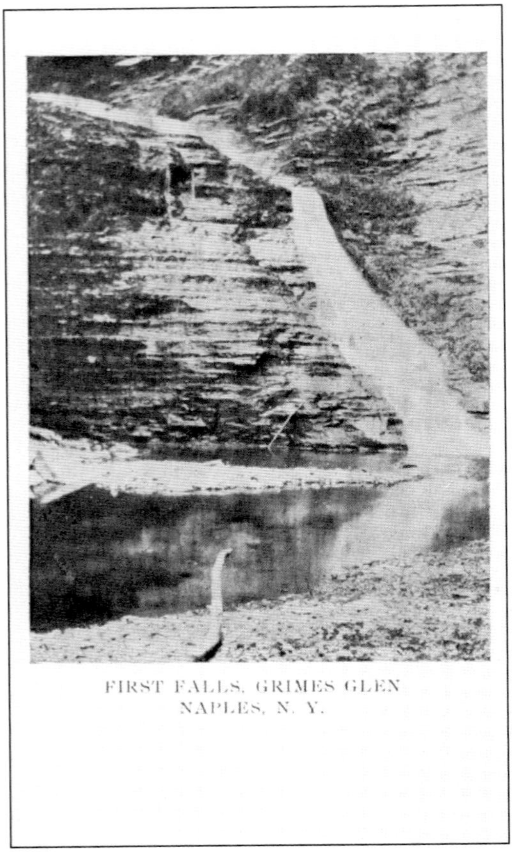

Grimes Glen contains a series of scenic waterfalls as the water of Grimes Creek descends the shale banks near the village of Naples and flows toward Canandaigua Lake. Long a private park open to the public, the glen has recently been given to Ontario County through the Finger Lakes Land Trust.

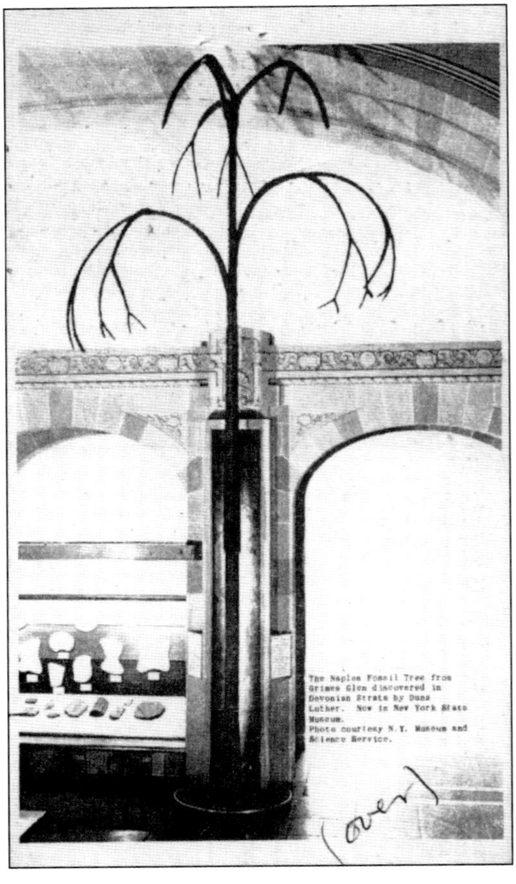

In 1882, D. Dana Luther discovered the Naples Devonian Tree in Grimes Glen. That fossilized tree is now in the collection of the New York State Museum in Albany. The publisher of this postcard is unknown. However, the image of the Devonian tree was produced by the state museum.

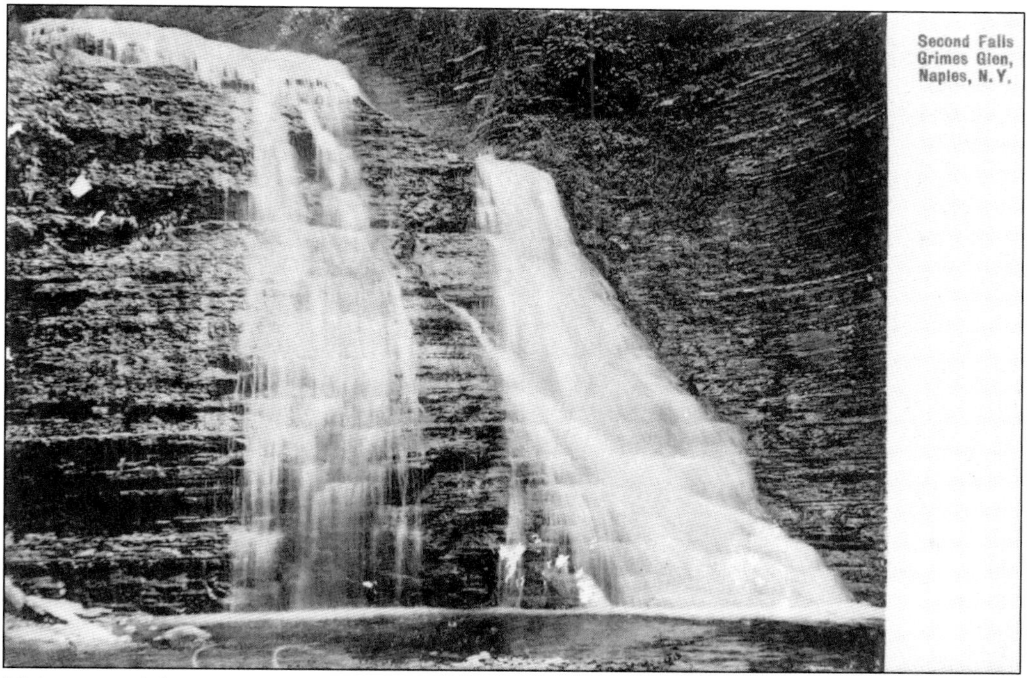

This view of the second falls in Grimes Glen provides an even better glimpse of the geology of this typical Southern Tier glen. The thick banks of shale represent the compressed mud of a prehistoric lake bottom.

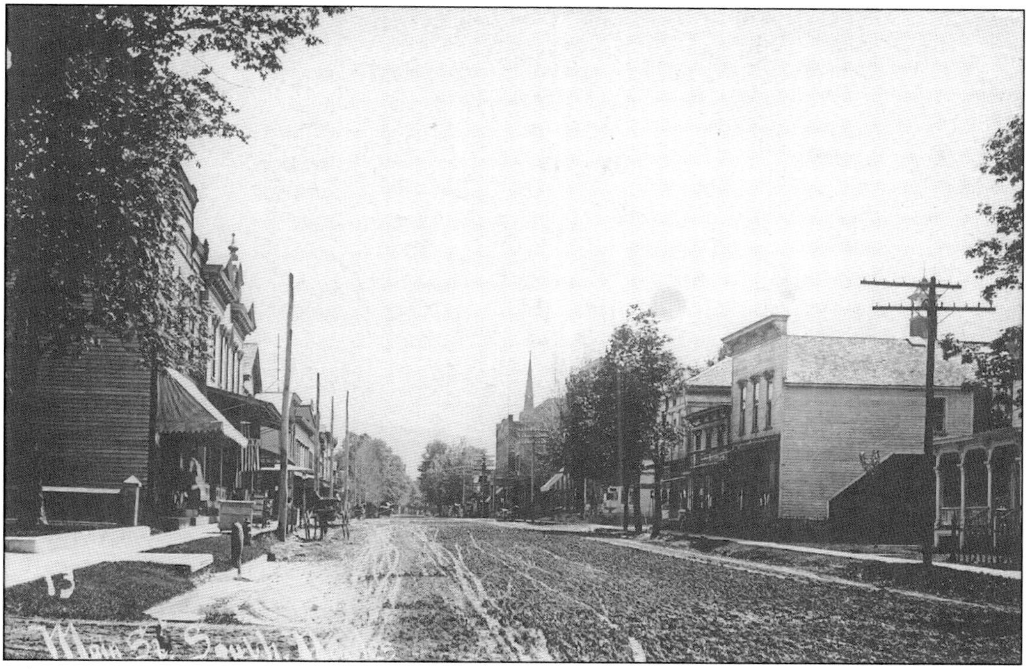

Like most small towns, Naples's Main Street changed rapidly at the dawn of the 20th century. Increased automobile traffic required smoother roadways. For its first 125 years of existence, Main Street was rutted and often muddy or thick with dust. This postcard shows Main Street in the last years of the horse-and-buggy era.

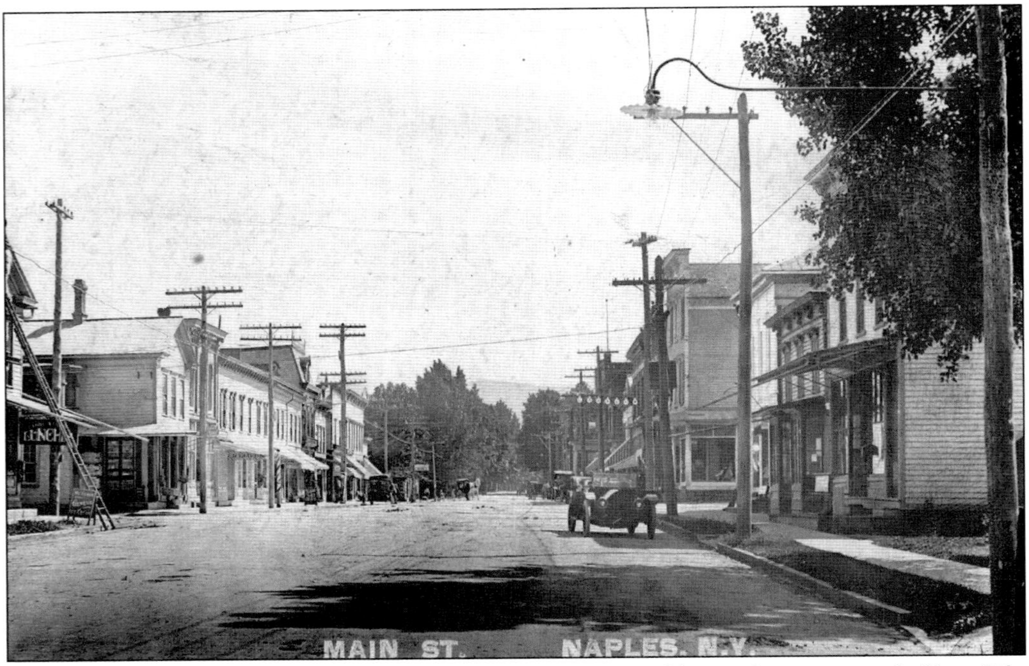

Just a few years later, Main Street was showing the progress felt in other aspects of village life. Both sides of the street show telephone poles and electric lights. Although a horse is visible in the far background, an automobile is parked next to the curb in the foreground.

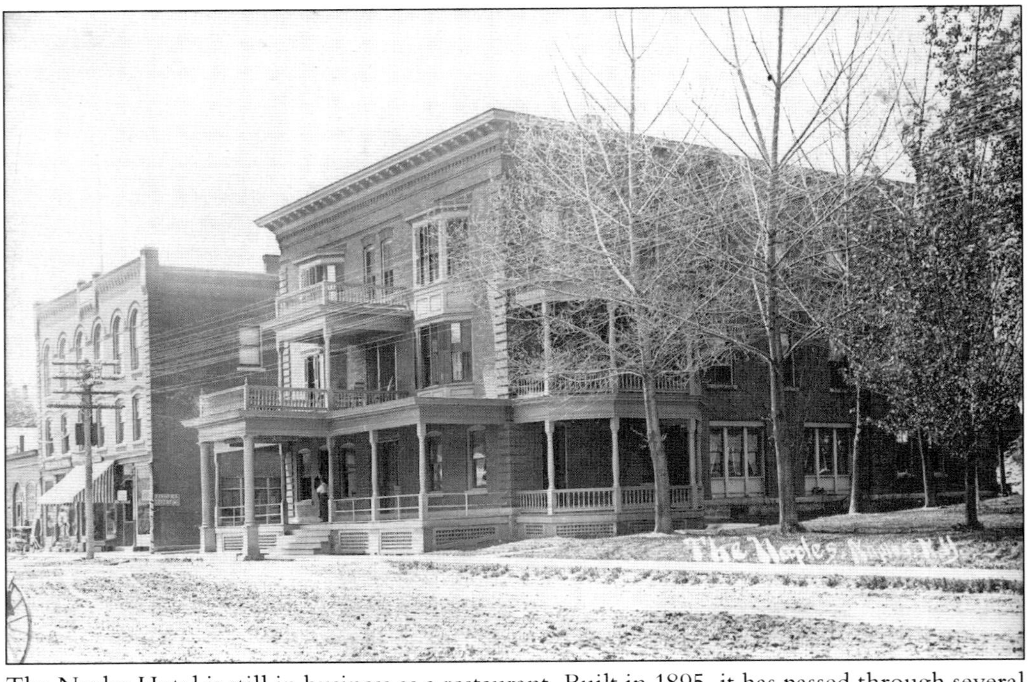

The Naples Hotel is still in business as a restaurant. Built in 1895, it has passed through several owners. J.T. Brown was its first proprietor. The hotel quickly became a center for dinners, weddings, and banquets, as well as a site for speeches by public officials. When this postcard was made, Main Street was still a rutted thoroughfare.

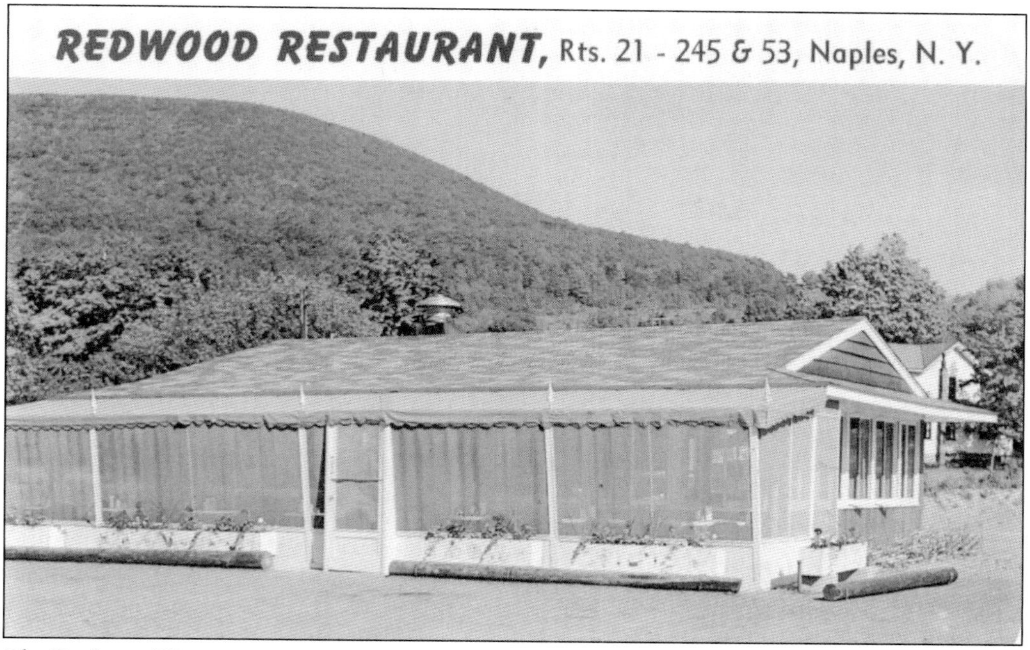

The Redwood Restaurant was opened in 1955 by Al and Frieda Hodges. The original restaurant was really just a refreshment stand with a counter and tables for 38 people. It has grown and prospered over the years, and a bar and cocktail lounge was added in 1963. Today, the Redwood also has banquet rooms. This postcard, probably dating from the late 1950s, shows the Redwood as it looked when it opened.

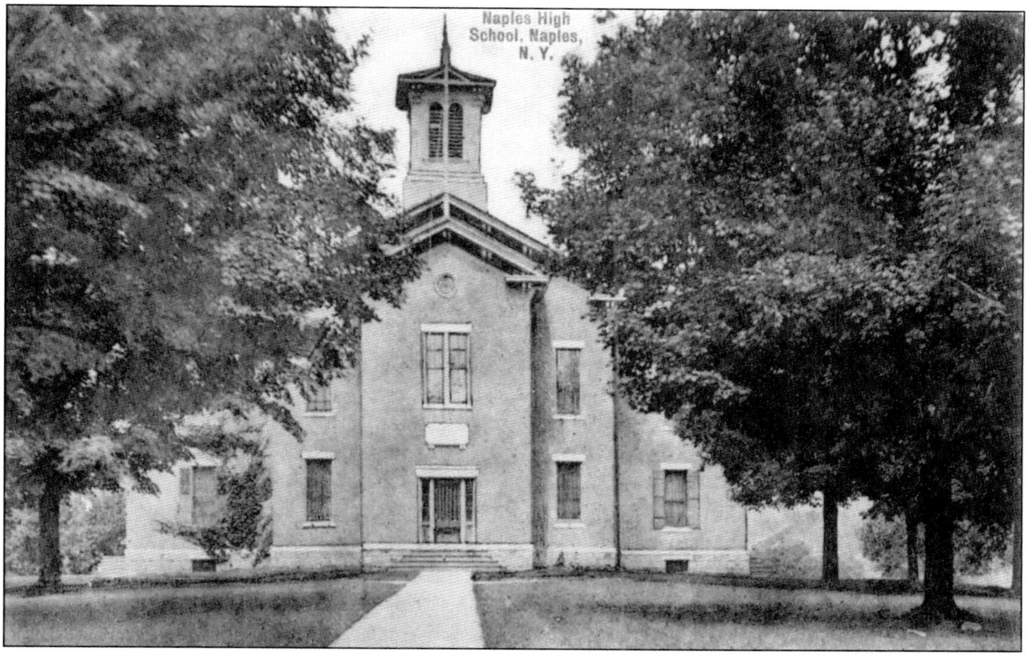

Chartered in 1859 as a private school for boys, Naples Academy held its first classes in 1861. It became a public high school in 1912 and included one of the first public libraries in Ontario County. It was located just to the north of the present high school. The old plaque over the front door rests on the lawn of the present high school.

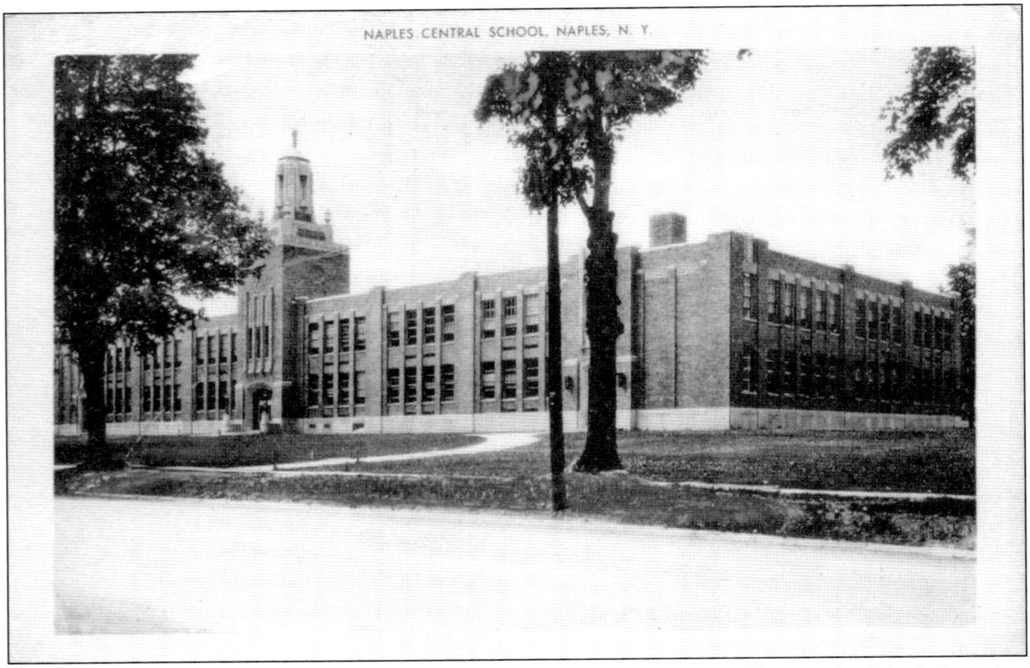

Naples Central School, housing the secondary grades, was built as a Public Works Administration project, and completed in 1940. Thirty rural school districts were consolidated in 1938 to create Naples Central School District. Located on Main Street, it was just south of the old Naples Academy Building. This postcard shows the school as it looked by the early 1940s.

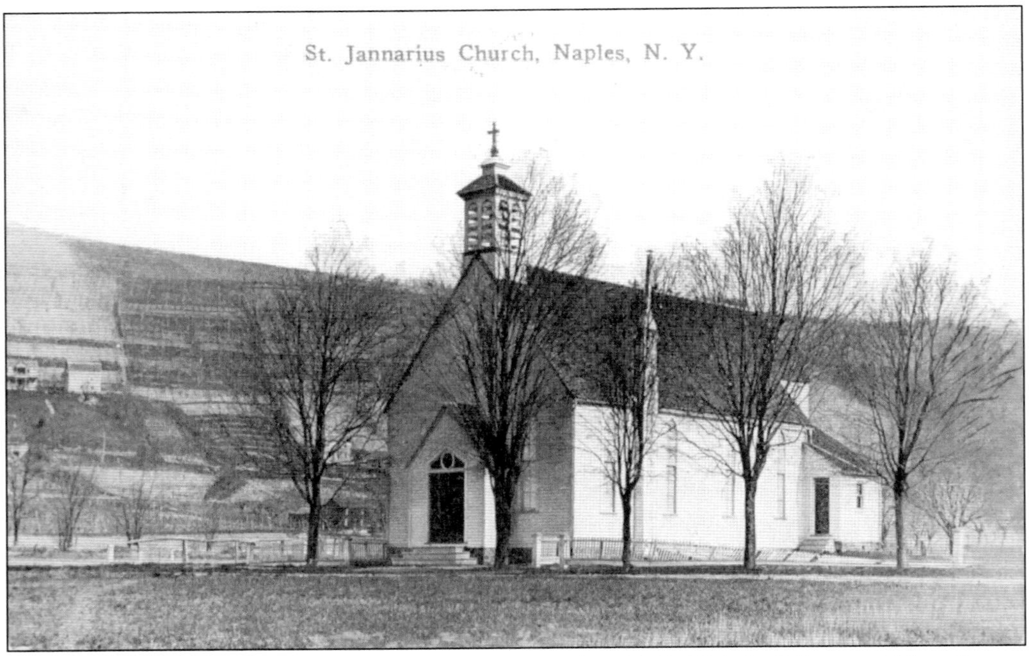

St. Januarius Roman Catholic Church was organized in 1876. This building on Tobey Street, near the Widmer Wine Cellar, was built in 1878. The church is named for Saint Januarius, Bishop of Benevanto, Italy, and a Christian martyr, killed in Naples, Italy, during the reign of Emperor Diocletian.

The Naples Methodist Church was dedicated in 1881. The presence of both telephone poles and gas streetlights illustrates the pace of change at the end of the 19th century.

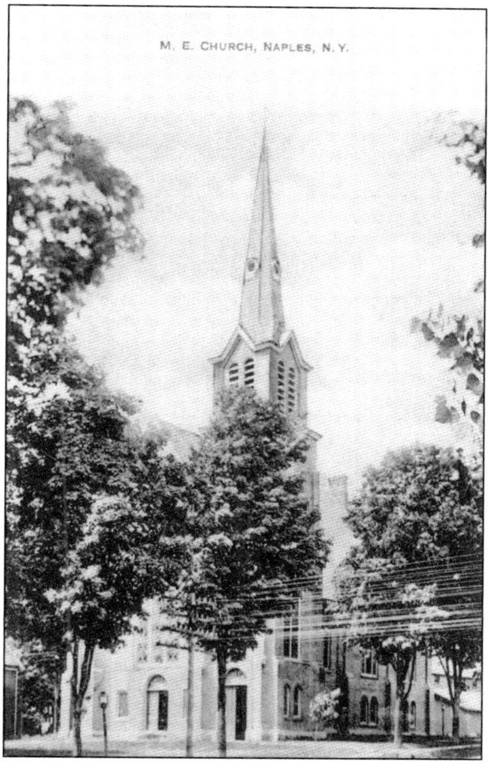

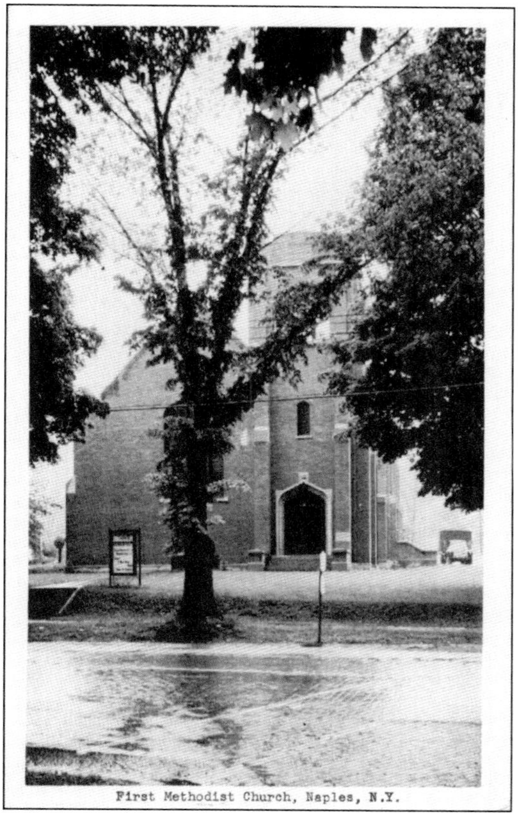

A 1922 fire destroyed the Methodist church built in 1881. It was replaced by this building dedicated by Bishop Leonard in 1924. This building became the home of the Bristol Valley Theatre in 1992.

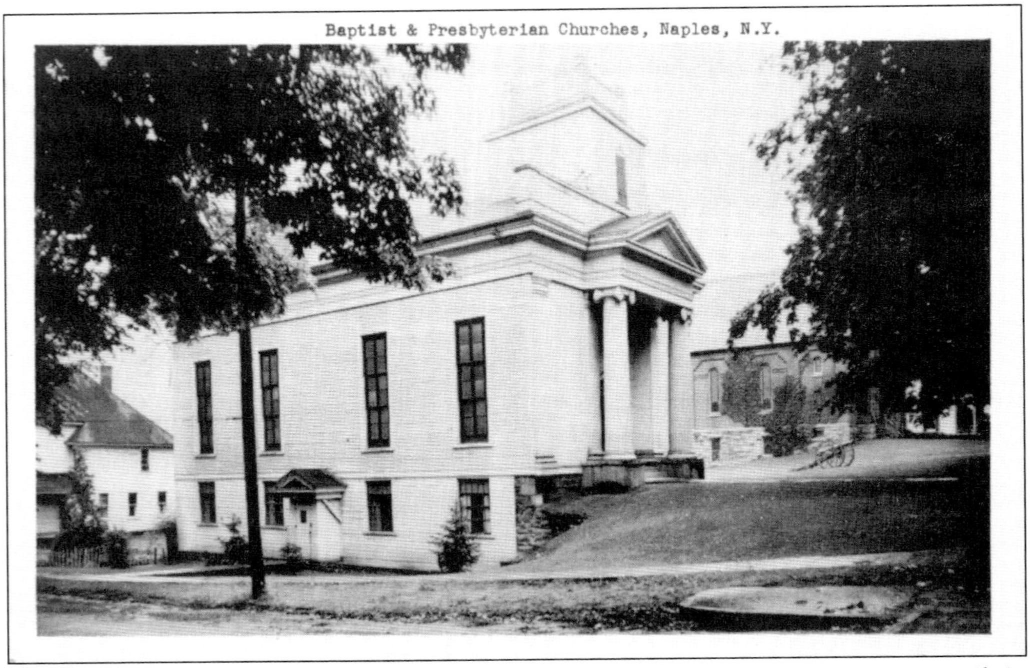

The Naples Baptist Church is located on Main Street at the corner of Monier Street. Built in 1854, this church once had a high steeple that was removed about 1900. The church was also well known for its high-toned bell.

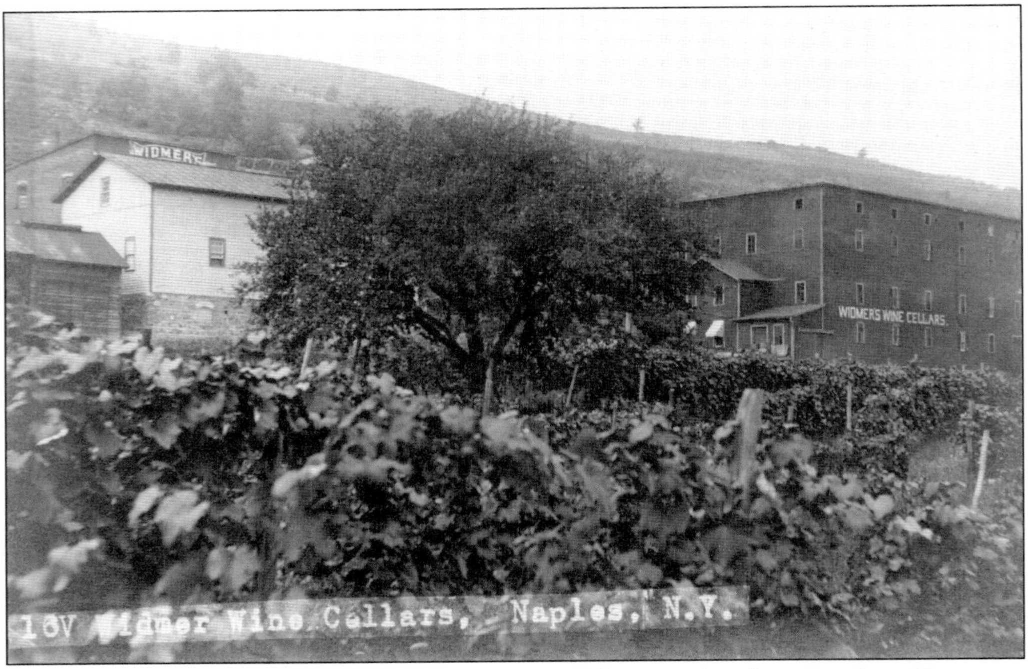

James L. Monier reportedly brought the first "Isabella" grape vine from Dutchess County to Naples in 1835. John Jacob Widmer emigrated from Switzerland in 1882. Widmer bought some vineyards and took the Naples area grape business to the next level, building the Widmer Wine Company. Widmer opened his first wine cellar in 1894.

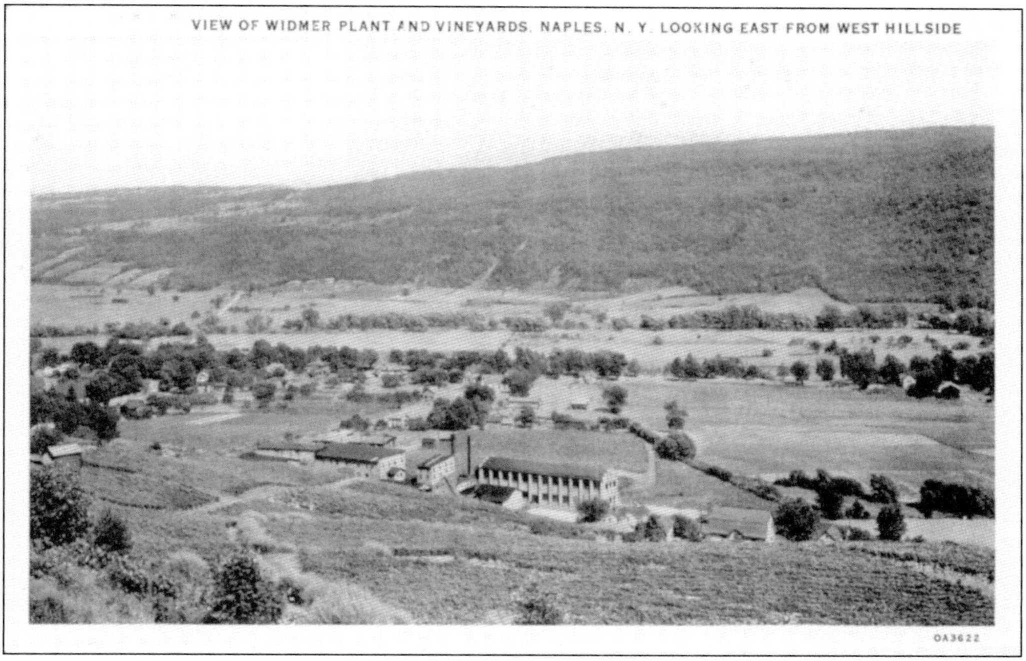

This view of the Widmer wine cellars was published prior to World War II. Looking east down the hill and toward Main Street, the extent of the vineyards can easily be seen.

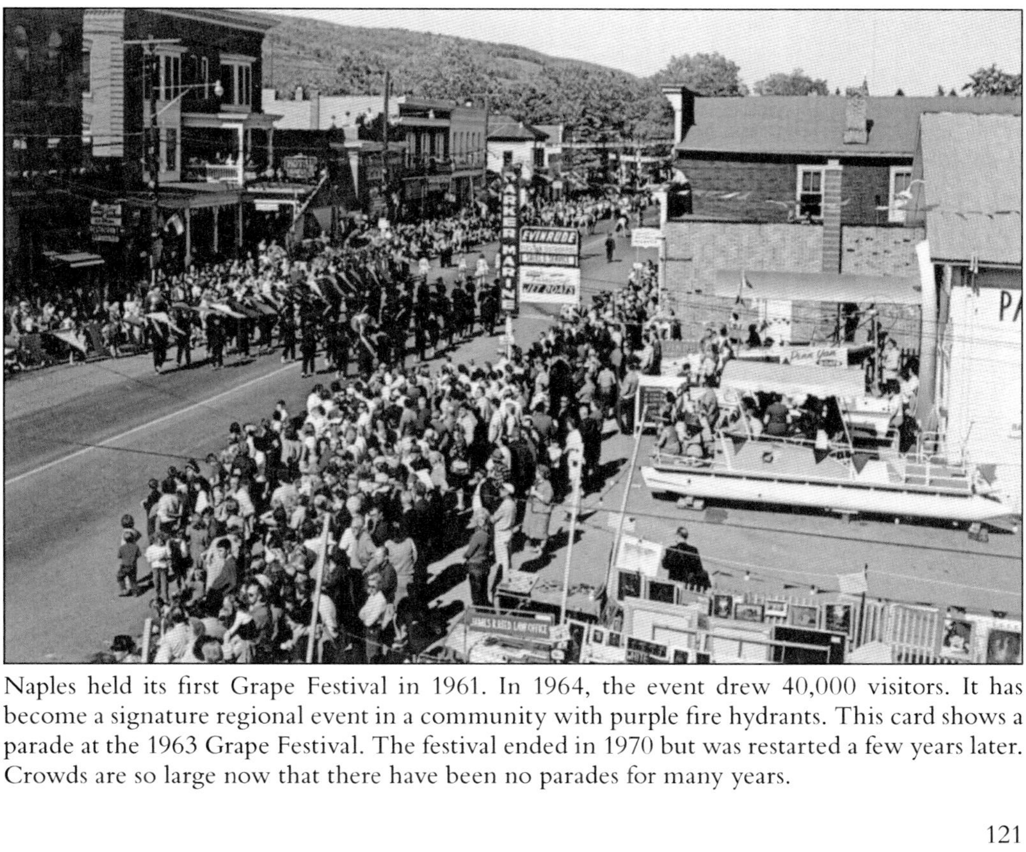

Naples held its first Grape Festival in 1961. In 1964, the event drew 40,000 visitors. It has become a signature regional event in a community with purple fire hydrants. This card shows a parade at the 1963 Grape Festival. The festival ended in 1970 but was restarted a few years later. Crowds are so large now that there have been no parades for many years.

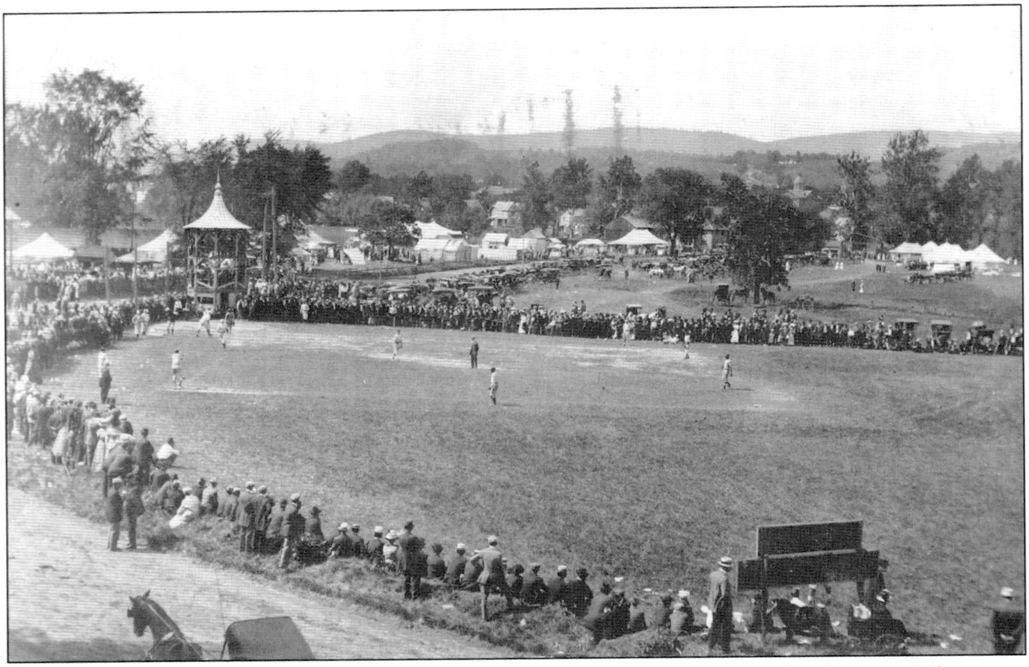

The Naples Fair, first held in 1857, was an important seasonal exposition for the area. Like many local fairs, the Naples Fair eventually ended as a result of competition from county fairs and changes in transportation that allowed people to travel farther. These fairgrounds along Naples Creek were first used in 1879. The final fair was held in 1941. This postcard is postmarked 1912.

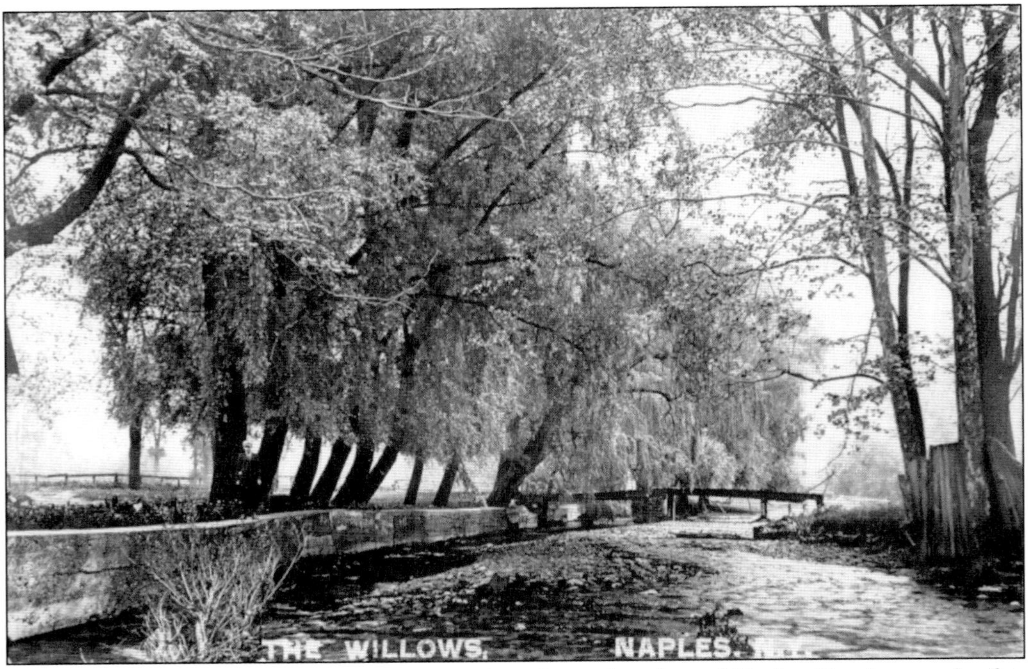

This postcard shows the willow trees growing along the edge of Naples Creek near the fair grounds. Here, one can see the bridge required to reach the fair grounds from Naples village. The fence along the racetrack can be seen in the lower left. This area has been the scene of many trout derbies since 1961.

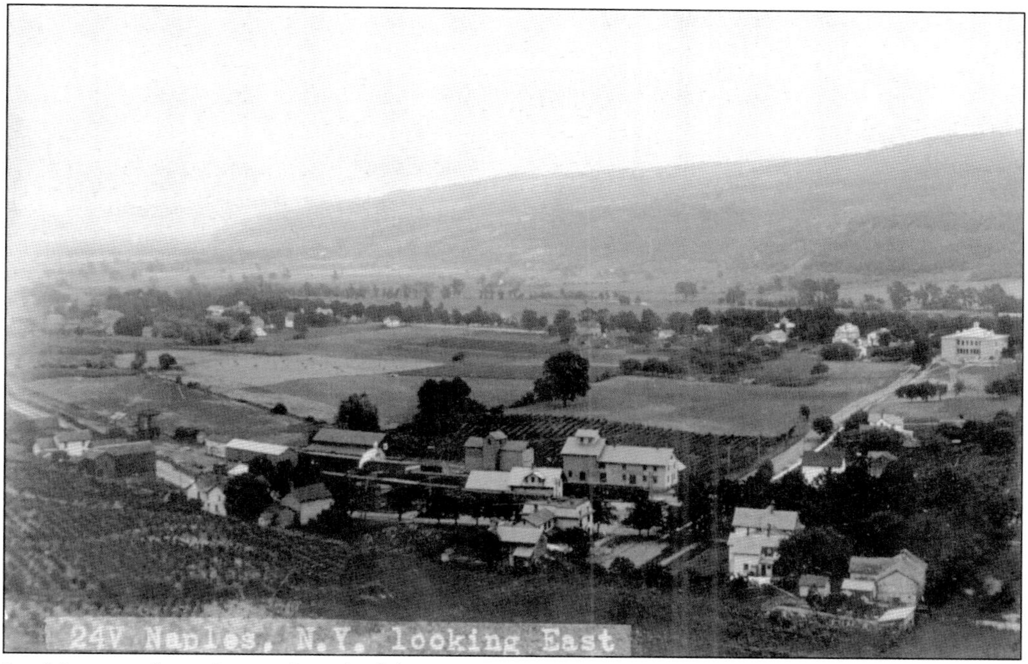

Looking east from the north end of the village of Naples, this postcard shows the Lehigh Valley Railroad station in the lower center. Along the middle of the right edge, the old Naples High School can be seen. Naples Valley stretches to the left toward Canandaigua Lake, which is not shown in this postcard.

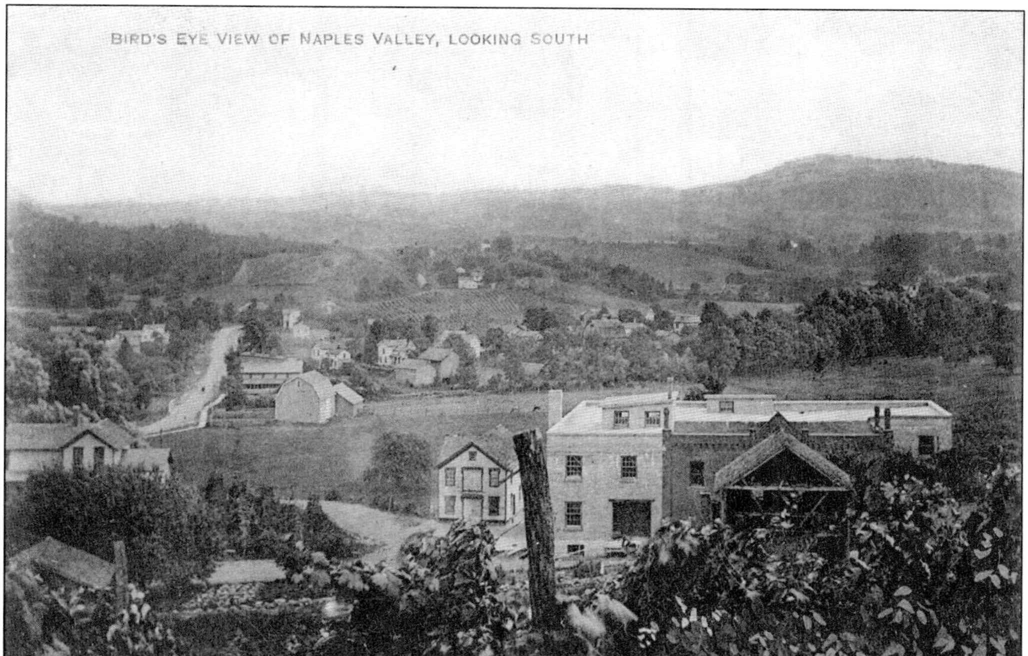

This view shows the south end of the village of Naples. The Maxfield Wine Cellar is in the right foreground. Hiram Maxfield and his son Denison established the Maxfield Cellar in 1882. Widmer Wine Company purchased it in 1920.

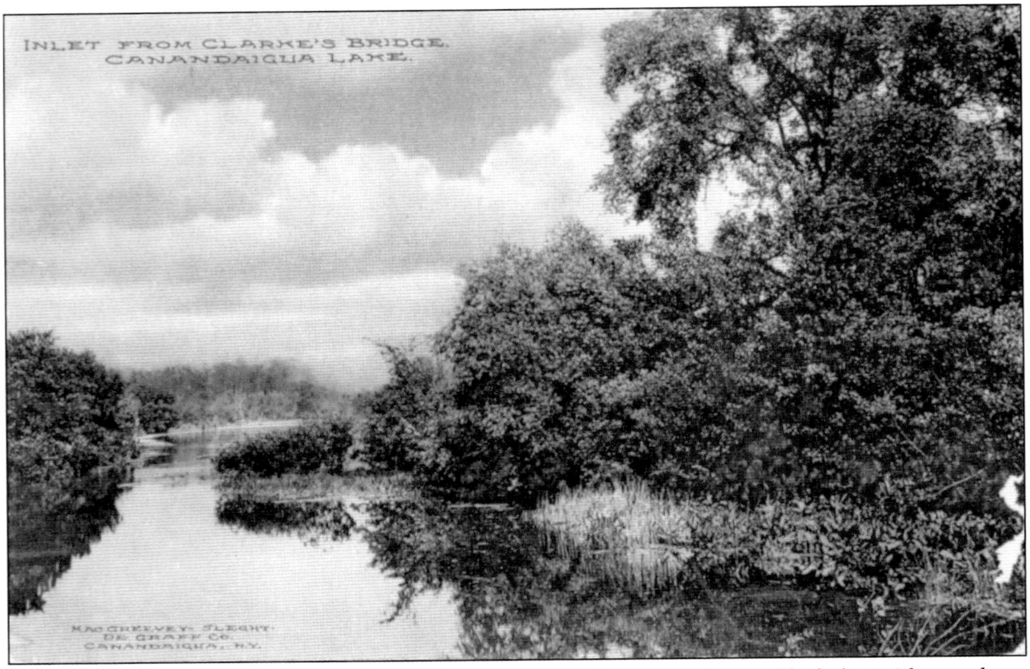

This scene along West River shows the stream and swamp from Clarke's Bridge, where Sunnyside Road crosses the river. That location is really inside the town of Italy, Yates County. It is called the Inlet because West River flows into Canandaigua Lake.

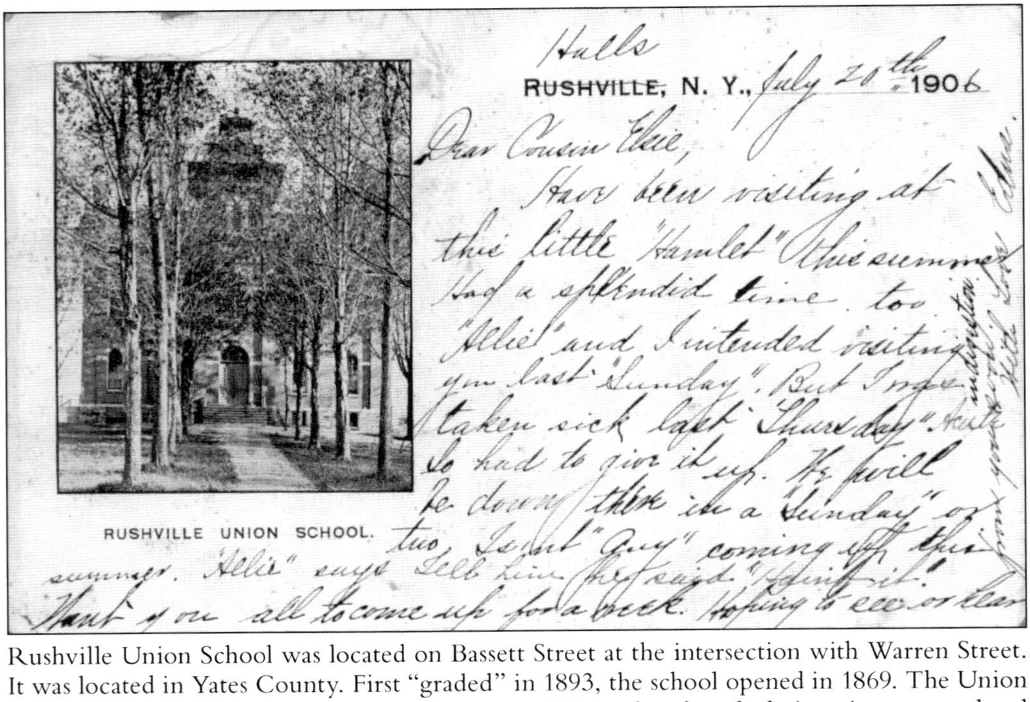

Rushville Union School was located on Bassett Street at the intersection with Warren Street. It was located in Yates County. First "graded" in 1893, the school opened in 1869. The Union School added high school grades in 1909. Prior to 1893, students' grade designations were related to the textbooks they used. Enlarged several times, Rushville High School was incorporated into Middlesex Valley Central School District in 1937.

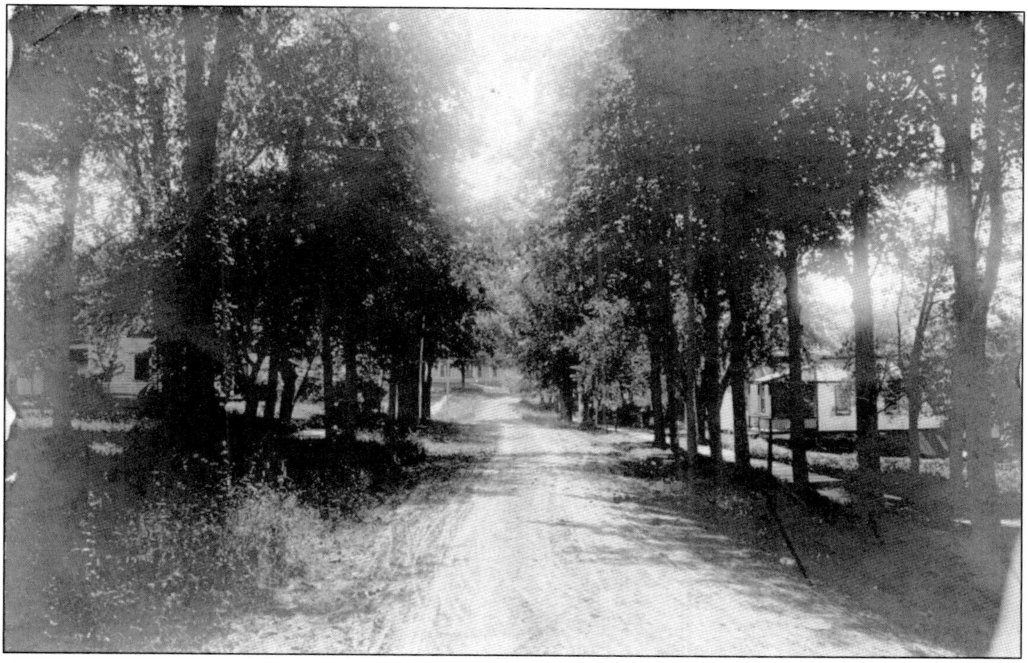

This postcard of the road into Rushville was produced around the time it was postmarked in 1903. The writer asked the recipient, "Do you recognize the other side of this card? It was taken before the Phillips girls had their walk made." It appears to be near the present intersection of New York Routes 245 and 247.

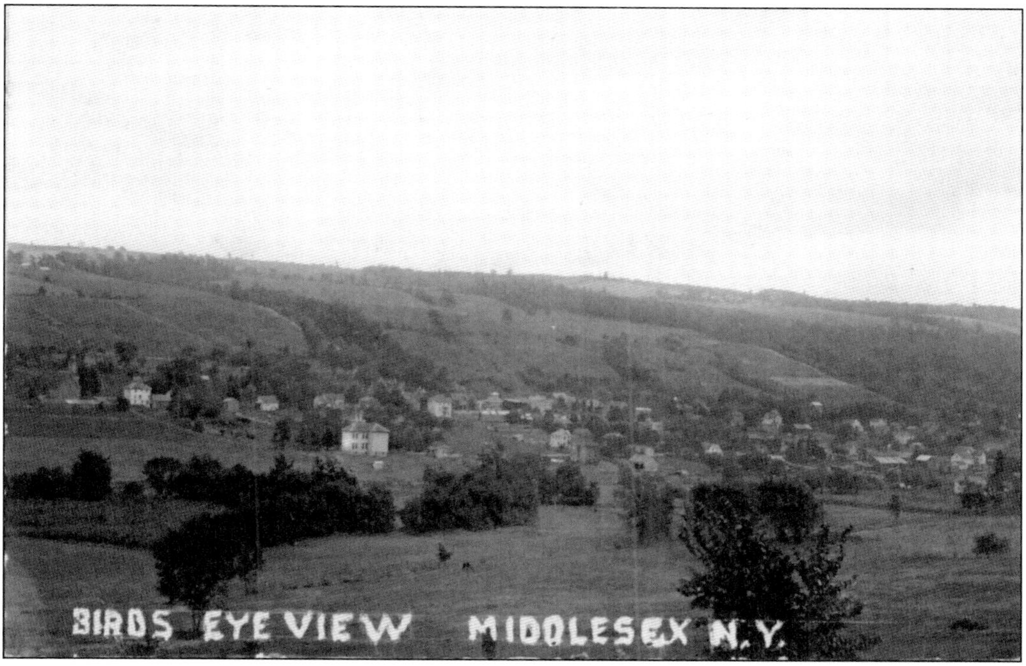

Just over the hill from Canandaigua Lake, the town of Middlesex is located on West River, the inlet for the lake. It was also a station on the Lehigh Valley Railroad. Postmarked in Middlesex, September 18, 1917, the sender was probably a woman. She wrote, "I have been having just a fine time." Her host took her to the Naples fair, then up to Rushville for an evening.

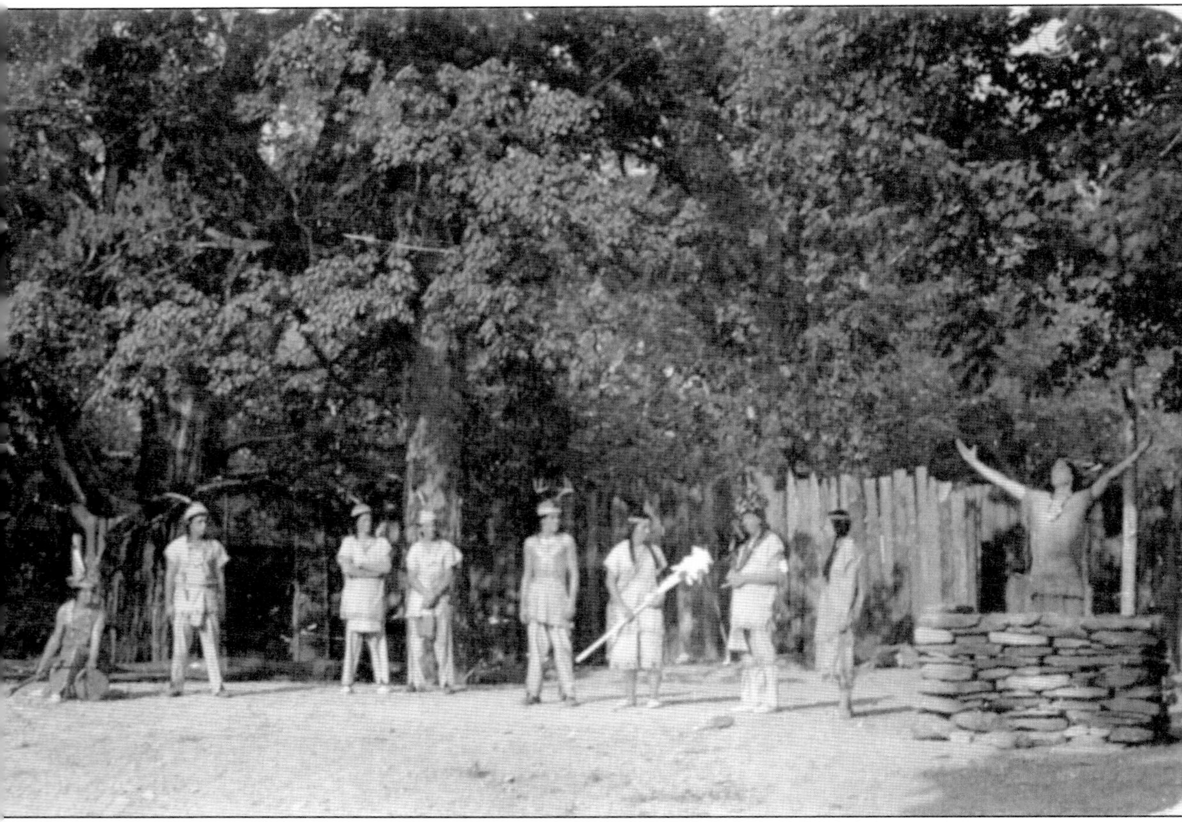

For many years after it was chartered in 1954, the Nundawaga Society for History and Folklore put on an outdoor pageant presenting "the authentic story of the Seneca Nation." The pageant grounds were on New York Route 245 between the villages of Middlesex and Naples. The pageant was a feature of Labor Day weekend. (Photograph by Margery M. Elling.)

About the Organization

Founded in 1902, the Ontario County Historical Society was chartered by the State of New York Board of Regents that same year. Its founding president and organizer was Charles Milliken, publisher of the *Ontario County Times*. A second-generation publisher, Milliken and his father Nathan had witnessed events in Ontario County since 1854. Their newspaper had a reputation for publishing local history articles that would last as long as the publication lasted. In 1911, Charles Milliken published the two-volume *History of Ontario County*, noted for its coverage of the political history of the county.

It was a time of colonial revivals and patriotic fervor that resulted in the founding of several patriotic and heritage societies. It was also a time when many veterans' monuments and historical markers were erected in Ontario County and around the nation. Many of the men and women who incorporated the Ontario County Historical Society were descendants of distinguished pioneers.

The first decade of the 20th century was also a time of great change. Waves of new immigrants entered the nation and the county. The first airplane flights took place during that decade, and the first flight over Ontario County took place in Naples in 1910. In 1900, local clothier F.W. Kinde brought the first automobile to Canandaigua.

The great changes taking place, and the passing of many residents who actually knew the pioneers, prompted the organization of the Ontario County Historical Society. Renowned architect Claude Bragdon designed the current museum building, built in 1914. Until 1972, the museum building also housed the Wood Library. Since that time, the entire building has served as a meeting place, educating the public about the history of the community. It also provides display space for artifacts and a growing research library.

Chartered to promote interest and appreciation of the history of Ontario County, the society and its museum maintain and enhance the historical collections, exhibits, and educational programs.

www.arcadiapublishing.com

Discover books about the town where you grew up, the cities where your friends and families live, the town where your parents met, or even that retirement spot you've been dreaming about. Our Web site provides history lovers with exclusive deals, advanced notification about new titles, e-mail alerts of author events, and much more.

MADE IN THE USA

Arcadia Publishing, the leading local history publisher in the United States, is committed to making history accessible and meaningful through publishing books that celebrate and preserve the heritage of America's people and places. Consistent with our mission to preserve history on a local level, this book was printed in South Carolina on American-made paper and manufactured entirely in the United States.

This book carries the accredited Forest Stewardship Council (FSC) label and is printed on 100 percent FSC-certified paper. Products carrying the FSC label are independently certified to assure consumers that they come from forests that are managed to meet the social, economic, and ecological needs of present and future generations.

FSC
Mixed Sources
Product group from well-managed forests and other controlled sources
Cert no. SW-COC-001530
www.fsc.org